A Guidebook to *Paradise Lost*

Also by Joe Nutt

John Donne: The Poems
An Introduction to Shakespeare's Late Plays

A Guidebook
to *Paradise Lost*

Joe Nutt

First published 2011 by
PALGRAVE MACMILLAN

Palgrave Macmillan in the UK is an imprint of Macmillan Publishers Limited,
registered in England, company number 785998, of Houndmills, Basingstoke,
Hampshire RG21 6XS.

Palgrave Macmillan in the US is a division of St Martin's Press LLC,
175 Fifth Avenue, New York, NY 10010.

Palgrave Macmillan is the global academic imprint of the above companies
and has companies and representatives throughout the world.

Palgrave® and Macmillan® are registered trademarks in the United States,
the United Kingdom, Europe and other countries.

ISBN 978–0–230–53665–4

This book is printed on paper suitable for recycling and made from fully
managed and sustained forest sources. Logging, pulping and manufacturing
processes are expected to conform to the environmental regulations of the
country of origin.

A catalogue record for this book is available from the British Library.

A catalog record for this book is available from the Library of Congress.

10   9   8   7   6   5   4   3   2   1
20   19 18 17 16 15 14 13 12 11

Printed and bound in Great Britain by
CPI Antony Rowe, Chippenham and Eastbourne

*For Tabitha, who is the most courageous person
I know*

Contents

Preface

I make no apologies for writing another book on *Paradise Lost* and adding to the critical work, of all shades and tones, that has steadily amassed in the three centuries since the most famous epic poem in the English language was published. Ironically, in a period when some scholars have commented on the emergence of something of a Milton industry since the formation of the Milton Society of America in 1948, the ability of ordinary students of English literature (if there are such creatures) to read Milton's epic poem with relative ease and understanding has diminished dramatically. Seismic shifts in cultural attitudes, mores and practice have pushed much of the literary and religious texts on which the poem is built out of the common educational experience of those very same students, to the point where Milton has become a truly *difficult* poet. The scale alone of *Paradise Lost* has always given readers pause for breath, if not always thought, but when to this is added all the complexity of Milton's immense literary, religious and political scholarship, and a sophistication of style that demands intelligence and effort from the reader, it is no wonder that contemporary students hesitate and even baulk at what should be one of English poetry's greatest delights.

The single purpose of this book, then, is to assist students willing to make the effort to a point where they assimilate ways of understanding Milton's thinking that do not rely on a strong grounding in classical or Christian literature and history, so that they can feel confident about reading and enjoying *Paradise Lost* independently. Through a blend of analysis, ranging from themes or techniques in individual narrative passages, to the highly detailed, close analysis of major sections of the poem, the book will encourage readers to engage with the poem as it is not unreasonable to suppose Milton himself would have wished, embracing all its awesome ambition, metaphysical complexity and religious sincerity.

All the detailed analysis will proceed on the principle that readers will have a limited Biblical or classical literary grounding; I will not seek to provide that through detailed annotation, which is the job of a scholarly edition such as Alistair Fowler's Longman Annotated Poets *Paradise Lost*, of which the 1997 second edition is the base text used throughout this book. Instead, my method will be to focus on the most central or poetically rewarding books, to summarise the narrative, yet also to expend considerable space and effort on persuading the reader of the high returns to be gained everywhere in the poem through a close analytical process.

Should the book succeed in this, the reward for the reader will be a way to understand and appreciate one of the most imaginative, remarkable and, most significantly, influential poems in the English literary canon. It was no accident that subsequent critics and poets of the standing and calibre of F. R. Leavis and T. S. Eliot went to some pains to undermine Milton's great epic, not least because they understood fully the profound influence it had had on later generations of poets and writers, an influence they found conflicted starkly with their own modernist ideology.

Less than a decade after its publication in 1667 as a poem in ten books, *Paradise Lost* had merited a second, revised edition in twelve books, in 1674, the year of Milton's death. This success of the poem occurred during a decade when the Restoration of the English monarchy under Charles II might have led one to expect Milton's popularity to have been at its weakest. As a famous and influential apologist for the regicides who had torn their country apart by executing Charles I in 1649, Milton's republican politics, loathing of tyranny and mastery of languages had initially brought him state office as Secretary for the Foreign Tongues, but it also brought him the enmity of Royalists who were in absolute control after the Restoration of 1660. Whatever the means and actions through which he avoided the death sentence meted out to other regicides – the influence of admirers, his blindness or merely keeping well away from the centre of power – it seems that there was, after the bloodiest period of English civil strife, something of an appetite for his unique blend of Protestant conviction and art.

Editors and critics throughout the intervening three centuries have dwelt on every image, stylistic trait, ambiguity and nuance they can find, overt or hidden in the 10, 562 lines of poetry in all twelve books. The serious student of Milton today is faced with a choice of critical works second only in scale and range to the works on Shakespeare, though it is not the aim of this book to help you define or work your way through your own reading list. Rather, by concentrating on the experience of reading and listening to the poem, like a staged production of a Shakespeare play, my aim is to ensure that you will never fail to be enriched by the mind of the poet you meet, face to face, in the work itself.

One of the goals of this book was to provide the twenty-first-century student with a genuinely helpful, practical guide through Milton's epic. Many of the poem's key dramatic events and passages relating to Milton's theodicy have been analysed in some detail, but there remain large sections of the poem untouched by any critical strategy. In the Exercises at the end of most chapters a number of less significant passages are picked out and a clear suggestion offered as to how students might explore them for themselves. There are of course numerous approaches that could be taken with untouched sections of the poem, and there is no suggestion that the ideas offered here are exemplary or even consistent. However, they do provide readers with a definite focus and approach that, if pursued, are likely to lead to both greater understanding and further valuable questioning.

JOE NUTT

Introduction: Milton and His England

It is difficult to become a serious student of John Milton without studying something of the tumultuous political and religious culture into which he was born in the unassuming Bread Street, in the City of London, in December 1608. Shakespeare wrote and produced *Corialanus*, *Timon of Athens* and *Pericles* at about this time, but had yet to write *The Winter's Tale* or *The Tempest*. The greatest period of Elizabethan drama was giving way to the Jacobean era of John Webster, John Ford and John Fletcher, with its taste for baroque plots and ingeniously contrived murder. A short walk over London Bridge, a mass of tall, crammed houses with a drawbridge still barring passage to the City at night on its southern end, would have taken Londoners to the greener setting of the Globe Theatre, then at the height of its popularity. Close by they would have been able to visit St Saviour's Church, today's Southwark Cathedral, where Shakespeare's brother Edmund would be buried together with the playwrights John Fletcher and Philip Massinger, and in which John Harvard (the founder of Harvard University) had been christened a year before in 1607. Almost on the doorstep of the inn where Milton was born, the Spreadeagle in Bread Street, was the overpowering bulk of the old St Paul's Cathedral, a building whose beauty had been praised for over 300 years but which, after fire and neglect, was in something of a decline. The cathedral was the focus of a range of lively commercial activity radiating from it, from respectable and scholarly booksellers to alehouses and brothels. Here, the metaphysical poet John Donne would soon be preaching regularly, after his appointment as Dean there in 1621.

London was undoubtedly, however, a capital city, though of a nation still warring with many of its Continental neighbours and still struggling with the Protestant identity Elizabeth had bequeathed it, together with the *Book of Common Prayer*, when she died after forty-five years on the throne, only five years before Milton's birth. Never far beneath the politics of Milton's era was the dominant religious divide that cloaked much of Europe: that between the Catholic and Protestant churches. Elizabeth's father, Henry VIII, had led his entire nation away from Rome, whereas elsewhere in Europe the split had been driven largely by disaffected clergy and theologians repulsed by the corruption and excess which seemed to characterise papal rule. Milton's father was born into an Oxfordshire Catholic family but he moved to London as a young man and established himself there both as a successful scrivener and a loyal Protestant. As a fully qualified scrivener who had served a lengthy apprenticeship, Milton's father would have produced a wide range of legal documents and managed an equally wide range of property and commercial transactions for customers.[1] He was also a musician of sufficient ability to have composed a number of religious pieces for publication, chiefly for voice and viol, and there is no doubt that musical performance formed a major part of his son's domestic life and education. Although members of Milton's Oxfordshire family clung to their Catholicism in spite of the financial penalties and even greater personal risks, Milton's parents brought their son up to be a Protestant believer whose adult literary and political writing exhibits a distinctly anti-Catholic zest.

Milton's father prospered in his chosen profession, but it would be unfair to characterise him simply as one of the many merchants who dominated City of London life, much as today's bankers do. He was also a musician and composer who worked with some of the most celebrated court musicians of his day and it would surely be churlish to assume that his interest in the Blackfriars Playhouse, London's first real indoor theatre, where he was a trustee, was disinterestedly commercial. Whatever the reasons, it is clear that Milton's parents invested a great deal in their eldest son's education. They provided John with a tutor, a Scottish Presbyterian called Thomas Young, who gave up his post to live in Hamburg when John was eleven, but left his mark on the young child, since they continued to communicate years later.

It is highly likely that Milton assimilated some of his strongest puritanical traits and his mistrust of the bishopric from the Presbyterian Young. Shortly after Young's departure, Milton began formal schooling at St Paul's school, the forerunner of the outstanding private school. In Milton's day, the school was close by the Cathedral and, although domestic conditions would have been harsh by today's standards, the academic quality and content of his studies could hardly have been matched anywhere in the country. Young would have already given Milton a strong grounding in Latin but at St Paul's he would also learn Greek, mathematics, philosophy and literature written in his mother tongue, English. Milton's skill as a linguist would win him high office later in life, but the early seeds of that talent would have been planted at St Paul's.

The twenty-first-century student fortunate enough to have studied Classics or Latin at school will, nonetheless, barely have touched on the texts and authors Milton was steeped in and taught to emulate. His was a schooling rooted in words, their power, beauty and history. Visual imagery was scarce, even more so since the Reformation and the establishment of a Protestant aesthetic in churches which substituted simplicity for artistry. Images had to be imagined.

Another major influence on Milton's education was Christ's College at the University of Cambridge, which Milton joined when he was sixteen in 1625. Offering a curriculum that was but a fraction of that of today's Cambridge, the focus of much of Milton's scholarly effort was again on Latin, speaking as well as writing and translating. Latin was the language of all serious scholarship, science, philosophy, theology and, most significantly, poetry. English was fashionable, evocative and popular but Latin was the tool of the poet who sought immortality and a place with the great poets of the past. One of the key uses of Latin for students was debating, and students were required to complete a number of formal academic exercises, or prolusions, which involved them often in raucous and passionate verbal exchanges in front of college audiences. Milton's skill in this practice came into its own when he came to write the debate in Pandaemonium.

Milton undoubtedly earned a reputation for his skill as a Latinist at Cambridge – eventually it became one of what today's employers would call the 'key competencies' – which led to his being appointed Secretary for Foreign Tongues in 1649 under the much reduced Parliament which Cromwell still led and which had recently executed Charles I. What this meant was that Milton was in effect a leading civil servant deeply involved in communication between the new Republican government in England and other European monarchies. It's tantalisingly impossible to know whether it was primarily Milton's linguistic talents that recommended him to Cromwell's government or his enthusiasm for regicide. Because the other great talent Milton possessed and amply demonstrated in the years after he left Cambridge was a talent for political writing.

Milton studied very successfully at Cambridge between 1625 and 1632. Although biographers have sought to unearth highly personal details of his life that relate to the nature of his close friendship with Charles Diodati,[2] who he knew from St Paul's, and a conflict he had with his tutor at Cambridge, William Chappell,[3] nothing is known for sure about either; but what is clear is that Milton chose to leave Cambridge in 1632 and went to live with his family in a small village called Horton, west of London. John's parents had left the City for what would then have been a far quieter, rural parish life. He was such a successful student, he might well have been expected to follow a university career, which at that time meant becoming a clergyman, but this was not the choice he made. Instead, he decided to continue studying, but under his parents' roof. He described this period of his life later in almost idyllic terms, since he had nothing to do but read and would occasionally visit London to buy books and meet friends. But anything an author writes about himself in retrospect has to be treated cautiously and five or six years is a long time for any young man to decide on a path in life he wishes to follow. Were Milton's parents perhaps over indulgent? His mother was Sara Jeffrey, the daughter of a successful merchant tailor in the City, and although there is no reason to think she may have spoiled her elder son, John's parents clearly financed his education without question. Added to the absence of any sign of familial conflict is the fact that he ended this period of intense scholarly indulgence not by taking holy orders – or, like his brother and many other well educated young men, moving to Lincoln's Inn to study law – but with a trip to mainland Europe, which must again have been financed by his parents.

He left England in May 1638, returning home in the summer of the following year, having travelled via Paris, Nice, Genoa and on into Tuscany, taking with him the letters of introduction which would be needed for him to meet the kinds of scholars, poets and intellectuals he clearly sought. There were strong reasons for his taking this early version of a Grand Tour. He did not go on a religious pilgrimage or on business, unless the business involved was the advancement of his own standing as a scholar and poet. He had distributed some poetry in Latin and English amongst friends at Cambridge and afterwards, including *L'Allegro* and *Il Penseroso*, and in 1634 he had been commissioned, and perhaps more importantly delivered, his masque, *Comus*, for Sir Thomas Agar, in celebration of his appointment as Lord President of Wales and the border region called the Marches, at his official residence, Ludlow Castle. As Milton approached his thirties, it seems likely that he had, if not publicly, decided that writing was the path in life he wished to pursue. In order to do that most successfully, he looked to the centre of the artistic and scholarly world, which in Milton's era was certainly not England, but Italy.

Milton spent a short time in Florence where he performed some of his Latin and Italian poetry at a few of the learned academies there. It was this brief but highly significant stay which above all allowed him to claim a reputation as an international scholar and poet when he returned to England. The academies were the intellectual salons of their day where leading Tuscan writers, philosophers and religious figures met to discuss and share their ideas and works. In his later prose work, *Pro Populo Anglican Defence Secunda*, published in 1654 and aimed at defending the regicides' actions and the right of the English people to sovereignty, he wrote about his visit to Florence in memorable terms:

> In that city, which I have always admired above all others because of its elegance, not just of its tongue, but also of its wit, I lingered for about two months. There I at once became the friend of many gentlemen eminent in rank and learning, whose private academies I frequented – a Florentine institution which deserves great praise not only for its promoting humane studies but also for encouraging friendly intercourse. Time will never destroy my recollection – ever welcome and delightful – of you, Jacopo Gaddi, Carlo Dati, Frescobaldi, Coltellini, Buonmattei, Chimentelli, Francini, and many others.[4]

Even allowing for seventeenth-century formalities of style, there is something irritatingly ostentatious about this expression of fellow feeling and gratitude, for what was in reality a mere two months' stay. The way Milton claims immediate equity with the elite, European, intellectual class, his readiness to praise Florence 'above all others' on the basis of his limited travel, strains credibility and may provide some insight into the central driving force behind Milton's entire career: his desire for fame. He was certainly accepted into several of the academies and there is evidence that his poetry was admired and he did stay in contact with Carlo Dati, who became an art historian of real importance.

From Florence Milton travelled on to Rome where, together with other English visitors, he stayed at the English College, which was a Jesuit seminary. Again, it is impossible to speculate about the manner in which he mingled with the Catholic intelligentsia of Italian society. The young men educated at the English College would have been dedicated to the restoration of the faith in their homeland and some would have deliberately returned home with that dangerous goal in mind.

A stay in Naples was followed by a second stay in Rome where besides hearing some of the latest music and opera he was invited to visit the Vatican library by Lukas Holste who was connected to the powerful Cardinal, Francesco Barberini. There is a sense in which this single fact tells us more about Milton's growing scholarly reputation than any number of letters to members of the academies complimenting each other on their poetry. The Vatican library held some of the most significant and rarest books in Europe and Holste eventually became the librarian there.

In August 1638, Charles Diodati died in London and several biographers conclude that this was a key reason for Milton ending his trip soon afterwards. He moved on to stay in Venice for a month and then to Geneva where he would almost certainly have had contact with some of Diodati's family, since his uncle was a resident. For any Protestant, Geneva was a place of immense importance for it was the heart of Calvinism and the nascent University there was a fount of Protestant theology and political influence. He left Geneva in June 1639 to return to England, at least able to describe himself as travelled and in possession of a wealth of useful scholarly contacts, as well as a greatly expanded library. His journey would also have exercised his linguistic skills constantly, but above all it had given him a much stronger appetite for poetry and some understanding of what it meant to live in a republic.

If the England Milton left in 1638 had been embroiled in religious and Scottish issues centring on the proper role of bishops and Charles I's right to rule over Scotland, the England he returned to was close to turmoil. Charles had failed to settle his control over his northern territory and his taste in ritual and ceremony worried many Protestants, aristocrat and commoner, who saw his Catholic wife's hand in the reforming actions of the deeply unpopular Archbishop Laud. Laud had risen through the ranks of the Protestant clergy, supported by powerful figures like the King and the Duke of Buckingham, to become Archbishop of Canterbury in 1633. His efforts to assert the authority of the church and of his bishops ran counter to much of the Protestant reforms Milton had seen in Europe, and many English protestants, Milton among them, were deeply suspicious of Laud.

In spite of Milton's first literary act being the publication of a Latin poem, *Epitaphium Damonis*, an elegy for Diodati, Milton's scholarly and authorial skills were equally quickly invested in this religious controversy and his contribution has been discovered in pamphlets ascribed to the group of anti-Laudian clergymen who gave themselves the acronym, Smectymnuus. Although the liturgical debate of the various pamphlets circulating at the time often verged on the arcane, the tone was frequently anything but and Milton was not at all averse to blanket attacks on Catholic clergy as drunks and crooks.

If Milton had chosen poetry as his life's path, the religious and political controversies of his home nation and capital city proved a seductive diversion. Besides settling into a new home in Aldersgate Street, which is on the north edge of the City of London still, he became energetically involved in the sudden outburst of political writing which accompanied the growth of parliamentary power and the abolition of censorship. But not before he had made some notes about a major drama he was planning to write that dealt with the tragic events in the Garden of Eden.

These are preserved in the Trinity Manuscript, a collection of early drafts for poems and works, which is still owned by Trinity College, Cambridge. It was some years before this idea for a drama was to become a poetic reality and outshine all the intensely felt, ardent, political pamphlets and prose writings which dominated the next decade or so of his life. It is of course also revealing that his initial creative thoughts about *Paradise Lost* were dramatic. In 1642 he also seems to have found time for much more than his career, having returned from a trip to Oxfordshire with a seventeen-year-old bride, Mary Powell. The lack of verifiable documentation about their marriage (we do not even know where they were married) causes biographers delight and dismay in equal measure, but what is certain is that their marriage was very quickly in trouble and Mary returned home to her parents after they had been together for only a matter of weeks.

There are some intriguing parallels to be drawn between the explosion of writing made possible by the cheap printing costs of pamphlet production in Milton's London and today's Web 2.0 world of blogging and social networking. Just as the internet has fuelled a level of public discourse that seems to have abandoned all boundaries of taste, privacy or veracity, so Milton's capital city was littered with writing characterised by immediacy, vehemence and, ultimately, its wholly ephemeral value. In the midst of this outpouring of polemic, Milton produced a work which gained him notoriety very quickly indeed. The *Doctrine and Discipline of Divorce* was published in 1643 and the mere choice of subject was enough to earn Milton a reputation as a dangerous liberal in a world where divorce was anathema to all decent Christian souls.

The creation of Eve in *Paradise Lost*, to be a fit and suitable companion for Adam, and the subtleties of their relationship which Milton plays out so intricately in Books 9 and 10, has a clear connection to this early religious tract and to Milton's own first experience of marriage with Mary Powell. Although it is easy to see Milton in this tract as a cosy liberal, well ahead of his time, it is as much about the tyranny of church law as it is about the tyranny of an unhappy marriage, and there is never the slightest suggestion anywhere, in either the first or second versions, of gender equality. When Milton discusses divorce, it is entirely for the benefit of man and in pursuit of that special quality of manliness he felt was so tightly linked to religious faith.

The book of Genesis plays a key part in the biblical scholarship that Milton deployed in order to defend the idea that divorce should be permissible, but there is little evidence that his argument convinced anyone. The tract is interesting to modern students of *Paradise Lost* since in it he displays a clear distaste for loveless, dutiful sex, in favour of a high minded image of marriage in which the woman is regarded as a kind of intellectual foil for the man. Companionship and compatibility are the key ideals Milton seeks in the good marriage, and their absence, he argues, creates an unbearable burden it would be better to remove than endure.

The turmoil in Milton's private and literary life was overshadowed by the political turmoil that the entire country was facing since Parliament and King Charles had ceased any meaningful dialogue. Parliament's most provocative step was to declare it lawful for Lord Lieutenants to raise armed forces in anticipation of an unspecified threat from the Catholics, who it appeared were always just itching to reclaim England for the Pope. In response, Charles denounced this new law and threatened any who acted on it with dire consequences. This didn't stop the creation of a substantial force of 8,000 parliamentary soldiers in London, and the stage looked set for a military conflict within the King's realm – a civil war. In the summer of 1642 Charles had established himself in Nottingham and issued commands for Oxford to prepare its defences. After a number of localised fights around the country, mainly aimed at gaining armaments or control of key military resources, the costly and indecisive Battle of Edgehill in the autumn left no one in any doubt that England was tragically at war with itself. Milton's seventeen-year-old wife, Mary, remained with her family in Oxfordshire while her husband resided right at the heart of parliamentary rebellion, the city which had ejected its king, London. Things were even more complicated since Mary's family were Royalists and her father was indebted to

Milton through a series of loans he had taken out some time before the war began.

The war shifted ground from north to south during the autumn and winter, with no side gaining a clear upper hand. Throughout, Milton continued his largely political writing, although he was also looking after and tutoring two young nephews, Edward and John Phillips, after his sister Ann had died in1641. This may well have influenced his decision to publish a less controversial tract which detailed his notions of how to educate young gentleman, *On Education*, in 1644. In the summer the English Civil War had become a thoroughly British affair since Parliament had formed an alliance with the Scots against Charles and his Irish Catholic supporters. The Scots Presbyterians were eager to win religious reform as a prize and, after a number of savage battles, the Royalists lost ground in the north and the unmistakable voice of Oliver Cromwell began to be heard above all others, just as the Queen, Henrietta Maria, left her realm for the Catholic security of France.

As the Scots Presbyterians grew in power, Milton found himself under attack from them for his stance on divorce, and Parliament appeared to be of a like mind. Their forces had suffered some major defeats and although the King was hardly in the ascendant – penned in at Oxford, his only remaining stronghold – neither was Parliament. Set against this uproar, Milton published his famous defence of free speech, *Areopagitica*, probably the most powerful and influential of all his political works since it so forcefully treated the right of free expression as a key feature of English culture. Throughout this period Milton was the object of a great deal of scorn and abuse for continuing to publish new editions of *On Divorce*, and was even made to answer charges of publishing without a licence by the House of Lords. It was also during this extremely dark period for the country that Milton's personal world too began to darken, as he began progressively to go blind.

As Cromwell prepared to seize power, Archbishop Laud, for such a long time the focus of Presbyterian fears about religious reform, was executed in an attempt to stem the growing sectarianism that was shattering the Presbyterians' hold on state religion. Milton's interest in binding his Christian faith to an ethical political life is evident in most of his writing at this time and he was unhappy about the way the Presbyterians had turned on what he believed were liberty and freedom, in favour of strict control and power. Cromwell's parliamentary machinations finally achieved their chief design and he became the unchallenged military commander, or Lieutenant General, of the New Model Army, the name given to the parliamentary forces.

Cromwell's success at the Battle of Naseby led to Charles's imprison-
ment, but more importantly it gave Cromwell the providential evidence
he craved of divine inspiration. His was a cause, like Milton's, driven by
God. With Charles in captivity, the principal reforming voices within
the army participated in a series of debates held at the Church of St Mary
the Virgin, Putney, Surrey, in October and November 1647. On one side
were the most radical ordinary soldiers, many of them Levellers, and on
the other the army commanders like Henry Ireton and Cromwell who
sought less radical change and some kind of settlement with Charles.
The Putney debates were chaired by Cromwell and evolved into one
of the most significant turning points in the civil war. Cromwell used
military regulations to control the most extreme voices clamouring for
individual freedoms and equality. On the verge of imploding, the New
Model Army suddenly found a cause that could reunite them. Charles
escaped from prison and all differences were forgotten in the face of
renewed conflict. Many critics have drawn parallels between the Putney
debates and the debate Satan holds in Pandaemonium, in Book 2 of
Paradise Lost.

At the heart of this crisis, for reason biographers are often left to speculate about, Mary Powell came back to London and moved into a house
in the Barbican to live with her husband, where she soon gave birth to
their first child.

For the next four years or so Milton's literary output is minimal and
is dominated by his publishing a collection of early Latin and English
poems as though he felt the need to confirm his status as a poet in
the public realm. The warring sides settled back into a confusing and
unsatisfactory stalemate until hostilities broke out again and the Second Civil War saw new heights of cruelty and violence. Charles had
new Scottish allies and for a while seemed capable of defeating the parliamentary forces until finally Cromwell put an end to all doubt at the
battle of Preston in 1648. Towards the end of the year a core of revolutionary parliamentarians, led by Colonel Thomas Pride, succeeded in
reducing the numbers willing to take a seat in Parliament to what the
public scathingly referred to as the 'rump', a hard core of republicans
who were determined to rid the nation of the King once and for all.
Charles was quickly put on trial for 'High Treason' and, in the midst of
this shocking and exigent process, Milton appeared to find a cause again
for which he was eager to lift his pen: regicide. In 1649 he published a
new polemical tract, _The Tenure of Kings and Magistrates_, which argued
without qualification for the execution of any tyrant. The title page itself
used the unequivocal phrase 'to depose, and put him to death', making

it absolutely clear what Milton thought of those whose revolutionary spirit might have paled at the final step: the trial and execution of a King found guilty of treason. Charles was indeed found guilty, after a brief trial that strained every muscle to claim credibility, and on 30 January 1649 the King was beheaded in Whitehall before a crowd torn between voyeurism and shocked disbelief.

The moment Charles I went to his death unrepentant and incapable of giving an inch to his enemies, the public mood changed and a new war began, this time between those who relished the power of a new regime and those who mourned a terrible crime against God. In using his literary skill on behalf of the regicides, Milton had bound himself to their revolutionary cause completely; and to have been so instrumental in the process, he must have been closely connected with some of the most powerful figures of the time. How closely is unclear, yet Charles I's death warrant was signed by the then Lord President, a man called John Bradshaw, who also happened to be Milton's lawyer. He was immediately rewarded with a post in the new republic's government. Less than two months after the death of the King, Milton was Secretary for Foreign Tongues, with a handsome salary and accommodation in Whitehall, responsible for representing the new regime to neighbouring nations, mostly monarchies, who were far from impressed by events in London. Much of the diplomacy of the period was, of course, in Latin.

In this highly charged political atmosphere, truly radical movements like the Ranters and the Diggers hoping for new freedoms were quickly suppressed by Cromwell's will and absolute authority. At this intensely dangerous moment, a small publication appeared which quickly gained a substantial readership and which threatened to stifle the new regime almost at birth. This was *Eikon Basilike* (*The King's Image*), which was first published on the very day Charles was executed, as the posthumous defence of the King, believed to have been written by the King himself, although later scholarship suggests it was not entirely his work.[5] The small volume proved so popular it was reprinted repeatedly that year and, through its pious, sincere tone, it seemed to build on the courageous faith he had displayed on the scaffold. Milton was asked to respond to it and did so in his *Eikonoklastes* (*The Image Destroyer*) in which he attempted to unravel the King's religiosity almost line by line. *Eikonoklastes* won the approval of many republicans and strengthened Milton's status as the most articulate voice of the new English regime, but the irony is that he may well have felt himself deeply torn by what he now found himself having to defend. For the Rump Parliament reintroduced censorship and sought to control the very freedom of expression Milton had so loudly championed in *Areopagitica*.

The unease abroad led to efforts to reinstate Charles's sons and Royalist exiles commissioned a famous French Classicist, Salmasius (full name Claude de Saumaise), to write a defence of Charles called the *Defensio Regia Pro Carolo I*, which was almost designed to provoke Milton. Milton's response was *Pro Populo Anglicano Defensio* (*The Defence of the English People*), which was published in 1651, and which pulled no punches in its vehement assault on Salmasius as a poor linguist and hen-pecked husband, though nonetheless it was not the most assured of Milton's many polemical tracts. However weakly or strongly one senses republican zeal at work in it, it was a highly popular publication which was publicly burnt as readily as it was purchased across Europe. It won him a level of notoriety on the Continent that outdid the notoriety at home created by his writings on divorce. Although his sight was failing, he was kept busy by the government he served, working with visiting ambassadors and drafting the correspondence which represented the new regime to the larger political world it was struggling to find a place in.

Meanwhile his personal wealth and property investments grew, along with his family which by 1651 consisted of two daughters and a son, also called John. But at what may have seemed like a high point in his material and literary career, in the space of a few months Milton lost both his wife Mary – who was only twenty-seven years old when she died within a few days of enduring the difficult birth of their fourth child, Deborah – and then shortly afterwards his son John, who was only fifteen months old when he too died.

The wider political landscape too was changing dramatically, and Cromwell was gradually stifling all dissent. In a reversal of operatic proportions, Cromwell seemed to be laying claim to the same divine right which Charles was so reviled for. Milton expressed his anxiety, over what to him must have felt like so much libertarian promise slipping away, in a sonnet sequence addressed to political leaders, amongst them Cromwell himself. By 1653 he was totally blind but still managing somehow to fulfil his official duties in Whitehall. What might surprise today's reader is that there would have been precious little sympathy for him, since the most common interpretation of any disability occurring later in life was as a punishment from God. For many observers, Milton's blindness would have been regarded as a very specific divine punishment for the key part he had played in the regicide.

Cromwell's patience at an end, he finally dismissed the Rump Parliament with a famous speech that ended, 'Depart, I say, and let us have done with you. In the name of God, go!': a speech given a new lease of life only recently in the frenzied Web 2.0 world to mobilise voters keen to express their anger with contemporary British politicians by 'Cromwelling' them online.[6] After a weak attempt at installing a puppet Parliament, Cromwell opted for the logical step and established himself Lord Protector of the Commonwealth on 16 December 1653. Whitehall became the new and lavishly furnished home for him and his close political associates, a sight Milton might well have been silently relieved he did not have to see. Although increasingly ill, he continued writing a mixture of poetry and prose, keenly pursuing a feud with Salmasius which did little to gain either writer credit but certainly fanned the flames that were slowly licking the ground towards this fragile new English government. Change had promised so much for Milton, but it had resulted ultimately in a theocractic and unashamed dictatorship that quickly moved to suppress all newspapers except the official *Mercurius Politicus*. How the author of *Areopagitica* reconciled himself to the repressive reality he had undoubtedly helped to bring about, one can only imagine. The archetypal targets of Puritanism were attacked with renew vigour and Cromwell's government, such as it was, provided for harsher punishments for anyone guilty of drunkenness, blasphemy, ignoring the Sabbath day and, that old staple of Puritan outrage, attending the theatre. Gambling and prostitution too became the subject of official attention and control.

In 1656 Milton remarried, most significantly not in church but in a civil ceremony. His second wife was Katherine Woodcock, who was only twenty-eight, a full twenty years Milton's junior. She gave birth to their first child, another Katherine, in October 1657, but was herself dead three months later, not yet thirty years old, the cause, tuberculosis. The daughter Katherine too died as a result of illness soon after her mother's death, before she was five months old. Milton, now twice a widower, was nonetheless the blind father of a family of three daughters, aged twelve, nine and five. However tragic and personally devastating the loss of Katherine and her daughter was to Milton, it would be eclipsed by the sudden death of Cromwell himself, five months later in September 1658, an abrupt and unforeseen event which ironically left the English Revolution once again at the mercy of primogeniture, since it was Oliver Cromwell's ineffectual son, Richard, who was made Lord Protector immediately after his father's death, much against both his inclination and political skill. His central role was short played as he found himself increasingly subject to the demands made by a revitalised army eager to seize some advantage for itself when the opportunity was so ripe. In May 1659, Richard Cromwell abdicated and the army was in control, but within a few short months, during which rumour and power swayed equally violently from one locus to another, the real power finally lay with one of Cromwell's most successful officers, General George Monck. Monck led his forces out of Scotland, where he had been in command, and south into England. All along he had been holding secret discussions with Charles I's son, Charles Stuart, in advance of a likely Restoration. The thing Milton, with an intellectual's privilege, feared most of all – that the ordinary people would slide backwards into the slavery of the past – was now happening; and in a very short space of time it had become commonplace to discuss the possibility of a return to the monarchy, unthinkable while Oliver Cromwell had held the reins of state. Later, in *Paradise Lost*, Milton voiced this fear in the debate in Pandaemonium, when Mammon argues passionately that it would be better to continue to fight than acquiesce into slavery:

> Let us not then pursue,
> By force impossible, by leave obtained
> Unacceptable, though in Heaven, our state
> Of splendid vassalage; but rather seek
> Our own good from ourselves, and from our own
> Live to ourselves, though in this vast recess,
> Free and to none accountable, preferring
> Hard liberty before the easy yoke
> Of servile pomp. (II, 249–57)

In the real world, Milton reacted with determination by hastily writing a new pamphlet, *The Readie and Easie Way to Establish a Free Commonwealth*, but he could not prevent the convening of a new Parliament favourably inclined, after years of turmoil and political ground shifting, to a return of the Stuarts embodied in Charles Stuart.

The new King entered London triumphantly in May. Having become a favourite target in print in recent months as the main apologist for the republic, Milton somehow managed to find a safe hiding place and remain hidden for several vital months. The most violent voices calling for his death burnt themselves out, even as his books were being gathered in and burned in public by the hangman at the Old Bailey. When the new King Charles II announced a general pardon, which of course excluded the most guilty parties – several of whom were, like Cromwell, already dead – John Milton's name was missing from those now living under penalty of death. Quite who spoke up for him is not clear. His nephew Edward Phillips reported that the poet, Andrew Marvell, who had worked with Milton in the civil service, was energetic in his defence. Whoever spoke up, it is undoubtedly surprising that the salaried and most articulate apologist for the revolution escaped with his life when, such was the sense of public shame, several of the dead regicides were exhumed and re-executed publicly, including Cromwell himself. Yet soon after Milton reappeared in public, he was arrested and imprisoned for two months, late in 1660, perhaps because the new regime could not quite permit themselves the luxury of complete forgiveness.

Milton left prison to spend the first half of 1660–70 in relative obscurity, as compared to the central role he had played in the former regime. The next few years were hardly pleasant for Milton or the nation at large, which was ravaged by plague and, eventually in 1666, the Great Fire itself, which destroyed so much of London, including St Paul's Cathedral and much of the book trade it had nurtured and protected. Milton, like other Londoners wealthy enough to travel, spent as much time outside of the City as he could at times of plague and was certainly healthy enough to marry yet again in 1663, to the twenty-four-year-old Elizabeth Minshull. In his early biography, Edward Phillips states that she was recommended to Milton by his physician, and it was not uncommon for older widowers to seek younger brides able to keep house and order.

Such a series of national misfortunes could barely be understood except as an indication of divine anger and, although the Restoration may not have pleased all, few had the appetite to renew political or religious conflicts that seemed to so many ordinary Englishmen and women to have led to the decimation of their people by disease and the destruction of their capital city through fire. The Old Testament provided ample models of God's catastrophic response to mankind's evil. It is during this uncertain and bleak period after 1655 and into the next decade that *Paradise Lost* was composed. Most scholars agree that Milton began it sometime after 1655, although there is little agreement about how it was composed. Milton would not have been short of young, religious or scholarly men willing to read to him or work for him, and the popular picture of his daughters carrying out this function for him does not appear to be founded on anything like credible evidence. The book was published in 1667 by one of the most successful and well known of the City's printers, the Simmons family, who had published many of

Milton's political pamphlets. It was sold widely by six different book-sellers and within a short space of time had won a reputation as art of the finest stature.

It is interesting to speculate where Milton's place in English literary history would have been without *Paradise Lost*. He had written a masque, which would have had only one live performance and as such remained obscure and unread; a small number of Latin and English poems, some of which might uncharitably have been described as obsequious; and a large number of political tracts that had more than anything else characterised his literary merit. He had travelled briefly in Europe and impressed a few Italian and French scholars with his own classical learning and carried out his job as a civil servant and Latinist efficiently, though to no great acclaim. Against this backdrop, *Paradise Lost* is something of an aberration. Yet in reading it, we can see so much that reflects the tumultuous political and religious climate Milton survived and, even at times, rose above. Woven through the very fabric of the text is his desire to see his nation transform itself into the God fearing, ephemeral home only a Protestant living under the constant shadow of the Second Coming and with a mind set on salvation could understand. And, more significantly, could earnestly seek.

1
Religious Mythology

Summary

The poem opens with the conventional call of an epic poet for divine inspiration, and it is worth investigating the nature of the divinity Milton calls upon. But the poem very quickly, and dramatically, adopts the present tense to take us to hell in the few moments after Satan and his followers have been cast out of heaven. Milton lets us see this new-found hell through Satan's eyes before he speaks to his companion, Beëlzebub, and in so doing begins one of the most discussed and fascinating strategies of the poem, the characterisation of Satan. Ironically, it is through Satan that we also first see heaven.

The exchange between Beëlzebub and Satan about what they should now do is one of the most important sections of the entire poem because it contains a wealth of information about Satan, his nature and motivation. This is followed by a regrouping of his fallen troops for what Satan calls a consultation, but which turns out to be nothing of the sort. Milton seems to relish describing Satan's appearance to us, as well as the obvious imaginative challenge of attempting to depict hell; and his infamously elaborate use of simile figures very prominently here. As in Classical epic poetry, Milton provides a catalogue of the combatants. In his case it is a list of Old Testament deities, each with their own peculiar vice, drawn up as a perverse antithesis of Christ's twelve disciples. These and all the vast host of the fallen gather round Satan, eager to hear him speak like Homer's Greeks before the walls of Troy.

Though only recently defeated and apparently trapped in this newly created hell, Satan nonetheless calls for war and rouses the spirits of his damned followers to such an extent they instantly set about the creation of a new and suitably glorious palace, the famously named

Pandaemonium. Again this is the perfect blank canvas for Milton to experiment with, and he seems to delight in describing the raw materials, construction and elaborately extravagant finish of this immense edifice. Book 1 ends with the devils gathered in silence for their 'great consult' (798).

The Invocation

Paradise Lost is such a huge artistic endeavour, such a difficult and challenging poem to read and study, it is nigh on impossible to do so without a careful and detailed consideration of how it strives in its first lines to engage the reader. For this reason we will begin this study with a detailed analysis of the invocation which opens the poem. In these first twenty-six lines, Milton promises much. The question of whether he delivers or not is one of the chief pleasures facing any student new to the poem.

If, like many contemporary students of English literature, you find almost everything about the lengthy statement of intent that opens *Paradise Lost*, grandiloquent and something of a shock, don't be either surprised or deterred. The latter half of the twentieth century has enjoyed and promulgated poetry in education that is, in even the simplest respects of length, syntax, structure and prosody, often the complete opposite of Milton's *Paradise Lost*, the greatest epic poem in the English language. In more complex respects too, the late-twentieth-century poetry that contemporary students are more likely to have encountered, following the English literature curricula set by examination bodies, is often self-consciously biographical, secular, political or introspective. It is worth noting that even in Milton's day, the sheer cultural scope and scale of his poem were extraordinary. And should you extend your studies into Milton's life, you are likely to conclude that this is undoubtedly what he intended and hoped. As I detailed in the previous chapter, he was a man of remarkable intellectual ability who, faced with an impressive choice of paths to follow, chose writing, and specifically poetry, as the form of expression best suited to convey his deepest held ideas and beliefs to a world he believed was in dire need of them.

Given the parameters of the historical knowledge you may have from the previous chapter and wider reading, about Milton himself, and the period of English political turmoil through which he lived and indeed figured prominently, the most effective way to study *Paradise Lost* is by engaging with it entirely on its own, astoundingly ambitious, terms. In these first few lines Milton declares his intention to 'justify the ways of God to men': to explain to a European audience made up of warring Catholics and Protestants, the very nature of God's will, as experienced by his greatest creation, man. The term critics most often use to describe this intention, 'theodicy', was coined by a close contemporary of Milton's, the German courtier and philosopher Gottfried Leibniz in his book *Théodicée*. This describes an attempt to resolve the contradiction that a good and kind God could either create or allow evil: a metaphysical dilemma as real for many Christians today in a troubled Global Village as it was in seventeenth-century Europe with half the planet yet to be discovered. If you doubt Milton's sincerity in this, the entire poem will only ever feel like a rather curiously drawn out fairy tale, or at best religious mythology.

The mythical quality and connotations of the poem are something students are often quick to observe and one can see why when, in these first few lines, Milton makes one biblical or classical reference after another. Although Oreb, Sinai and Siloa may seem entirely unfamiliar, the prevalence of both biblical and classical references throughout the entire poem should impede neither your engagement with its ideas nor your enjoyment of it as poetry. Milton was a man completely steeped in the languages and literature of his era, the Greek and Latin of ancient playwrights, historians, poets and philosophers, the Hebrew of the Bible and the emerging strength of English as a language able to articulate difficult concepts previously reserved for these more ancient tongues. He was, without doubt, a brilliant Latinist.[1]

Milton consciously chose to create, in English, a poem to equal the great epics of Virgil and Homer, and the later European epics like Spenser's *The Fairie Queene* and Dante's *Divine Comedy*. Allusion to classical and biblical writing is the invisible warp thread on which the visible, intricately beautiful tapestry of the entire poem is woven. Without its poetic antecedents, *Paradise Lost* could not exist, and a serious student of Milton will undoubtedly at some point feel the need to read and study those great works too. However, our immediate need is to find a way to read this delicate, complicated tapestry with understanding and pleasure, and, at this point, the opening passage.

One of the difficulties readers of Milton experience is his use of lengthy, convoluted sentences that challenge you to keep pace with the flow of ideas and imagery as clauses and phrases build and play with one another. Through the work of talented editors like Alistair Fowler, whose edition of *Paradise Lost* is the text used in this book, we have the advantage of consistent and insightful punctuation to guide us through. Poetry is a kind of music, and however odd it might seem to you as a student, there really is no better way to relate to a poem than as a listener. In the absence of an audio version,[2] or someone reading aloud, it may be helpful to read through difficult sections or sentences aloud to yourself. However you choose to approach your study practically, what matters is that the fundamental unit of meaning – which Milton's education had equipped him to construct with great skill and art – the sentence, does not dissolve into a series of vaguely or intuitively related clauses or phrases more in the manner of an impressionist or mannerist poem.

One of the most successful tactics I have used when teaching poetry to students who are used to far shorter, self-contained sentences than the first sixteen lines we have to deal with here is to concentrate on using the punctuation as an entirely trustworthy guide. You might not fully understand or even partially understand the verse at first, but by trusting to the conventions of skilful editors and the often subtle effects of English punctuation you will find that some sense or a particular meaning will often suddenly strike you, when a less disciplined reading will have failed. More precisely, what this technique often uncovers, in sentences made up of several dependent clauses, is the main or dominant verb, in this case the 'Sing' of line 6. So the poem opens not only with a clear statement of its grand subject matter, the Fall and consequent possibility of Christian salvation, but with the epic poet's conventional appeal for divine inspiration familiar to readers since Homer. But 'Sing heavenly Muse' (6) also conflates the poet and Muse in one united voice, a striking claim for the reader's attention and respect. If we view this epic merely as the imaginative construct of a particularly creative and literate, seventeenth-century scholar and republican, then we underestimate both the poem and the man. *Paradise Lost* is Milton's great project. Although he began writing poetry as a very young university student, and continued until his death aged sixty-six in 1674, *Paradise Lost* sits at the heart of his life's work and his religious faith.

The poem's magnificent scale and ambition is acknowledged by Milton in this opening passage where he calls it 'advent'rous' (14) and then asserts his intention

> . . . to soar
> Above the Aonian mount, while it pursues
> Things unattempted yet in prose or rhyme. (14–16)

Mount Helicanus, the Aonian mount, was the home to the Greek Muses, so through this desire to 'soar/Above' it, and his preference for sacred biblical sites, Oreb, Sinai and Siloa, Milton affirms the ambitious nature of his project.

Although we can see Milton consciously weaving biblical and mythological sources together, his appeal for external help is immediately given a preferential focus by a reference to the Holy Spirit, 'And chiefly thou, O Spirit' (17), emphasising how profoundly Christian this artistic enterprise really is. If we look now at the second lengthy sentence that comprises this opening passage as a single unit (16–26), and read it in isolation using the punctuation again to steer us through its less difficult structure, this preferential focus is clearly justified. It seems clear that Milton appeals to the Holy Spirit as a Muse superior to his classical antecedents. The Spirit 'from the first/Wast present' (19–20), and through a simile in which Milton makes what is more usually a symbolic relationship between the Holy Spirit and the peaceful, white dove, literally the

> Spirit becomes the father *and* mother of all creation.
> Dovelike satst brooding on the vast abyss
> And mad'st it pregnant: (21–2)

Milton's classical Muses are placed in a clearly inferior historical relationship to this profoundly intimate, quintessentially Christian relationship between the poet and his personal God. This qualitative judgement is underscored most eloquently in his earlier claim that the Spirit 'dost prefer/Before all temples the upright heart and pure' (17–18) that the Holy Spirit's 'temple' is the human heart itself.[3] Understanding the way in which he perceives his plea for divine inspiration is genuine and can be a valuable balance for modern, secular readers possibly alienated by what they perceive as the narrowness of Milton's purely Christian enterprise:

> what in me is dark
> Illumine, what is low, raise and support; (22–3)

Apart from the humility of this stripped away, simple appeal, enhanced by a rhythm which dwells pensively on the word 'Illumine' and then stresses both 'raise' and 'support', the words carry some poignancy when one recalls that Milton was blind[4] and, in the period of the poem's composition, under the regime of a recently restored Charles II, a regicide, imprisoned briefly in 1660 and who was lucky to escape with his life, let alone his freedom.

All of this spiritual and artistic resource, he asserts, is to be marshalled together to answer the single most important question of all in his seventeenth-century universe,

>   That to the height of this great argument
>   I may assert the eternal providence,
>   And justify the ways of God to men. (24–6)

It's not unusual for today's students to feel utterly baffled by what they regard as the outrageous ambition of this claim, and if that is your reaction then resist it and accept that Milton *means* it.

The first question Milton asks his muse, the Spirit, is to name 'what cause' (28) turned Adam and Eve from God's will and lost them the joys of Eden; but before waiting for a response he qualifies the question himself to what person, or figure, 'Who first seduced them to that foul revolt?' (33), and in so doing introduces one of the poem's most fertile grounds for literary criticism, the personification of evil as Satan. And he does this in a manner which is itself unusual and critically provocative. The precise question, 'Who first seduced them...?' is immediately followed by a precise answer, but with no formal or conventional indication by the poet that the narrative voice has changed from poet to muse:

>   Who first seduced them to that foul revolt?
>   The infernal serpent, he it was, whose guile
>   Stirred up with envy and revenge, deceived
>   The mother of mankind, (33–6)

What we hear is a seamless blending of the poet with his muse, as invisible a transition as possible between the two voices. Immediate evidence if you like of the success of Milton's opening appeal for divine guidance. One way of thinking about why Milton might have chosen to do this is to imagine the effect of the corollary, of his having clearly distinguished between them. As we study the poem, we will encounter a wide range of voices and characters, each with their own set of questions and issues.

Discovering Hell

Possibly the most memorable voice in *Paradise Lost* is Satan's and certainly a number of leading poets and critics over the past 300 years have been at least drawn to Milton's character, if not actually seduced by him. Most famously William Blake, if often quoted as having thought Milton an unconscious supporter of Satan without his actually being aware of it, and there is undoubtedly a strong strain of criticism on *Paradise Lost* which regards Satan as far more dynamic, exciting and attractive than either God, Christ, Adam or Eve in the poem. If you are tempted to view Satan in this way, it's valuable to consider some of the poem's historical context, especially the seventeenth century's acceptance and abhorrence of witchcraft, which was essentially their way of understanding how evil manifested itself in the real world. The early twenty-first century lacks such an easy tool with which to interrogate evil acts or phenomena.

This section deals with Satan's fall from heaven and his discovery of hell, surrounded by his followers. Artists throughout the ages have been fascinated by the challenge presented in depicting the experience of damnation and hell, and Milton, like Dante,[5] is arguably one of the most successful of these. It is in passages like the one which discovers Satan 'rolling in the fiery gulf' (52) that Milton's skill as a poet and imaginative thinker are most in evidence.

If you read the twenty-four lines beginning 'Nine times the space that measures day and night' (50) you will notice they form a single, lengthy sentence. Its structure is determined by a very logical, dramatic sequence. After nine days during which Satan and his followers have lain, trapped and inactive, 'Rolling in the fiery gulf/Confounded' (52–3), following their fall from heaven into hell, Satan is the first to regain some level of conscious action. His first act is to look around him and take in his new surroundings, and this act allows Milton to describe those surroundings, and their origin and purpose. That punishment is pre-eminent among these is clear when Milton makes Satan's immortality no defence against God's will, 'but his doom/Reserved him to more wrath' (53–4). A terse way of making it clear that Satan's doom is *eternal* punishment.

Alert to his condition now, Satan is made acutely aware both of the 'happiness' he has lost and the 'lasting pain' (55) he has gained, a realisation that in the literal sense 'Torments him'. The malignant, 'baleful eyes' (56) that we would expect to see also give witness to the 'huge affliction and dismay'(57) Satan feels on waking to eternal damnation, and in the very first move towards characterising Satan, Milton adds to this potentially sympathetic image of Satan's gaze 'obdúrate pride and steadfast hate' (58). What these paradoxical eyes see is in some ways an entirely conventional vista of hellfire and sulphurous darkness, but at first sight Milton's hell is less conventional and far more interesting in its psychological, than in its apparently physical, consequences. The first thing to note is the sheer vastness of the place. Something conveyed succinctly by Milton reminding us of Satan's angelic status on the scale of being. The second thing perhaps to note is the way the psychological

conditions are linked so tightly to the physical as to be almost inseparable, so that what Satan 'views' is a 'dismal situation' (60), an almost
invisible pun:

> At once as far as angels' ken he views
> The dismal situation waste and wild, (59–60)

More conventional images, 'dungeon horrible' (61) and 'one great fur-
nace' (62), follow, but one of the first things students of the poem can
start to expect as they begin to work with it thoughtfully is Milton's
penchant for the surprising or contrasting detail, seen here where hell's
flames give out 'No light, but rather darkness visible' (63). Although
the paradox itself is not original, and there are numerous literary precedents, it is the stark use of the oxymoron 'darkness visible' which may
surprise the reader whose imagination has been lulled into a kind of
gentle indolence through the short sequence of conventional images.
And Milton continues to surprise. Ambiguity is in some respects almost
a *sine qua non* of all poetry. Students of poetry grow used to looking for
the subtlest of echoes, the most literary of connotations and sometimes
startling potential for meaning that great poets seem able to embed in
the simplest of phrases or images, such as Edgar's 'Ripeness is all'[6] or
Othello's 'Put out the light'.[7] In describing what Satan sees, Milton's
skill with ambiguity is evident in a single word picked out in bold here
to help make the point:

> A dungeon horrible, on all sides round
> As one great furnace **flamed**, yet from those flames
> No light, but rather darkness visible (61–3)

If we hear 'flamed' as a verb, then there is almost a closed unit of meaning in these three lines and we should expect a full stop to conclude
them. But it is impossible to use a full stop here because of the enjambment (the flowing over of sense from one line to the next) that connects
the idea in the next line with 'Served' and indeed well beyond that.
What we cannot avoid hearing is the grammatical link between the
subject 'darkness' and the verb 'Served' in line 64, such that the oxymoronic 'darkness visible' is the means by which Satan is made to feel
the full psychological horror and misery of his 'situation', heaping irony
on top of paradox. Milton piles on the miserable images that Satan's
eyes take in for another six lines of verse; 'sights of woe' (64) combines
with 'Regions of sorrow, doleful shades' (65) and 'a fiery deluge' (68).
All have their psychological counterparts in 'where peace/And rest can

never dwell' (65–6) and 'hope never comes/That comes to all' (66–7), while Satan and his crew must endure 'torture without end' (67). It is a dismal prospect indeed and one yet to be capped.

The account of Satan's new domain concludes with a reminder that hell has been created by God as a 'prison' for 'those rebellious' (71) as a place of 'eternal justice' (70). But the cruellest punishment of all is the one reserved for the end of this description, before Satan begins to discuss their plight with Beëlzebub. Hell, we learn, is

> As far removed from God and light of heaven
> As from the centre thrice to the utmost pole. (73–4)

And although there may be an invitation to dwell on the scale or distance, or to make comparisons with earlier accounts of hell's relationship to heaven, what should strike us most deeply is the idea that the removal from God's presence, in a prelapsarian sense, is the utter and complete absence of joy. The worst conceivable punishment for the fallen angels and for Satan is this removal from God's presence for all eternity.

Satan Speaks

If we exclude the poet's own voice and his blurring of that into the Holy Spirit as muse, that we noted in lines 33–4, then, when Satan begins to speak to Beëlzebub at line 84, his is the first voice we hear. Milton's account of mankind's loss of paradise reaches as far back as it possible for him to go in search of an explanation that will justify God's actions, and in later books we will encounter crucial events even preceding Satan's discovery of being in hell. Critical debate about Satan and Milton's portrayal of him is often fierce and partisan. The way you react to him as a student of *Paradise Lost* cannot help but be influenced to some degree by one's own preconceived religious or secular beliefs. Milton's Satan is literally and historically a prince among devils, something of a tour de force in the canon of devilish literature. You should now read lines 84–124, Satan's first complete speech addressing his chief lieutenant, Beëlzebub, before continuing.

Something that might strike you is how quickly and abruptly Satan appears to get distracted from his train of thought. 'If thou beest he' (84) would most conventionally be followed by a conditional clause or phrase beginning with 'then' or a consequent fact relating directly to Satan's having recognised Beëlzebub, but this is not what immediately happens. Satan is distracted immediately by the sight of his

companion – we might assume because he is so shockingly transformed – and by the light and darkness that follow aptly on from the
vision of hell Satan has just taken in:

> Who in the happy realms of light
> Clothed with transcendent brightness didst outshine
> Myriads though bright: (85–7)

Having noted the dramatic change in Beëlzebub, Satan is able to return
to his first thought but Milton's use here of ellipsis, simply missing
out extraneous words, to pick up the image can cause confusion and
mean we lose its full impact. This means 'if he whom mutual league'
(87) is more fruitfully understood as 'if you are he whom...', then
Satan's realisation that his rebellion has brought equal damnation to
his companions has greater impact, at last delivering the consequen-
tial outcome we expected when he began his speech with 'If'. For
seventeenth-century readers, Beëlzebub's fate is probably of considerably more interest than for many contemporary students. Those who
ally themselves with Lucifer in life, share his fate of eternal damnation
in death. Again, this key meaning can elude the careless reader who
hasn't learnt to trust Milton's often elaborate sentence structure and
work out the precise relationships between subject and verb, as well as
what is often a question of hierarchy between them. In this case the
issue revolves around 'joined' (90), a word used at the start and end of
the line but in each case relating to a different subject. Picking the word
out again in bold type, illustrates this clearly:

> if he whom mutual league,
> United thoughts and counsels, equal hope
> And hazard in the glorious enterprise,
> Joined with me once, now misery hath **joined**
> In equal ruin: (87–91)

In the first instance it is Beëlzebub who has 'Joined' with Satan in the
rebellion, but in the second it is 'misery' who has 'joined' Beëlzebub,
and all the fallen angels, to Satan in 'equal ruin'. This latter meaning is
the most powerful and provocative because in any half decent human
it would give rise to feelings at least of sympathy, if not of deep regret
or self-mortification towards those they have dragged down with them.
Not so Satan.

He has already referred to their rebellion as a 'glorious enterprise' (89)
and no sooner has he admitted that he has led a host of fellow angels

to this 'pit' than he denies any regret whatsoever, displaying an almost childish level of denial when he asserts 'till then who knew/The force of those dire arms?' (93–4).

It is worth reading the next sentence of Satan's speech, lines 94–105, as one, since it will help you become used to managing Milton's eloquent syntax and bring to light more evidence of Satan's complex characterisation. Satan is utterly unrepentant. He continues to defy God, undeterred by the suffering inflicted so far, 'nor what the potent victor in his rage/Can else inflict' (95–6), and denies that he has changed in anything but outward show, proudly exhibiting the same 'fixed mind/And high disdain' (97–8) which led to this disaster. The way this sentence builds; its use of powerful, warlike diction; words like 'lustre' (97), 'mightiest' (99) and 'fierce contention' (100), leading up to the huge, climactic boast, 'And shook his throne' (105), made emphatic by Milton's use of a caesura (an abrupt break in the middle of the line), as well as the choice of four single syllable words of equal stress – all this combines to convey the very essence of Satan's weakness: his pride.

Yet many of Milton's admirers have found in this kind of language and conviction much to admire about Satan. There is no doubt about the force with which Satan expresses his enmity here, and elsewhere, but what is at issue is how we respond to that expression as characterisation in a narrative poem. *Paradise Lost* tells a story. Milton might have argued it was the greatest story ever told, but it is nonetheless a story, and for it he has to create a number of characters. That process of characterisation inevitably provokes an aesthetic response in the reader and that response is often the perfect vehicle for students eager to go beyond the narrative into the profound philosophical and religious questions this great story poses.

A good example is provided by the next section of Satan's speech where he explains why he remains, even as he endures God's wrath, incapable of penitence. 'What though the field be lost/All is not lost' (105–6) introduces a list of things, as it were saved. Besides his 'unconquerable will' (106) and the predictable thirst for 'revenge', we find 'immortal hate' (107), 'courage' (108) and the weakly catch-all phrase 'And what is else not to be overcome?' (109). All of these Satan believes are worth defending to the point where he unites them all under the one term, 'glory' (110), a prize he will never award the victor of the heavenly war, 'To bow and sue for grace/With suppliant knee, and deify his power' (111–12).

We are invited to make our own judgements on what this tells us about Satan, and possibly about ourselves. Do we hear the courageous spirit of a free soul, determined to resist the cruelty of a tyrant, or do we hear the bitterness of an incurably envious soul, enraged at his own impotence in the face of his creator's implacable opposition? Whatever our response, Satan uses one word which seems to imply some kind of rationality lies behind his determination to fight on. His use of 'deify' (112) might be taken to suggest he simply refuses to accept God is divine, preferring instead to see him as his equal, in spite of all the evidence to the contrary. The evidence for his holding this view is slight indeed. Satan implies that, such was the violence of his rebellion, God was forced to doubt he could maintain his divine status, 'Who from the terror of this arm so late/Doubted his empire' (113–14). We have only Satan's word for this, and as the poem develops we hear a very different account from God himself.

The idea that Satan has a very different understanding of his relationship to his creator than we do is developed shortly after he rejects surrendering as 'low indeed' (114), an 'ignominy and shame beneath' (115) even the hellish depths to which they have already sunk. It is clear that he believes himself and his fellow fallen angels are immortal, 'since by fate the strength of gods/And this empyreal substance cannot fail' (116–18). The 'empyreal substance' is his own shape and form and what is noticeable is that he denies that he owes its existence to a single, almighty God, bowing instead to fate and ranking *himself* as a god.

As his first speech comes to a close, Satan makes every effort to lift his own and Beëlzebub's hopes, employing the kind of spirited rhetoric of a military commander looking for advantage in a hopeless situation. He argues, without conscious irony, that their downfall has in fact proved a blessing, that the experience has left them no worse off in strength of arms, and in fact 'in foresight much advanced' (119), better equipped to continue the struggle 'by force or guile' (120). This final decisive statement has immense narrative significance for man, and more precisely for Adam and Eve. Satan's choice to wage war, 'Irreconcilable to our grand foe' (122), will ultimately engulf them and mankind as a whole.

There is a final revealing use of language in Satan's conclusion. Although he imagines God triumphant and 'in excess of joy' (123) because he is what he is, he cannot avoid what contemporary students might immediately term a Freudian slip where this joy is translated into the image of God holding the 'tyranny of heaven' (124). Later in the poem[8] Milton uses the viewpoint of the archangel Raphael as a stark counterpoint to Satan's envious imaginings here.

Satan Rouses Himself

Satan barely pauses to reflect on Beëlzebub's plea for respite, if not com-plete acquiescence to God's will (128–55) before proclaiming his own implacable goal in simple language which leaves no room for further debate or discussion. What Satan commits himself and all his followers to is eternal guerrilla warfare with their maker:

> But of this be sure,
> To do aught good never will be our task,
> But ever to do ill our sole delight,
> As being contrary to his high will
> Whom we resist. (158–62)

Why, we might want to ask ourselves, considering all the evidence of his senses and intellect, does Satan reach this conclusion without any seri-ous reference to Beëlzebub's entirely rational objections? He gives us an intriguing reason himself which should provoke even more questions. Doing 'ill' he regards as the only pleasure, 'delight' (160), available to them, and it is a 'delight' for the sole reason that it defies God's will and gives them the only way to continue to resist. Resistance is a dif-ficult concept in the early years of the twenty-first century, since the preceding century was marked in the West by two catastrophic wars that overwhelmed entire populations and left resistance the only option to many. This means that to many ears it can connote courage and deter-mination, fidelity to fine ideals and just moral causes. But it is Milton's use of the word 'will' (161) that is more revealing. We have heard the plight Satan and all his followers are in, described in some detail, heard the lucid arguments put by Beëlzebub for acquiescence, and heard all these dismissed by Satan in favour of a 'delight' in evil that we are likely to struggle to comprehend as pleasurable in any sense whatso-ever. It may be God's 'will' as to why Satan is punished, but it is Satan's that he continues to create evil. Milton makes absolutely sure we see Satan in possession of the single most significant gift God is to give to Adam and Eve: free will.

In Milton's time there was considerable Protestant theological debate centring on the works of John Calvin[9] and his concept of uncondi-tional election, an idea which came to mean to many Protestants that their souls had, or had not, been chosen by God for salvation, regard-less of their worldly endeavours or behaviour. It is easy to see how this notion creates all sorts of difficulties when brought into contact with the conventional Christian notion of free will, that our moral choices and the impacts we have on our fellow man are our own. As we will see again and again in this study of *Paradise Lost*, Milton is a firm believer in free will. He makes it a central tenet of his theodicy.

In purely philosophical terms, you might object to this account of Satan's actions here on the grounds that, as God is omnipotent, Satan can only ever be his instrument and whatever choices he appears to make here are not choices at all. Almost as though he has anticipated this objection, Milton introduces it himself by having Satan confirm the legitimacy of his decision even in circumstances where God's will might turn their evil to good ends:

> If then his providence
> Out of our evil seek to bring forth good,
> Our labour must be to pervert that end
> And out of good still to find means of evil; (162–5)

Milton appears determined to assert Satan's own determination and capacity to do evil, in effect, to dramatise this free will.

When Satan lifts himself off the burning lake to alight on what he describes as a 'dreary plain, forlorn and wild' (180), Milton lets his imagination itself take flight and, mingling classical mythology with vivid physical description, produces a richly baroque picture for us to enjoy and ponder. If we stop for a moment and think about the questions Milton must himself have faced, having decided to plunge into this description of Satan as a physical creature, a being we can visualise, what might strike us is how reserved he actually is. Satan is, after all, the personification of evil. But before he launches into the lengthy and much quoted simile beginning at line 200, in which Satan is compared to a whale against which an unsuspecting mariner anchors 'some small night-foundered skiff' (204), Satan is compared to Briarios and Typhon, classical mythological figures linked mainly by their immense strength and size, but also because they challenged Jove or Zeus and, in so doing, warred with heaven. Of all the possible features Milton could have chosen to describe in characterising Satan, he opts for size and, by implication, strength.

Similes of this complexity and length are common in *Paradise Lost* and are often so complicated, intricate and lengthy that critics themselves are often encouraged to write at undue length about them. Rather than fall into that trap, what I am most interested in introducing here is the idea of you taking the time and trouble to re-read and consider these similes almost as little cameos of artistry sitting inside the complete work. Some are more successful than others, but they always reward the pensive student and at their best, like this one, are essential stylistic and aesthetic features of the epic form. It is also valuable because it gives us a good opportunity to practise analysing Milton's elastic sentence structure. It is, for example, quite difficult to read this Leviathan section of the simile coherently. Try it:

> or that sea beast
> Leviathan, which God of all his works
> Created hugest that swim the ocean stream:
> Him haply slumbering on the Norway foam
> The pilot of some small night-foundered skiff,
> Deemed some island, oft, as seamen tell,
> With fixèd anchor in his scaly rind
> Moors by his side under the lee, while night
> Invests the sea, and wishèd morn delays: (200–8)

The crux, I would argue, focuses on the inconsistent use of the past tense for 'deemed', where we ought to expect 'deems', in agreement with the tense used for 'slumbering', 'moors', 'invests' and 'delays'. But Milton has dreamed up a complex image, shifting chronologically from Satan rising off the hellish waves before the Earth was even formed, through classical mythology to biblical narrative and finally contemporary maritime myth (a seventeenth-century equivalent of our urban myth). Adding to this difficulty is the immense distance between us and seventeenth-century science, informed by Darwin, which renders the image of a whale mistaken for an island to be almost ludicrous. All that before we even try to imagine the poor creature's 'scaly rind' (206).

However, look what happens if we read and consider the simile (192–208) with its first comparison (Satan with the Titans of classical mythology) intact. By connecting the phrase 'as huge/As whom' (196–7) with 'or that sea beast' (200) we can isolate the separate parts of the simile and expose its determining structure. Suddenly, the Leviathan and the unfortunate sailor anchored to his great bulk can be understood as separate, but coherent, parts of this complex simile which flow logically on from the description of Satan as a massive creature. The hard lesson to be learned here is perhaps that reading Milton not only demands a great deal of concentration, but he is the kind of artist who writes in expectation that he will get complete engagement and commitment from his reader.

To be fair to Milton, he does show signs of being aware that this stylistic trait can lead the reader astray and picks up, pretty much where he left off, with the phrase 'So stretched out huge in length the arch-fiend lay' (209). The lengthy, drawn out stress on 'huge', lifted out of the rhythm by the two short stresses of 'in length' that immediately follow, is a fine example of Milton's gift for linking sound to meaning. However, yet another lengthy, dense section follows, and we should note that after seventeen lines we are still in the midst of a single sentence that has another twelve lines to run.

Though lengthy and dense, these additional lines contain some of the most crucial concepts within the entire epic and can provide the perceptive student with a rich source of information to exploit. Firstly, Milton makes it clear that it is only with God's permission that Satan is able to escape the burning lake and the chains that bound him to it:

> but that the will
> And high permission of all-ruling heaven
> Left him at large to his dark designs, (211–13)

Why? Once defeated and imprisoned, why on earth would God release Satan to bring evil into the world? This is a question that goes to the heart of the poem's theological aim and which is immediately followed with a clear and unambiguous answer. God releases Satan, Milton suggests, because in doing so he creates the circumstance in which Adam and Eve will be tested *and* will fail, because by doing so they allow God to show his 'infinite goodness, grace and mercy' (218). And there is a quite terrifying irony to this which is easily overlooked by the casual reader. Milton states that no matter what evil Satan may loose on or cause to others, ultimately the effect is to 'Heap on himself damnation' (215) and to witness again and again, for all eternity, God's love for his creation man. Damnation is, quintessentially, the absence of God and God's love.

One of the most febrile discussions you will encounter from critics of *Paradise Lost* is that relating to the nature and behaviour of Milton's God. If you now go back over these last few lines and concentrate solely on the diction Milton uses, you may notice that there is a very Old Testament tone to 'the will/And high permission of all-ruling heaven' (211–12). Words like 'Heap' (215), 'enraged' (216), 'wrath' and 'vengeance' (220) all contribute to this picture of an anthropomorphic, vengeful tyrant. Modern sensibilities are often deeply offended or repelled by what they regard as his overt cruelty, something they find difficult to reconcile with his 'infinite goodness' (218). But it is worth reminding ourselves of the era in which Milton lived and wrote. Civil war had almost ruined a proud, confident nation state just beginning to find its own intellectual feet in post-Renaissance Europe. Yet at the same time witchcraft was an unquestioned reality that led many unfortunate souls to cruel and merciless deaths, and the plague still periodically cut down tens of thousands of healthy people with little warning, no scientific explanation and even less no apparent justice. In this kind of dangerous cultural climate, Milton's angry, Old Testament tyrant might not seem so difficult to understand.

Better to Reign in Hell?

In parallel to critical debate about the nature and behaviour of Milton's God, which you will undoubtedly come across in your critical reading, an even more excited and intense historical debate has centred on the reader's response to Satan. Milton, like Shakespeare, is such a rewarding and intellectually stimulating poet that a number of academics have made him their life's work and built substantial reputations on their analysis of his poetry, life, and political and religious significance.[10] For some, this has led to a fascination with, and critical focus on, Satan, and in the case of Neil Forsyth's[11] provocatively titled, *The Satanic Epic*, even a complete work. But this book assumes readers who are relatively new to Milton and to *Paradise Lost*, so you need to build for yourself an informed view of Satan based on what he says and does, before you can get the most out of that wider critical controversy. To help achieve this goal, read Satan's imperious speech (242–70) and, as you do so, concentrate on the rhythm of the verse as well as the sense.

This guide intends to show you practically how to begin to unravel and sometimes even begin to enjoy Milton's ornate verse. The first thing you may notice reading this speech by Satan is how unusually heavily punctuated it is and how many sentences there are in such a short space. The passage also contains a number of distinct caesuras – clear breaks in the middle of the poetic line that disrupt the flow of the verse for emphasis or poetic effect. If we take the first of these, in line 245, and ask the questions 'Why is it here?' and 'What is its effect?' we can use it as a model to analyse other such instances when we come across them. The crisply staccato phrase 'Be it so' (245) that follows the caesura, before the flow of meaning is picked up by the more languid sounding 'since', adds to the broken effect considerably. Above all else, I would suggest that Milton uses the technique here to signal Satan's decisive bravado, although there is also perhaps a bitterness or even anger dependent on the contrast Satan creates between the 'mournful gloom' (244) and the 'celestial light' (245) before he accepts the loss of the latter after the caesura.

You can also profit by asking yourself what is Satan really doing here? The rest of the fallen angels are still bound on the burning lake, as is clear from lines 264–6, and Beëlzebub is the only audience for this speech. Having discovered the nature of their new hellish domain, understood their plight and found a space to contemplate it, Satan is predicting his future eternal struggle with God, but at the same time clearly seeking to re-establish his own power and authority. He constructs a step-by-step, rational argument for Beëlzebub that begins by accepting God's greater physical strength, 'whom . . . force hath made supreme' (248) but betrays his quintessentially sinful nature through his almost imperceptible claim that God's victory has been over 'his equals' (249). That claim to equity with his maker, his astonishing presumption that mere force distinguishes God from him, goes right to the heart of Satan's character, the pride that is conventionally his downfall. This is a good example of how important it is to be able to think outside of the cultural norms we might find ourselves tempted to impose on poetry written for a different age, and for dramatically different sensibilities. Much of contemporary political life and social exchange is underpinned by a faith in the value of equity that is almost too taboo to question. Milton's England was far less interested in equity of any kind.

The next step in his carefully constructed argument sees him bid goodbye to heaven forever, 'Farewell happy fields/Where joy forever dwells' (249–50), and then apparently to embrace fully his new lodging with something akin to relish, 'hail horrors, hail/Infernal world' (250–1). Satan seems to be trying to convince himself as much as Beëlzebub that this catastrophic change of fortune has its good side as he lays claim to 'profoundest hell' (251) as its 'new possessor' (252). Another caesura at this point introduces the next step. And to those readers, or indeed listeners, who have the ability to respond to the verse in the same, intimate and often emotional way most people are more familiar with through their experience of fiction, this moment might provoke anything from a wry smile to a pause for sincere reflection. Satan here asserts something superficially insignificant. He tells Beëlzebub that his mind remains unchanged, 'one who brings/A mind not to be changed by place or time' (252–3). And in any other circumstance this might not merit much attention, but it is a statement of immense importance if we are to build our understanding of his character and, through that, of Milton's entire theodicean project, because Satan's next logical step is really quite brilliant:

> The mind is its own place, and in itself
> Can make a heaven of hell, a hell of heaven. (254–5)

That Milton uses rhythm as well as syntax to separate this statement out so vividly from the surrounding verse may well indicate how important a statement of belief it was for him. For students well informed about Christian art and theology it should release a whole flood of questions about responsibility, guilt, conscience and ultimately free will. The existence and nature of free will, and particularly its relationship with predestination, in many ways formed one of the very central theological battlegrounds between Catholicism and Protestantism. A wealth of scholarship has gone into trying to describe Milton's own religious views in terms of historical, and especially seventeenth-century theological, debate, and theologians such as Jacobus Arminius,[12] John Calvin and Hugo Grotius[13] are all studied and cited in support of individual critical standpoints. But although a serious and skilled student can, and indeed should, entertain that level of detailed research, it is an intellectual exercise that can take you a long way away from the poetry itself, and I would urge readers to bring their own spiritual and cultural experience to bear on these questions in the first instance.

To emphasise his tremendously powerful idea, that somehow our minds free us from any relationship with God, Satan elaborates a little for Beëlzebub, asserting that geography is irrelevant when what really matters is that he remains unchanged in essence, and only less than God in the single characteristic of power. Once again there is something almost amusingly human about Satan's argument, a petulance bordering on the childish in the way he appears incapable of accepting defeat *gracefully*. Having embraced hell as his own and then denied its ability to influence or affect him, through appealing to the concept of free will Satan takes another astounding leap of the imagination and decides that, in hell, they are in fact free. 'Here at least/We shall be free' (258–9) More persuasively perhaps, he justifies this to some extent by stating that hell has not been created by God for his own entertainment or pleasure and therefore he 'will not drive us hence' (260).

By a series of ingenious dialectic steps, Satan has turned an utterly calamitous situation into one replete with advantage and gain which concludes with this infamously egotistical claim:

> Here we may reign secure, and in my choice
> To reign is worth ambition though in hell:
> Better to reign in hell, than serve in heaven. (261–3)

Given Milton was one of the most eloquent public voices, whose personal and ideological attacks led ultimately to the death on the scaffold in 1649 of King Charles I, we ought to sit up and listen, at least a little, when he employs the royal 'we' as he makes Satan do here. Although Satan's 'we' may appear to be generously inclusive, it is almost immediately negated by his use of the first person 'in **my** choice', and is in fact a smokescreen for his own utterly selfish, ambitious ends. The word 'reign' itself implies sole exercise of power, and from the pen nib of an unrepentant regicide this reverberates uncomfortably. The next logical question is to ask ourselves how we respond to Satan's final sententious remark, 'Better to reign in hell, than serve in heaven'. Our answer is very likely to guide much of the way we respond to Satan as we read on.

The drama of the next few lines, in which Satan appears suddenly to recall that his entire army happens to be lying forgotten and chained to the burning lake, is perhaps as close as one will ever get to comedy in Milton's epic. The moment of forgetfulness, or more precisely recall, is a conventional one in drama and can vary in effect from the downright funny or melodramatic to the genuinely suspenseful and even pathetic. The most easily referenced examples you are likely to have encountered as a student of English literature may have come from Shakespeare: the poignant way in which, after the intense joy of reconciliation, Olivia suddenly remembers with sadness Malvolio's reported distraction in *Twelfth Night*,[14] or the agonising wait the audience has at the close of *King Lear* until Albany recalls that Lear and Cordelia had been captured and imprisoned by Edmund, 'Great thing of us forgot',[15] illustrate the emotional scope the technique can cover. Though this is verse and not drama, the parallel holds and some of us may be tempted to smile at Satan's apparent short sightedness. But if we analyse the language he uses closely, we may see other possibilities.

Satan is still talking to Beëlzebub and makes the connection between the argument he has just cleverly concluded and his fallen 'friends' absolutely unambiguous through this phrase, 'But wherefore let we then' (264). Implying that somehow there may be something in his previous words to benefit his army. This idea is enhanced in the next three lines where not only is the fallen host described as 'associates and copartners' (265) but Satan reprimands himself for not calling them to 'share with us their part' (267). The structure and the diction combine to depict Satan almost slapping his own forehead with frustration at not having remembered earlier to tell them the good news! That the news is not so good is beautifully and bathetically conveyed in the single adjective 'unhappy' to describe their new 'mansion' (268), almost an unconscious slip of the tongue, since Satan follows it immediately with a vacuous call to arms:

> or once more
> With rallied arms to try what may be yet
> Regained in heaven, or what more lost in hell? (268–70)

Faded Glory

When Milton returns our attention to Satan, it is to dwell for a moment on his appearance in front of his followers. The shift of point of view is signalled by a caesura in line 587, but the phrase which, by its positioning and sonority, most arrests us is the 'dread commander:' of line 589. Although his followers are diminished in stature when set against him:

> he above the rest
> In shape and gesture proudly eminent
> Stood like a tower; (589–91)

Whatever admiration they may feel is tinged with the fear conveyed so emphatically in the harsh 'dread'. The blind poet then turns to imagery of light and dark to describe much more than Satan's visual appearance. Satan retains some of his 'original brightness' (592) but Milton puts an intriguing distance between Satan's presence and his physical appearance by using the word 'form' (591) and switching its gender through the use of the personal pronoun 'her' (592). This has the effect of extending the terms of his description to much more than mere looks: it is a way for Milton to capture something of Satan's essence, perhaps even his soul. And that this is the case becomes clearer as he employs two cleverly complementary similes to refine the notion of dimmed splendour, 'the excess/Of glory obscured' (593–4). The first involves the sun; the second, the moon:

> as when the sun new ris'n
> Looks through the horizontal misty air
> Shorn of his beams, (594–6)

It is a poignantly beautiful, natural image, and one which may perhaps have been more accessible to readers of Milton's era than our own. Most of the readers of this book will have experienced life living in urban communities of one kind or another, and opportunities to observe the natural world in the way that was a regular feature of life for a seventeenth-century Englishman are few and far between. You need something of a vista to experience the type of misty dawn scene Milton alludes to here, and cities are, by their very nature, visual barriers. The hurdle is one worth remembering as you continue to study the poem because, once Milton takes us into Eden, nature is a hugely important source of imagery and symbolism.

The complementary simile follows almost seamlessly through his use of 'or' in the middle of line 596 rather than what we might expect, which is 'or as', the more conventional means to launch a simile. The moon as a poetic image is replete with connotations, especially from classical literature, but Milton doesn't choose the moon itself, or even moonlight, to convey Satan's diminished state. He opts for something more unusual, potent and provocative by continuing his use of sunlight:

> or from behind the moon
> In dim eclipse disastrous twilight sheds
> On half the nations, and with fear of change
> Perplexes monarchs. Darkened so, yet shone
> Above them all the archangel: (596–600)

This time it is the strange darkness produced by a total eclipse of the sun which Milton exploits. In classical literature it is of course an ominous indication of calamity, social disruption or war. If we pause to remind ourselves that this is a simile, and what it describes is Satan's faded glory, then there is something maimed as well as ominous about Satan, something aberrational and even unnatural. These are useful points to deploy in any discussion about Satan as romantic hero.

Sometimes it is hard to keep up with Milton's imagination, and from the metaphysical he now plummets to the mundane, sketching for us the marks on Satan's face: the 'deep scars of thunder' (601) and the 'faded cheek' (602). Although he maintains an epic balance by countering these wounds or signs of weakness with:

> but under brows
> Of dauntless courage, and considerate pride
> Waiting revenge: (602–4)

What happens next, before Satan begins to address the fallen army, you may find confusing or surprising, or indeed both. At the sight of this mass of 'millions of spirits' (609) 'condemned/Forever now to have their lot in pain' (607–8) Satan appears to feel something akin to guilt, 'signs of remorse and passion' (605). Since he has so far appeared utterly implacable in his hatred of God and of goodness, this empathy might strike us as odd or insincere. Before you decide either way, it is important to grasp the source of this apparent empathy. Satan observes this mass of damned souls and realises that they have only merited damnation for following him:

> Millions of spirits for his fault amerced
> Of heaven, and from eternal splendours flung
> For his revolt, (609–11)

Milton repeats the idea in the short space of these three lines, emphasising the point and laying blame precisely at Satan's door. When Satan travels out of hell and encounters Sin and Death, Milton's views on the precise nature of Satan's fault are given far more space and poetic energy. This hiatus allows Milton to shift Satan's point of view a little further and produces the comparison of the fallen angels with 'forest oaks, or mountain pines' (613) that have been struck by lightning yet still stand on the 'blasted heath' (615). These images are doing much the same job as the sunlight similes we have already looked at that helped us to understand Satan's diminished stature. But if you ask yourself how they differ, you will probably notice that, instead of light and dark, Milton has chosen quite different contrasts to describe the reduced state of Satan's followers. You may even feel that the comparison is one drawn by Satan himself and not by the narrator because it works so much in Satan's favour. Whatever your own response may be here, Milton does seem to want us to perceive a link between Satan's 'remorse' and the faded glory of his 'faithful' (611) followers.

A caesura in line 615 marks his attempt to speak, at which the entire army folds around him as though in close attendance, eagerly awaiting his speech, 'attention held them mute' (618). Then, perhaps in mockery of the three days Christ took to rise from the dead, or the three times St Peter denied knowing Christ on the eve of the Crucifixion, Satan tries three times to speak and has to fight back the tears. Besides considering the literary precedents for this – such as the king of Persia, Xerxes, crying when he considered the imminent death of the vast army he had arrayed against the Greeks – you might ask yourself the key question: how does Milton want us to view these tears?

A New Type of War

Once he has fought back the tears, Satan addresses the fallen host in a lengthy single speech, lines 623–62. Like many talented orators, Satan opens with a little flattery, 'O powers/Matchless, but with the almighty'

(622–3), and is very quick to praise his companions for all their recent efforts on his behalf, 'that strife/Was not inglorious' (623–4), possibly because, given the reality of their current status, it would be dangerous in the extreme not to do so. If we consider the position Satan faces as leader of, not just a defeated, but an eternally damned army, it is, to say the least, an unenviable, and even paradoxical, situation. The truth is that his leadership has brought them to this 'dire' (624) state, a word Satan himself repeats. For Milton to carry out his great theodical project, he must investigate and expose for us not just how Satan acts, but how he thinks. Exploring and analysing the very nature of Satan's mind is one of the key means through which Milton attempts to explain to us how man stands in relationship to God and to salvation. Satan acknowledges defeat, 'As this place testifies, and this dire change/Hateful to utter' (625–6), but, crucially, does not *accept* it.

His first justification for not accepting defeat continues the flattery but individual readers may have very different responses to it:

> but what power of mind
> Foreseeing or presaging, from the depth
> Of knowledge past or present, could have feared,
> How such united force of gods, how such
> As stood like these, could ever know repulse? (626–30)

On one level you may find it an almost childish piece of rhetorical reasoning; 'who could have possibly known?' Satan appears to be saying. At another level you may privilege the flattery above the argument and view these words as skilfully manipulative, even Machiavellian, simultaneously illustrating the quickness of mind and presence that has made him the leader of such 'myriads of immortal spirits' (622). The repetition of the phrase 'how such' and especially the eulogistic 'As stood like these' (610) undoubtedly contribute to the effect this speech has on his fellow angels, since when he finishes they unsheath their swords as one and clash them in true epic style against their shields, in defiance of God (663–9). But it is precisely the difference between how they react, and how we as readers react, that constitutes the debating platform upon which Milton is able to work out his argument. How we respond to Satan goes a long way to determining how we react to Milton's own faith and to his epic attempt to influence our own beliefs.

We can pursue this further by analysing the next step in Satan's speech. Continuing his technique of using rhetorical questions (for who among his listeners would have denied the praise he has heaped on them?), Satan poses quite a remarkably bold question, considering the current state of affairs:

> For who can yet believe, though after loss,
> That all these puissant legions, whose exile
> Hath emptied heaven, shall fail to re-ascend
> Self-raised, and repossess their native seat? (631–4)

It is quite a dramatic leap to move from 'no one could have foreseen' to 'who can doubt?'. Alert students will also notice that in his efforts to flatter the angels he adds hyperbole to his rhetorical armoury by stating that their defeat 'Hath emptied heaven' (633). The truth is quite different as Raphael tells Adam in Book 5, namely that Satan in fact 'Drew after him the third part of heaven's host' (710). But although it might seem so at first sight, this is not yet a crude declaration of renewed war. Satan has some way to go before he reaches that point. Ironically, he calls on 'all the host of heaven' (635) to witness the truth of what he asserts and reminds them all of his own courage by suggesting loss of hope will not be because of 'danger shunned/By me' (636–7), though implying it might be as a result of 'counsels different' (636). In effect, Satan is neutralising his critics before they speak.

In the next few lines Satan paints a picture of God as King of Heaven, and knowing as we do Milton's antipathy for the monarchy, it may seem a counter productive image. But Milton allows the image to say more about its maker than it does about its object, since God is 'upheld by old repute/Consent or custom' (639–40), not loved or worshipped in the way Adam and Raphael are later to relate, and Satan even implies cunning or cowardice on God's behalf through this revealing phrase, 'but still his strength concealed,/Which tempted our attempt, and wrought our fall' (641–2). There is even a richly ironic use of the regal third person since it was Satan who was tempted, and Satan who tempted others to join '*our* attempt' and participate in '*our* fall'. (Only a few lines earlier Satan was using 'me'.) Appreciating God's power fully now, 'Henceforth his might we know' (643) means they can avoid provoking him or being provoked to renewed fighting. Satan has better advice. His recommendation is that they continue the conflict covertly, 'To work in close deign, by fraud or guile' (645) with the aim of achieving 'What force effected not' (647). It is at this climactic point in the argument he has been developing that Satan makes a brilliantly sententious remark, which although understated is nonetheless pregnant with menace. By following his advice, Satan asserts, they will eventually triumph and

God will learn 'who overcomes/By force, hath overcome but half his foe' (648–9).

In pursuit of this new guerrilla war, Satan introduces the Earth as battleground for the first time by mentioning a rumour, 'a fame in heaven' (651), that not only was God intending to create a new world, but to populate it with a race to rival their own:

> A generation, whom his choice regard
> Should favour equal to the sons of heaven. (653–4)

It was noted earlier that Milton cannot reasonably fulfil his grand aim without articulating for us the mind of Satan. That mind is very clearly at work in the envy that gives rise to this observation. Why else would Satan raise the question of equality if not because it rankles? It is why he chooses Eden as his first goal, even if only to spy, that he believes it worth the effort, 'Thither, if but to pry, shall be perhaps/Our first eruption' (655–6). But with consummate rhetorical skill, he takes that slight word 'Thither' as his cue to begin the conclusion of this epic address. In utter denial of the hellish reality of their current abode, or of the vast gulf through which they have fallen nine days and nights from heaven, Satan declares that nothing can contain them and adds hyperbole to the flattery:

> For this infernal pit shall never hold
> Celestial spirits in bondage, nor the abyss
> Long under darkness cover. (657–9)

And although he pays lip service to the idea of discussing this with his commanders, 'But these thoughts/Full counsel must mature' (659–60), he immediately dismisses any possibility of dispute or disagreement with another rhetorical question that none but the most foolhardy lieutenant would dare answer, 'For who can think submission?' (661). By this stage Satan knows he has won back his audience and he can safely declare, 'War then, war/Open or understood must be resolved' (661–2), which is the signal for his followers to burst into noisy approval, lighting up hell with the fire of their swords and clashing metal against metal in true Homeric fashion.

Pandaemonium

Satan's army responds to his redeclaration of war with admirable energy and enthusiasm considering their recent combat experience. So many blazing swords are unsheathed they 'Far round illumined hell' (666) and the noise created by the mass of those swords clashing against so many shields, Milton calls with certainty the 'din of war' (668). Words like 'raged' (666), 'fierce' (667) and 'hurling defiance' (669) contribute to the epic tone, echoing not only the vast scale of the army fielded against Troy in Homer's *Iliad*, but the combined sense of epic enterprise and overt courage of individual combatants to be found in all of the poem's epic models.[16] And if we miss or underestimate the violence of the devils' reaction, we risk underestimating the threat they present to God's plan for earth and for man, and ultimately for our own immortal souls. It is when Satan determines on a course of eternal opposition and enmity with God that humanity becomes the innocent means to that end. Milton signals the power of this moment syntactically by making it a single, clearly distinguishable sentence (663–9) sitting between Satan's oratorical speech and the frenzied activity that goes into the creation of a palatial parody of heaven, Pandaemonium, by the devils.

The conventionally placid and introductory phrase, 'There stood a hill' (670), leads us into the final section of Book 1, a section of the poem which some students may find morally puzzling. Even a cursory appreciation of baroque architecture, without any knowledge of terminology, is probably enough for a reader to engage imaginatively with the intricate and architecturally detailed images of Pandaemonium Milton produces; and although a modern sensibility may not respond with awe at the ornate richness of what is essentially a baroque aesthetic, it does still tend to value the skill and art which has gone into its construction. Put more simply, Milton presents us with the paradox of creative devils.

The first thing to note is that the 'hill not far whose grisly top' (670) is the source of the devils' building materials is in every sense an ugly and disturbing place. It 'Belched fire' (671) and the sibilant alliteration of 'Shone with a glossy scurf' (671) seem apt for devils even before we witness Satan adopt the serpent as a disguise in Eden, or the entire host of fallen angels transformed into snakes in Book 10 (504–47). The second thing is that the 'numerous brigade' (675) that speeds to the site, and like a well disciplined band of sappers begins to dig furiously in search of the 'metallic ore' (673) they expect to find inside the hill, is led by a named individual, Mammon. Even by Milton's time the name was synonymous with wealth or luxury, and it is one of the few biblical references most likely to be instantly accessible to contemporary students. Milton chooses to characterise him through a very significant use of antithesis, calling him 'the least erected spirit that fell/From heaven' (679–80), since his attention was always drawn down towards 'The riches of heaven's pavements, trodden gold' (682). The antithesis works on the most superficial level through opposing Mammon's desire to look down or up, to be upright or stooped. But this simple opposition is emblematic of a far more sophisticated one where the desire for material riches is set against the desire to worship God. Mammon had rather devote himself to the physical material of which heaven is made than seek for a better understanding of God 'In vision beatific' (684), the joyful sight of God which was the first step a saint could take on the road to canonisation. Mammon leads the devilish sappers, just as according to Milton he led mankind to exploit the mineral wealth of the Earth, and by doing so creates the conditions for wealth and luxury to corrupt mankind further:

> by him first
> Men also, and by his suggestion taught,
> Ransacked the centre, and with impious hands
> Rifled the bowels of their mother earth
> For treasures better hid. (684–8)

The image of mankind violating the maternal figure of mother earth is a particularly cruel one, but one in keeping with Milton's whole treatment of the physical planet here, and one many modern readers, perplexed by the politics of climate change, will respond very easily to. A little earlier we are told that the very masculine hill attacked by the devils' eager spadework hides the metallic ore in 'his womb' (673). This apparent confusion of gender may be less awkward when placed in the context of classical literature in which fertility is not necessarily a uniquely female attribute. The sense of violation is continued in the image of 'ribs of gold' (690) before Milton seems unable to resist a characteristically puritanical dig himself at mankind's proverbial love of material wealth by interjecting a sententious aside (690–2) which echoes the proverbial (though originally biblical, *Timothy* 6:10) view of the love of money as the root of all evil.

Milton then adds two more working parties of devils to that which has ripped open the earth, and whose combined skill and energy produces 'in an hour' (697) a construction to belittle the most magnificent monuments armies of mortal men have been able to produce. It is difficult not to admire a poetic imagination which pictures the devils exploiting the very substance of their suffering, fire, to create a kind of liquid ore before channelling it into 'boiling cells' (706) which, instead of cooling, rises miraculously to the accompaniment of music to form the palatial structure which Milton is soon to christen Pandaemonium, and in so doing gift to the English language a word which subsequent generations have delighted in employing, ironically to describe a state of chaos or confusion, whereas one could hardly imagine a more disciplined, purposeful crew than Milton's demonic engineers.

The palace rises from the earth to the accompaniment of music, 'dulcet symphonies and voices sweet' (712) and this apparently slight detail has some interesting connections for the thoughtful student to pursue. If we reflect on the Renaissance habit of linking music and architecture in terms of proportions and design, Milton appears to be investing Pandaemonium with some highly admirable qualities. If you now read the remaining lines describing the palace itself, up to line 730, you can ask yourself the provocative question, how do I respond to this imaginary building? Rather than pre-empt your answer, I will simply point here to just a few of the words and phrases worth dwelling on and relating to each other, and to what you already know about the Puritan mind and aesthetic. The 'temple' (713) has 'Doric pillars' (714), a 'golden architrave' (715) and roof of 'fretted gold' (715), which neither Babylon nor ancient Memphis (Alcairo) could compare in 'wealth and luxury' (722), and its 'ample spaces' (725) are lit with 'starry lamps' and 'blazing cressets' (728) almost as brilliantly as the heavens themselves, 'As from a sky' (730).

However you answer this question, the devils themselves are hugely impressed 'and the work some praise/And some the architect' (731–2), of whom the latter Milton names as 'Mulciber' (740), the Latinate version of the Greek God Hephaistos whose mythical role combined the use of fire with metalworking and the physical skills relating to the making of artefacts. Milton reminds us that it was he who had built 'many a towered structured high' (733) in heaven itself, before one of the most famous of all classical allusions in *Paradise Lost*, the expulsion of Hephaistos from Heaven by Zeus. Satan then summons a council which begins with the vast numbers of devils all besieging their new 'high capital' (756), which starts a lengthy sequence of images relating to scale and number that all add to our growing sense of the threat Satan and his followers present. The precise nature of that threat has not yet been articulated, but by juxtaposing the vast numbers against the vast space, and nonetheless creating a sense of overcrowding, Milton sets humanity clearly in the shadow of these immense beings:

> they anon
> With hundreds and with thousands trooping came
> Attended: all accéss was thronged, the gates
> And porches wide, but chief the spacious hall (759–62)

This sense of immense scale then takes a surprising turn as Milton uses the verb 'swarmed' (767) to introduce a complex and even difficult image, comparing the devils to bees. Your own edition of the poem will no doubt point you towards some of the least accessible connotations, such as the popular use of bees as images for the clergy which Milton's readers would have readily appreciated, or the notion of the hive as a highly organised, hierarchical community. However, I would also like you to consider the effect of shifting so suddenly from images of great scale and size, spatially and numerically, to an image of such an intensely local, even parochial focus. How do we react to this subtle antithesis? Milton's bees are not swarming in anger:

> they among fresh dews and flowers
> Fly to and fro, or on the smoothed plank,
> The suburb of their straw-built citadel,
> New rubbed with balm, expatiate and confer
> Their state affairs. (771–5)

The witty oxymoron, 'straw-built citadel', need not rely on little pigs to make its point, but it does somehow render the devils less threatening, and this poetic effect is abruptly and startlingly energised as Milton exploits the ability of angels to metamorphose, in a poetic instant, his Titanic devils into dwarves (775–80).

The dwarfish devils are then compared to pygmies and fairies in turn, each of these similes carrying far more relevance than the most immediate one of size. For Milton's readers, pygmies were just as elusively intangible as fairies, something clearly conveyed by his locating them somewhere 'Beyond the Indian mount' (781). But in his overtly conscious reference to Shakespeare's A Midsummer's Night Dream,[17] where Oberon's 'moonlight revels' become 'midnight revels' (782), we might gain a glimpse of his age's own views on such unscientific phenomena. Milton's 'belated peasant sees,/Or dreams he sees' (783–4) these moonlit, fairy revels, yet his reaction eloquently captures the consequent ambiguity: 'At once with joy and fear his heart rebounds' (788). It is as though his world view has not taught him which is the appropriate reaction, and consequently both exercise equal effect.

As Book 1 draws to a dramatic close, the most powerful devils preparing for their conclave and retaining their immense stature while the rest are diminished to a mob, Milton's use of 'infernal court' (791) reminds us of his own political views and anticipates the quality and politics of the debate we will soon witness in company with the mass of ordinary devilry.

Exercises

Lines 128–55. If, like a military commander facing overwhelming odds and imminent defeat, Satan expected to hear his first lieutenant, Beëlzebub, offer unqualified and enthusiastic support, joining in his rallying cry, he is immediately disappointed. Read Beëlzebub's reply, and by picking out the different stages of his response, assess to what extent he remains loyal to Satan.

Lines 271–587. Beëlzebub's brief speech here echoes his master's own inflated image of himself, flattering him and reassuring him that the fallen army will rush to his side as in former times and battles. But it never pretends to form part of a discursive conversation and is quickly followed by Milton's famous description of Satan moving across the burning lake to the shore, in which both classical and biblical imagery abound. This is a rich section of the poem for you to study independently in terms of extended simile, as Milton employs several that you may find challenging even just to isolate as similes, and which are understandably very famous. Ask yourself whether there are any common qualities these similes tend to exhibit and, if so, what they contribute to your impression of the events you are witnessing.

2
Epic Voyage

Summary

Satan opens the consultation in Pandaemonium with words of
encouragement and immense confidence, as though the creation of this
new palatial structure is evidence of all he previously said of their continuing resistance. Moloch, the most ferocious of Satan's deputies, is the
first to enter the 'debate' (42) and calls for open defiance and continued
war with God, preferring to risk God's greater anger and consequently
their possible extinction, in an attempt to overthrow the Almighty once
more, rather than their continued suffering. Action of such an aggressive
nature he feels is at least a form of 'revenge' (105). Next to speak is Belial,
in many ways Moloch's corollary, since all his fine appearance and manner hides nothing but vice and deviousness. He questions Moloch's logic
and the false choice he sets up between revenge and extinction. Belial
does not believe God will ever destroy them since he has saved them to
punish them eternally but he does believe that, over time, their suffer-
ings might lesson and so counsels against war fought either openly or
covertly, preferring instead to bide his time and do nothing.

After Belial, it is Mammon who contributes to the discussion by arguing that the war has not in fact been with an omnipotent God, but
between fate and chance. Mammon imagines a situation where God has
granted them his 'grace' (238) only to reject it on the grounds that such
a hypocritical existence would be impossible. Having already improved
their lot through their own energies, his preference is, like Belial, to bide
their time inactively, and hope for an amelioration of their suffering.
Mammon's words meet with mass approval from listeners who have not
long been free from the pains of battle and have no appetite for more
suffering. Beëlzebub speaks next, and since his authority is second only

to Satan's, he gains immediate respect and quiet. In his view, the war has never ended, and they delude themselves to think hell is some kind of safe, new realm, since God has determined to punish them eternally. Acting as the mouthpiece for Satan, Beëlzebub then argues that there is a better way to fight than renewed battle, and a better, safer battlefield. Reminding them of God's plan to create a new world and a new race of godlike creatures, that he will favour highly, Beëlzebub argues that they should seek to learn more about the new world and new race in order to corrupt and ultimately destroy them since by doing so they will be gaining some kind of revenge and satisfaction.

Beëlzebub's words win the debate and all vote in support of his plan before he continues his speech by asking who will take on the task of journeying to this new world to discover how they might effect their plan to corrupt and destroy its inhabitants in pursuit of their enmity against God. When none volunteer, through fear and cowardice, Satan stands triumphantly to claim the role he has engineered via Beëlzebub. He seizes the opportunity to reinforce his superiority and instructs his followers to make the best of their new abode while he risks all in a terrifyingly risky journey he says he undertakes selflessly, on their behalf. Roaring approval, the legions then disband and explore the hellish landscape while Satan flies to hell's gate where he is confronted by his own incestuous children, the grotesque figures of Sin and Death. When Satan and Death seem intent on conflict, Sin intervenes and Satan is made to recognise his offspring before he persuades Sin to unlock the gates of hell, opening the way for them all to reach earth. Satan hurls himself into the vast space between heaven and hell, Sin and Death following on, building a permanent causeway behind him.

The Outcome of the Great Consultation

A number of devils figure in the great consultation which ultimately reaches the conclusion Satan had already intended for it. Moloch, Belial, Mammon and Beëlzebub are all given impressive set piece arguments to deliver which relate directly to their character and roles within Milton's demonology, but once they have spoken, it is Satan who outshines them all in rhetorical skill and cunning. At line 430 he continues his flattering approach to those he considers his inferiors, making sure he doesn't chide or reprimand any of his followers for their apparent silence and cowardice when Beëlzebub asked for a volunteer. He makes no grammatical distinction between himself and his followers, 'With reason hath deep silence and demur/Seized us' (431–2), directing all their minds more persuasively towards the reasons for their stasis: 'Our prison strong, this huge convex of fire' (434) and the 'gates of burning adamant' (436) which 'prohibit all egress' (437). It is not too difficult to discern the rhetorical tactic he is using here. Also stressing the severity of their incarceration and the magnitude of the prison walls God has created to contain them allows him to stress his own courage and superiority in attempting to breach them. But before we examine how he refines this rhetorical figure further, there is one statement he makes which will repay some further probing: 'long is the way/And hard, that out of hell leads up to light' (432–3). If you ask yourself the question, how would a Christian contemporary of Milton's respond to this apparently factual statement?, you should find yourself wondering at what level it is meant to operate. Escape from hell is nonsense to the practising Christian, yet the descriptive terms Satan uses suggest a difficult ascent for sure, but hardly one that is theologically insurmountable. Are we to read this as a sign of Satan's astounding arrogance or is Milton seeking only to describe the various components of a prelapsarian universe in formulating his own theodicy? Those questions can safely be held unresolved while we get further into the poem and Satan refines his thinking for the benefit of his troops.

Between lines 438 and 444 Satan outlines what he perceives as the dangers to be faced by anyone attempting to escape from hell; and besides the rather easy way to express 'unknown dangers' (444) to be found in an 'unknown region' (443) he is perhaps most effectively intimidating when he describes 'the void profound/Of unessential night' (436–9) that threatens 'utter loss of being' (440), since this admission of vulnerability is strikingly at odds with his faith in immortality. Like many a braggart to come after him, Satan has given himself something of a big build up because what he is really interested in is in preferring himself above all others and advancing his plan to continue his war with God. This overtly political, hierarchical objective becomes clear if we examine the next complete sentence, lines 445–50, and list some of the key terms he employs. He speaks of his 'throne' (445) and his 'imperial sovereignty' (446), the language of absolute monarchy, but mingles this with the gratingly democratic phrase, 'judged of public moment' (448), as though to remind his listeners of the mandate he has recently won from them.

Satan's next, quite obviously rhetorical question, is so convoluted it is almost impenetrable, playing cleverly with the possibilities of 'refuse' (451) as well as a sonorous antithesis he creates between 'hazard' and 'honour'. 'Wherefore do I assume/These royalties' (450–1), he asks, if

I do not simultaneously accept 'as great a share/Of hazard as of honour' (452–3). But he doesn't stop there. The real quality of this deft piece of rhetoric is in the concluding remark, which is surely of great value in any critical discussion of Satan's character. In creating a proportionate link between 'hazard' (danger) and 'honour' (public approbation) he opens the way to assert his immense superiority over his followers. In cruder terms, Satan argues that such immense danger can in fact only be faced by someone of equally immense courage:

> ... and so much to him due
> Of hazard more, as he above the rest
> High honoured sits? (454–6)

before he slams the rhetorical door on any potential opponent with the starkly imperative 'Go therefore mighty powers' (456).

His instructions are plain. Stay at home, do what you can to make hell 'More tolerable' (460) and stay alert for any renewed assault by God. He, meanwhile, will undertake the immensely dangerous journey he has outlined so graphically for them, 'Through all the coats of dark destruction' (464). Why? To find 'Deliverance for us all' (465) and, just in case there is a member of the conclave still unconvinced, Satan's imperial tone reasserts itself: 'this enterprise/None shall partake with me' (465–6).

There are a number of avenues of thought worth pursuing here in discussion or critical commentary. In what sense will Satan *deliver* them? Milton's Catholic or Protestant readers could not fail to connect his choice of verb to the final plea in The Lord's Prayer.[1] How are we meant to respond to his extreme, autocratic manner? These are the kinds of questions that will help you to build up a personal view of Satan and equip you to understand why Milton's anti-hero has stimulated such a wide variety of contrary critical opinion over the years.

At Hell's Gate

In stark contrast to the dramatic realisation of the hellish conditions the 'adventurous bands' (615) discover and experience as they explore the furthest reaches of hell, Satan is free to attempt his escape alone, but his discoveries will be no less dramatic as he sets off on his flight to the gates of hell. Milton's linking God and man, as he does here, 'Meanwhile the adversary of God and man' (629), is worth noting because, as the narrative develops, the relationship between Adam and God becomes more and more significant and central to the reader's experience of the poem. Having taken the decision to continue his war with God by other means, Satan has logically also become mankind's implacable enemy. In a secular age ill at ease with the entire concept of sin, it is all too easy to overlook this danger, but for Milton and his contemporaries the Devil's desire to seduce and corrupt man's soul was a constant threat capable of manifesting itself in every aspect of daily life. Milton's sense of the dramatic is evident in the way he has Satan ranging like some vast hawk across the whole expanse of hell's firmament in his eagerness to escape and wreak havoc on earth. The build-up of alliterative 's' sounds as he 'shaves' and 'soars' (634), that help convey this sense of flight and sweeping movement, is abruptly broken by a trio of single syllable words and guttural sounds, 'Up to the fiery concave' (635), which mimic the abrupt change of direction as he seeks to break through the zenith of his prison.

By now the appearance of the phrase 'As when' (636) should alert you to expect a typically Miltonic simile, although the digression is comparatively brief. In comparing Satan to a far distant fleet of exotic merchant ships, there is scope to explore why he has chosen imagery from commerce, but there is a risk that you lose the highly visual foundation to this simile, through which sea and sky become almost indistinguishable and the reader's eye is cleverly aligned with the narrator's.

The impenetrability of hell's 'thrice threefold' (645) gates is emphasised through their composition: iron, brass and the almost alchemical 'adamantine', which was a word of ancient origin used to describe an unbreakable or very hard rock, including diamond. They are also, paradoxically, surrounded 'impaled' (647) with fire that cannot destroy them, 'Yet unconsumed' (648). A caesura marks the point at which we, like Satan, are made to pay more attention to the figures guarding the impenetrable gates than the gates themselves, and with just cause. In Chapter 1 we discussed the difficulties surrounding the concept of theodicy and the sheer ambition of what Milton attempts. Once again, differences in historical and social perspective can throw a twenty-first-century student new to Milton off track if you are not careful. The entire vast genre of science fiction was unthought of in the seventeenth century, so it easy to fall into the trap of not appreciating just how imaginative is Milton's handling of the two guardians Satan confronts.

The first quality we should note of the first guardian is her quintessentially deceitful nature which is conveyed with admirable economy in the words 'The one seemed woman to the waist, and fair' (650), where the rhythm dwells heavily on 'seemed' before the assonance of the subsequent lines – 'foul', 'fold' (651) and 'voluminous' (652) – roll away in the same way that her body coils into the shape of a huge serpent. This is the kind of image that feminist critics of recent years have been drawn to, together with Milton's entire treatment of Eve, to open up discussion on the politics of gender. Like the characterisation of Satan, this aspect of the poem, the way in which femininity is treated and positioned, is one full of potential for the student seeking to assimilate or pursue critical disagreements.

Besides the duplicity inherent in the way Milton conjugates beauty with ugliness, the as yet unidentified figure appears to be the mother of a 'cry of hell hounds' (654), a pack of ferocious dogs whose 'hideous peal' (656) is only muted by the shocking habit of their returning to her womb, their barking and howling still audible from deep inside their grotesque kennel. In this description, Milton is exploiting a wide range of mythology and earlier literature which depicted the guardians of the underworld as terrifyingly deformed monsters, central amongst them being Cerberus, in Greek mythology the three headed dog who guarded the entrance to Hades. As so often the case with great storytellers, it is in the differences from their sources that they reveal their own interests. These hounds he makes more abhorrent than those that 'Vexed Scylla' (660) or those which were thought to hunt with Hecate, the 'Night-hag' (662) queen of the witches in popular mythology, who was synonymous with the murder of infants. A scholarly edition of the poem will provide the detailed glosses to these external characters; what I would prefer to direct your attention to is Milton's purpose in emphasising their monstrous form. He avoids any real physical description or detail, concentrating on the sound they make, and on linking them to witchcraft, the nearest thing his world had to Satan's visibility on earth. The Salem witch trials[2] in the nascent state of Massachusetts, for example, took place almost thirty years after *Paradise Lost* was first published.

If the first figure is confusing or puzzling, then the second is even more challenging. If you read the eight lines (666–73) in which the second figure is introduced in isolation, you should see there is little physical description for us to engage with apart from it having something resembling a 'kingly crown' (673) on 'what seemed his head' (672), although at least we have the comfort of knowing its gender. If it has one dominant characteristic at this point it is its indescribability. It appears to lack both 'shape' (l 667) and 'substance' (669), partaking more of shadow than of form, yet through Milton's clever wordplay apparently exhibiting aspects of both, 'For each seemed either' (670). However we respond to its amorphousness, Milton is clear that it is to be greatly feared, linking it through a trio of similes to night, hell and the ancient

Greek goddesses of vengeance, the Furies, before making the pointed reference to monarchy. His intense aggression is conveyed by the 'dreadful dart' (672) he shakes at Satan. Milton uses the word 'dart' in a variety of ways in *Paradise Lost*, often to describe the action of striking out, as well as the weapon itself, which we might interpret here as a javelin, spear or even dagger; but if this monster is designed to frighten the reader, it has a more surprising effect on Satan.

Unperturbed, even as the monstrous form advances on him with 'horrid strides' (676), Satan is moved to admiration rather than fear, addressing it 'with disdainful look' (680) and in his own belligerent terms making it clear that he will not allow it to prevent him passing through hell's gates. There is a resoundingly hollow irony in his dismissive claim that the being should know better than to 'contend with spirits of heaven' (687). It is clear that the monster is in no doubt about the identity of his opponent, describing him as 'that traitor angel' (689), 'Who first broke peace in heaven and faith' (690), but also showing no sign of backing down. On an elegantly rational level, he reminds Satan that this is hell, the very place designed to punish him and 'the third part of heaven's sons' (692) who followed him, and that to 'reckonst thou thyself with spirits of heaven' (696) now flies somewhat in the face of reality. We then come a little closer to an understanding of who this figure is when he explains this is his kingdom, 'Where I reign king' (698), and that so far from being intimidated by Satan, he is in fact his 'king and lord?' (699).

Sin Speaks

The account which Sin now gives Satan of her origin, and of the ties that bind her to him, and both of them to Death, is a highly significant section of the poem. Through it we learn a great deal about Milton's theodicy. *Paradise Lost*, like other great works of an epic nature, is in some respects an intricate, complex structure of ideas as much as a lengthy or detailed narrative. While the narrative presents us with a sequence of interrelated actions, some of which we may know already from other sources such as the temptation of Adam and Eve in Eden in the book of Genesis, what we might term the philosophy or ideology of the poem is based on far less familiar foundations. It is therefore important to understand and trace the connections between major concepts in the poem, if we are to feel confident in our understanding of it. It is difficult to imagine how we can really appreciate or critically analyse Satan's character, and especially his interaction with Eve in Book 9 of the poem, if we fail to understand the unholy trinity[3] Milton describes for us here in Book 2.

There is undoubtedly something of the rejected lover's tone in the opening few lines of Sin's great speech 'Hast thou forgot me then' (747), created partly through alliteration and the plaintive opposition that Sin voices between 'fair' and 'foul' (748) when describing Satan's changing attitude towards her, echoing the Witches' chants in *Macbeth*. Sin accuses Satan of failing to recognise her, even though she played such a central part in their public rebellion against heaven 'with thee combined' (750). The length of the sentence here (746–67) may cause you some difficulty, and especially since the abrupt change of direction signalled by 'All on a sudden' (752) takes us away from Sin's stance as rejected lover to a dramatic image of her own birth. It is easier to deal with if we appreciate that Milton is interested in connecting three things. Firstly, the shocking revelation (at least for Satan) that this hideously ambiguous creature is his daughter; secondly, that he was, until now, ignorant of this; and thirdly, the Greek myth of the birth of Athene, who sprang, fully formed, from the head of Zeus.

Alliteration and a contrast between dark and light permeate the description of Sin's birth. As the 'miserable pain' (752) wraps Satan in darkness and dizziness, Sin herself bursts from his flaming head 'shining heavenly fair' (757) with 'countenance bright' (756). Sin is literally, as well as metaphorically, Satan's brainchild. It is easy to underestimate the implications for Adam and Eve and the religiously grounded reader. Milton's use of Greek myth here perverts the good effects of the original myth, since Athene is most commonly a figure of wisdom and calm, a beneficent goddess, largely sympathetic to human endeavour. Sin's appearance, like Athene, as an armed goddess resembling her father, 'Likest to thee in shape and countenance bright' (756), surprises and frightens the other angels, an effect underpinned by the staccato sounding 'back they recoiled' (759). But such is Sin's nature, that it is not long before they are captivated by her beauty, an effect elegantly conveyed through the use of the sinuously sounding 'pleased' (762) which lingers on the reader's tongue almost indecently.

Sin then recounts how she succeeded in winning over even 'The most averse' (763), but above all it is Satan who she has most effect on, and for good reason. It is worth your reflecting on her noting that it was Satan's observation, 'Thyself in me thy perfect image viewing' (764), that led to his falling in love with her. That is if we accept 'Becam'st enamoured' (765) as indicating love. It certainly indicates at the very least lust, since 'in secret' (766) Satan and Sin have sex, the result being the wittily ironic 'growing burden' (767) Sin has to carry and then deliver. There is plenty of scope for critical analysis here that examines the version of events Sin tells. Milton makes sure, for example, that we understand Satan's interest in Sin was a narcissistic fascination, seeing himself reflected perfectly in her. He also avoids any obvious puritanical temptation he may have felt to equate their union with the cardinal sin of lust, instead using the word 'joy' to describe the act of sex between them, but it is a noun qualified by the redolent verb 'tookst' (765), hinting at rape rather than mutual pleasure. And of course, this all took place 'in secret' (766). There is clearly something rakish, even (most appropriately given Milton's republican background) *Cavalier*,[4] about the way Satan appears to have used or abused Sin.

A typical use of a caesura after 'burden' (767) marks the shift of Sin's narrative to the wider conflict in heaven, which ends in the defeat of the rebel angels and their fall into hell, a fate Sin says she shared with them, and the point in the story at which the entire poem began. However, given everything we have heard from Satan in Book 1 about these events, in his discussions with Beëlzebub and others we might be surprised by the parenthesis Sin uses, '(For what could else)' (769), to imply their defeat was always inevitable. This reminds us starkly of God's omnipotence and when to that is added detail like the fact that in her fall she was given the key to hell's gate (774–5) we also start to appreciate God's omniscience. Sin has been instructed to 'keep/These gates for ever shut' (775–6), we can only assume by God himself, and her assertion that 'none can pass/Without my opening' (776–7), which also ends in a caesura, can be heard as a dramatic ploy, since it immediately invites the alert reader to consider what might take place to bring about the forbidden act of opening. Milton's readers were well aware that hell's gate opened one way only.

The next part of Sin's account describes in some detail the delivery of her 'growing burden' (767), how she gave birth to Death, and how she has exchanged a brief state where she was 'Pensive' (777) and 'Alone' (778) for an existence of constant fear and horror, eaten from within by her own incestuous brood of hell hounds and perpetually glowered at as tempting prey for Death. The description owes something to Greek and Roman precedents, but whereas those accounts tend to focus on the danger and ferocity of hell's guardians from the point of view of mere mortal interlopers, like Orpheus,[5] Milton's personification is far more interesting because of its psychological detail and hint of empathy.

Sin describes her birth pangs as 'Prodigious motion felt and rueful throes' (780), the choice of 'throes' and the assonance of the lengthy 'o' and 'ue' sounds combining to imply a writhing movement or violence which culminates in the horrifying discovery that Death was in fact not born at all, but instead 'Tore through my entrails' (783). The consequence of this horrible distortion of the natural birth process is that Sin's previously beautiful and godlike form is now 'Distorted' (784) and she is left with the grotesquely ugly form below the waist, 'nether shape' (784) Satan found so repugnant earlier. But the horror doesn't stop there, and as soon as he is 'born' Death brandishes the symbol of his entire function, 'his fatal dart' (786), which Sin recognises is 'Made to destroy' (787) before she flees from him crying out his name, a name so hideous that hell itself 'trembled' (788) and echoed back the sound 'From all her caves' (789). If you reread the few lines in which this part of Sin's tale is told, you should be able to see how much force and energy Milton invests in that single word, Death. It seems almost to echo itself at the end of line 789 where a heavily loaded full stop halts the urgency of her account.

However you find yourself responding to Sin up to this point, the next part of her tale seems absolutely calculated to provoke. Although Sin fled her horrific offspring, she describes in rather abstract terms (especially considering the physical detail she has provided so far) how Death pursues her out of 'lust' rather than 'rage' (791), easily overtaking and then raping her, the term Sin herself uses to describe this sexual act, and *not* the term she used of her earlier congress with Satan. The result of this rape was the 'yelling monsters' (795), the 'hell hounds' first described in lines 653–66 as 'Cerberean' (655). Like a number of mythological figures punished by the gods, Sin undergoes a constantly repeated cycle of torment. For stealing fire from Olympus and giving it to mankind, Prometheus is chained to a rock by Zeus where, daily, his liver is eaten by an Eagle, only to regenerate to provide a new meal for the bird the following day. Sin's systematic torture is to have her litter of monsters return to her womb 'hourly' (796) where they feed on her 'bowels' (800) only to 'vex' (801) her so routinely that she can find no kind of ease or rest, 'That rest or intermission none I find' (802). Although we might find the idea of their being 'hourly conceived' (796) a little strained, Milton appears to be using the word to emphasise their return to the womb as the source of nourishment, 'their repast' (800). It is the kind of bloody, nightmarish detail, worthy of a painterly imagination like Goya's or Fuseli's, and not the least Puritan.

Sin's tale of woe concludes with a final, ironic and unnatural twist. Not only does she endure this ceaseless torture, eaten from inside by a pack of hellish hounds she has given birth to herself, but her own son, Death, sits 'in opposition' (803) as her constant enemy. The tersely compact paradox 'my son and foe' (804) beautifully encapsulating her own appreciation of that irony. Sin knows that Death yearns to 'devour' (805) her and refrains only because he understands fully that their fates are linked, and her end is his own. Fate has dictated this, and in this assertion is more, clear evidence of Milton's omnipotent God, always one stride ahead of his enemies. Besides the sardonic food imagery that Sin chooses – herself as a 'bitter morsel' and Death's ultimate 'bane' (808) – it is easy to overlook a particularly significant phrase, 'For want of other prey' (806). In this universe empty of mankind, before God has created Adam, and the whole race of mankind to follow, Death is metaphorically starving. The only means to ease his hunger is his own mother. Eternal torment is the ineluctable condition of all who inhabit Milton's hell.

Sin's original motivation for speaking here was to intervene in what seemed an imminent battle between Satan and Death. Milton neatly rounds off her speech by returning to that theme and having her issue Satan with a deliberate and unambiguous warning not to fight with Death, since to do so would have consequences as yet unknown to anyone but herself. The cautious, broken rhythm of 'But thou, O Father, I forewarn thee' (810) emphasises her sincerity. There is even a kind of dark wit in her choice of adjective to describe Death's symbolic weapon, his 'deadly arrow' (811), since it is literally true in the purest sense. In warning him not to trust the 'bright arms' (812), the 'heavenly' (813) armour he still wears to protect him, she echoes the Homeric heroes, preparations for war and oracular declarations that Milton's readers would have been very familiar with. But Sin's final assertion is coldly precise and unequivocal. Only God, she insists, can withstand Death's 'mortal dint' (813).

Satan's Promise of Plenty

Sin is so successful in her attempt to prevent a fatal conflict between father and son that Satan's earlier state of titanic rage and nascent violence (704–20) is transformed to devious civility. Milton again opts for lengthy syllables and sibilant sounds to help convey Satan's untrustworthy cunning, exemplifying how sophisticated he can be in his use of sound and rhythm. It will be worth your spending a few moments discovering examples for yourself from this next section in which Satan convinces Sin to open the gates of hell (814–49):

> She finished, and the subtle fiend his lore
> Soon learned, now milder, and thus answered smooth. (815–16)

That 'smooth' answer lasts for twenty-eight lines, (817–44), and is a single, skilfully shaped sentence. The kind which for many students is dauntingly difficult to unravel, even though the word Milton uses to describe it, 'smooth', is in common, and not dissimilar, use in colloquial English today.

The practical method this guide recommends in such cases is to reread the sentence as one, trusting to the editor's punctuation as your guide and consciously trying to keep hold of the relationships between subject and verb as you go. It may take two or more attempts before those relationships become clear, but once you begin to see how the sentence works, how it is structured, you will be far more able to discuss or write about it for yourself. In this case, connecting 'Dear Daughter' (817) to the verb 'know' (821) as its subject is the first step to understanding the overall structure. Similarly, connecting Satan's 'I go' (826) with the infinitive 'To search' (830) will help elucidate his purpose and, therefore, part of the reason why Sin opens the gate for him.

Satan's smoothness can be seen in the language he now selects to describe his relationships with Sin and Death. His 'Sight more detestable' (745) has been replaced by 'Dear Daughter' (817) and 'fair son' (818) and the disturbing account Sin has given of her own conception and incestuous intercourse is transformed into a 'dear pledge/Of dalliance' and 'joys/Then sweet' (818–20). You may also notice that Satan cannot resist excusing the condition all three now find themselves in. Complete denial of any responsibility is characteristic of all his accounts of the rebellion and their 'dire change' (820) 'unforeseen, unthought of' (821) directly contradicts Sin's own earlier assertion in lines 769–71 that God's victory was never in doubt.

That the devil is cunning is a commonplace of Christian literature and thought, and there are several points in the narrative where Milton invests Satan with extraordinary skill and intelligence in this respect. His manipulation of Sin and Death here is a very strong example. On top of his 'smooth', flattering address, he adopts an obsequiously conciliatory manner in sharp contrast with his earlier belligerence and assures both Sin and Death that he is not their enemy. On the contrary, he positions himself as their friend and even liberator, his declared aim to set them, and all the rebel angels, free from hell. It is easy to make an unsupported claim: the cunning is in the way in which Satan makes such claims sound so convincing. Here he builds on his successful manipulation of the council of devils and stresses that he is acting not only on their behalf, 'from them I go' (826), but with admirable selflessness, 'and one for all/Myself expose' (827–8). His 'lonely steps' (828) and 'wandering quest' (830) sound more Arthurian knight than corrupt angel. Satan is more honest in his subsequent claim to be seeking earth, 'a place of bliss/In the purlieus of heaven' (832–3), and in it mankind, 'A race of upstart creatures' (834).

In an age where sin is no longer a concept to stir profound fear or loathing, and far from being a dirty word is even a term of approval in the world of film or advertising, it is very easy to miss some of the most interesting aspects of Milton's characterisation of Satan. In this case, his almost incendiary display of one of the deadliest of sins, envy. His use of 'upstart' betrays his predisposition towards Mankind, and his fear that they might supplant himself and the rebel host in heaven is clear, 'to supply/Perhaps our vacant room' (834–5), but the qualification he adds, 'though more removed' (835), can only indicate envy, as he himself admits he has no idea of what God's plan might be and he is anxious to discover it if he can:

> be this or aught
> Than this more secret now designed, I haste
> To know... (837–9)

His cunning is evident again as he turns this part of his explanation into the most enticing of promises to Sin and Death, assuring them he will return to bring them both to this new world. The imagery he uses to describe their new life on earth contrasts dramatically with the nightmarish existence Sin has previously described. He promises them they 'Shall dwell at ease' (841) invisibly, and in what may seem a very curious phrase, they will 'Wing silently the buxom air' (842). An earlier meaning for the word 'buxom' was plaint or supple, but its more conventional meaning seems almost as apt, since other language here points to fullness or plenitude. Although we may find ourselves being on the one hand pointed towards the future depiction of Eden, we are also as readers to some extent victims of Satan's cunning, since the way he ends his speech also carries something of a shock. Satan promises Sin and Death their hunger will be satiated in a world where 'all things shall be your prey' (840). We realise, even as Satan promises Sin and Death their fill, that we are, like every other living thing on our planet, metaphorically, on the menu.

Satan's cunning works its designed effect, and while Death imagines his eternal hunger, eternally sated, Sin speaks conspiratorially for them both. In this lengthy section (850–97) Sin reminds us first of the 'command' (851) she has been given by God to keep hell's gate locked, while Death stands guard to slaughter any who seek to escape. But she rejects God's command in a series of rhetorical questions ending in her acknowledgement of Satan as her true father, her original source of being. The sense of hurt and indignation she voices is also clearly fuelled by a loss of status when she angrily describes herself as 'Inhabitant of heaven, and heavenly-born' (860). The loss of divine status, what it entails and means to be exiled from God's presence, is a concept we first encountered in Book 1, and it is something Milton returns to again and again throughout the poem.

Milton's cosmology is a unique area of scholarly study and the section of the narrative which sees Satan battling through the void to reach earth is typical in the mix of classical literature, personification and science he brings to the task of building his own universe. Why Milton makes him pause, and why he then expends so much energy on Satan's desperate flight, his battling with the huge elemental forces to find his way, are questions worth time exploring independently, and where your answers lead you will influence how you respond to Satan as a dramatic character.

Chaos and Ancient Night

If you read the conversation Satan has with 'Chaos and ancient Night' (970), with the specific intention of distinguishing one interlocutor from another, you will almost certainly notice, even at the most superficial level, the differing sentence length. Milton exerts himself to mould Satan's speech in an entirely different form and tone to that of Chaos. Satan's single, elastic sentence occupies some nineteen lines of verse, and while Chaos's response also occupies some twenty lines, he takes three sentences to reach his unambiguous conclusion, and in a noticeably less convoluted way.

Although Milton uses the adverb 'boldly' (968) to describe the manner in which Satan addresses the formidable figures of Chaos and Night, in comparison with the belligerence he displayed in front of Death earlier in Book 2, his tone is mild, even placatory. Satan's chosen form of address is formal and measured, reminding the reader of the suppliant forms of address used by numerous figures in classical literature who are forced into seeking divine help. A more modern, cinematic reading might respond to the words as incantatory, but their true roots are in Greek tragedy and the epic poetry of Homer and Virgil. The formula involves using the person's title before naming them, 'Ye powers/And spirits of this nethermost abyss' (968–9), a sign of respect and even deference, and as such it ought to prompt you to ask why Satan adopts such a tone. Chaos and Night do not threaten him, but he is nonetheless in need of their assistance.

As his speech continues, what he wants does become clear, but it is not easy to discern amidst the complex sentence structure. You are probably more likely to gather a general sense of what Satan requests at first, which is their assistance in locating earth, than a clear understanding of how he makes the request; but by working your way through his speech in stages, you will be able to see exactly what he asks and where.

As if to disarm any potential challenge, Satan quickly follows his polite address with an assurance that he is neither a 'spy' (970) nor a threat of any kind to them, and that in fact he has been forced into their territory 'by constraint' (972), which is only partially true, and typical of the subtle quibbling he frequently employs to get what he wants. He may indeed have been at the mercy of the elements, but it was entirely his choice to attempt this journey. Having assured them of his innocence, he then proceeds to seek their sympathy, 'Wandering this darksome desert' (973), as he terms their realm, 'Alone, and without a guide, half lost' (975), before adding further assurance in that he seeks only the 'readiest path' (976) – in other words, the fastest route out to the border with heaven. It is at this point where a caesura indicates an abrupt but difficult change in tack. After 'Confine with heaven' (977), Satan pauses conditionally, using 'or' to steer his listeners his way, and if when you read aloud you give this pause sufficient length, you will be able to connect 'the ethereal king' (978) with the verb 'possesses' (979) and with its object, 'some other place' (977). Besides Satan's subtle use of language, you might find yourself thrown by his referring to earth in this vague, ignorant way, as though he knows little or nothing of it. This feigned ignorance is another characteristic trait of Satan's which is designed to manipulate others, as is his suggestion that the creation of such a place has been a territorial loss for Chaos and Night, 'From your dominion won' (978).

Another caesura in line 980 is your best guide to understanding precisely what Satan is after. The rhythm of the verse here isolates the single clause, 'thither to arrive/I travel this profound' (979–80), and that single statement is possibly the most valuable key to understanding the whole sentence. It is also, ironically, the truest thing Satan says, and is immediately followed by his request 'direct my course' (980), or in simpler terms, 'show me the way'. A less skilful mind might have stopped there, but Satan is delightfully more subtle and challenging than that and instantly makes them an offer, we might even say here, a tempting offer, 'Directed, no mean recompense it brings' (981). The incentive he offers them is possibly less clear, but again a thoughtful look at the relationship between subject and verb can help. Satan lists a number of actions he intends, all relating to earth, 'that region lost' (982), the slice of territory he argues God has stolen from Chaos for his latest experiment. In Satan's (not Milton's) cosmology, Chaos and 'ancient Night' (970) seem to possess a kind of chronological superiority to God himself, since he describes God's annexation of their territory as a 'usurpation' (983) and the first action he promises is to expel the usurpers, who we can safely predict will turn out to be Adam and Eve. Secondly, he promises to 'reduce' (983) the territory gained 'To her original darkness' and restore the authority 'sway' (984) of Chaos. Like the victorious figure he always fancies himself to be, he can then reclaim the earth for Night, 'Erect the standard there of ancient Night' (986), where 'standard' is simply an outmoded word for flag. And as though he anticipates the obvious question, what's in it for you?, he concludes with a neatly phrased antithesis, 'Yours be the advantage all, mine the revenge' (987). That, at least, is honest. The parenthesis in line 985, '(Which is my present journey)', serves to reassure his companions of his innocent presence in their realm as well as drawing together the various actions he has listed into one, grand project.

The whole speech is an admirably professional sales pitch, acknowledging the client's sensitivities, anticipating objections and articulating perfectly the benefits. In contrast, Chaos, who Milton intriguingly calls 'the anarch old' (988), responds with 'faltering speech' (989) and words that reflect his immense age and possibly even anarchical nature. He wastes no time on niceties, telling Satan immediately that he both recognises him and has witnessed, 'I saw and heard' (993), the rebellion Satan led. His phrasing is simple and direct, 'I know thee, stranger, who thou art' (990), in contrast with Satan's elastic syntax, and there is no deceiving him, in spite of Satan's skilful efforts. He chooses harshly unambiguous alliteration to underscore the outcome of Satan's grand rebellion, 'ruin upon ruin, rout upon rout' (995), adding the finely wrought and eloquent phrase 'Confusion worse confounded' (996), before pausing to follow up Satan's humiliation with a powerful image of the scale of God's response, as the victorious host of angels 'Poured out by millions' (997) through heaven's gate in pursuit of the defeated. A caesura after 'Pursuing' (998) marks his turning to his part in events, and the resignation he now shows might not be easily understood on an initial reading. After defining the limits of his realm, 'I upon my frontiers here/Keep residence' (998–9), Chaos uses ellipsis, the conscious omission of a word or phrase, to explain his reaction to these events, 'if all I can will serve' (999), where we might expect to hear the verb 'do' after 'can' to complete the sense. 'That little which is left' (1000) picks up on Satan's idea of God's creating hell and earth infringing on their more ancient territory, 'Weakening the sceptre of old Night' (1002) through the expansion below of 'Your dungeon stretching far and wide beneath' (1003) and above 'Now lately heaven and earth' (1004), by which he means the Earth and *its* sky and not paradise, which is clear because of the different reference to 'heaven' in line 1006. His choice is to settle for 'residence' (999) by which he appears to mean he will defend only that territory which God has left to him and to Night. Quite what Chaos, or Milton, is thinking of in his bitter allusion to 'our intestine broils' (1001) is yours to debate, but it is clear that his use of 'our' and not 'your', when Chaos has clearly had no part in the rebellion or its failure, begs some attention.

Although we can now see Chaos is not unduly swayed or impressed by Satan's rhetoric, he nonetheless finds reason to give Satan precisely what he has asked for in the final part of his speech. In an almost prosaic twist, 'If that way be your walk, you have not far' (1007), he nonchalantly points the way with the encouragement, 'go and speed' (1008), where 'speed' holds the older meaning of 'succeed' that you may be familiar with from studying Shakespeare. His reason? 'Havoc and spoil and ruin are my gain' (1009), where repetition of the conjunction 'and' not only signals the end of his speech, but emphasises his delight and anticipation. He is, after all, true to his anarchic nature.

Chaos's silence is Satan's cue to continue his journey with renewed vigour and speed, and in doing so he literally and figuratively paves the way for Sin and Death to enter 'this frail world' (1030). Although, as before, Milton makes Satan's journey a difficult and laborious one until he gains sight of heaven, and like a ship after a storm, gains some respite in calmer, coastal waters, he is also at pains to assure us that his success and the escape of Sin and Death from hell is 'the will of heaven' (1025). A key question to address here is about the compatibility of these two aims. Is Milton chiefly interested in characterising Satan as heroic, or in pursuing his overarching theodical mission? Are the two mutually exclusive? It does seem somewhat illogical to admire Satan for his strength and determination in undertaking this arduous journey if all the time he is merely a pawn in God's far greater plan.

Exercises

Lines 1–429. Book two opens, as promised, with the secret consultation between those select few closest to Satan in power and influence. Satan opens the 'debate' (42) and his first words are dense and riddled with conditionality, but his determination to continue the struggle against God is clear enough. Four others speak at his invitation, Moloch, Belial, Mammon and Beëlzebub, each given a distinct character by Milton in keeping with the multifaceted conceptualisation of evil common in Christian thought. Moloch seeks continued war and espouses a (literally) devil-may-care attitude, while Belial in comparison seems almost to have become a pacifist through his recent suffering. But it is Beëlzebub's words (310–78) that are most significant since they are, by Milton's design, Satan's own, and the entire 'debate' is proven to be a sham. Read through the debate and assess how successfully Satan manipulates the outcome.

Lines 466–628. Once Satan has gained the unanimous agreement he desired from his inner conclave of devils, he sets off on his mission without hesitation and with little concern for those he leaves behind. It is left to Milton to describe their state of mind and he does so in a lengthy digression rich in classical literary references, and one which contains a challenging example of a lengthy Miltonic simile for you to work through and analyse for yourself (488–95). You can also examine the various activities Milton ascribes to the devils and ask yourself to what extent Milton wishes you to respond to these figures as heroic.

3
Redemption and Free Will

Summary

Book 3 opens with a new invocation, 'Hail, holy light, offspring of heaven first-born' (1), in which Milton once again seeks divine help in this epic, creative enterprise. In moving the action from hell to heaven, Milton expends time and energy on setting the new scene for us and preparing the way for God's voice and the voice of the Son. The complicated way in which imagery connected to light and seeing permeates this entire opening is made of particular critical interest because of Milton's frank examination of his own blindness. While Satan seeks a way out of chaos, God sits surrounded by the heavenly host of faithful angels, with the Son at his side, watching Satan's action at the same time as he watches Adam and Eve on earth below.

God invites the Son to see what he sees, which is not just Satan's escape from hell, but his entire plan of action, his motives and all that will occur as a result. This speech contains the core of Milton's theodicy: God's own account of the existence of sin and death. The Fall, and Satan's part in it, is accurately and fully predicted and God's omnipotent timelessness given a narrative meaning. The Son asks a number of highly pertinent questions concerning man's ultimate fate and God's intentions to which his Father replies with Milton's own interpretation of Protestant theology how, through the divine gift of grace, mankind can seek salvation. The Father adds that, for justice to be done following Adam and Eve's Fall, someone must be punished in his stead; and just as Satan asked for volunteers to undertake the dreadful journey out of hell, God asks for volunteers amongst the heavenly host willing to become mortal and to die so that mankind might live eternally. As Satan was met with silence, so is God, until the Son speaks, who out of his inestimable love accepts God's challenge and sacrifices his own immortality in order to grant mankind theirs, knowing that in time God will resurrect him and give him leave to destroy both hell and death at the Last Judgement, bringing eternal peace and joy to heaven.

At God's affirmation of the Son's prediction, the heavenly host bursts into spontaneous praise and celebration, a direct contrast to the miserable way the fallen angels break up and explore hell after the great consultation. In heaven, the angels' words reiterate God's great plan and the role both mankind and the Son will play in it, and form hymns of praise and worship to both God and the Son. Meanwhile Satan lands on the very edge of the world and discovers Limbo, a place Milton satirises as replete with fools and religious heretics, mostly Catholics. From this vantage point Satan is taunted with the sight of distant heaven's gate but he also sees what he has come to find, the newly formed earth, and instantly covets it for its beauty. Flying earthwards, Satan arrives at the sun and encounters the archangel Uriel. Disguising himself as a youthful cherub before he speaks to Uriel, Satan tells the unwitting archangel he has come to seek out God's latest and greatest creation, man, in order to admire him and so praise God all the more. Unable to discern Satan's 'Hypocrisy, the only evil that walks/Invisible' (683–4), Uriel points out the way to earth and Satan immediately continues his journey, finally alighting on the summit of Mount Niphates.

The Voice of God

The opening to the third book of *Paradise Lost* poses many questions, not the least of which is: whom is Milton addressing in his opening invocation? 'Hail, holy light, offspring of heaven first-born' (1), which, the moment we recall the poet's blindness, becomes considerably more complex. A second, more fascinating question could be asked around Milton's choice of noun to describe his journey thus far, 'while in my flight' (15). Although it is the same, conventional, invocatory term he employed in the opening of Book 1 (14), and we recognise that everyone's poetic muse is prone to moments of aerial display, after spending so much time in the previous book with Satan on the wing as it were, is there a deliberate or unconscious alignment here between poet and anti-hero?

The opening section of the third book is one of the most useful passages to focus on if you are interested in understanding the way Milton appears to direct our response to Satan. After the opening invocation, Milton is quick to shift our point of view and the poem's milieu from hell to heaven.

With Satan held firmly in our sight and God's 'Coasting the wall of heaven' (71) and seeking a firm place to alight his 'wearied wings, and willing feet' (73), Milton shifts the focus of his narrative from the hellish to the divine, giving a voice to his God in strikingly human terms. When God addresses his 'Only begotten Son' here, he does so with familiarity and shared knowledge, calling Satan 'our adversary' (81), before commencing on a detailed and enlightening account of some of the key events and actions we have witnessed in the first two books. God's monologue (80–134) contains some of the most significant concepts in the entire epic, seeking as it does to account for the paradox of God's omniscience and Satan's evil.

The first thing worth noting is the scope of the single viewpoint that Father and Son share. The opening sentence, 80–6, is a rhetorical question, the focus of which is Satan's 'rage' (80) and irrepressible desire for revenge. It is *not* a practical query aimed at finding out if the Son too can see Satan's actions. But if Father and Son share the same viewpoint, part of the paradoxical nature of the Holy Trinity is that they do not share the same mind, so, before revealing more of his own, the Father situates Satan's current actions against the entire backdrop of creation and, more pertinently for Milton's readers, mankind's place in the universe. Fans of Satan are quick to decry Milton's God as a vengeful, Old Testament tyrant, but if we take that view to heart too uncritically, we risk missing a richer picture. The Father is not without wit, as his use of 'Transports' (81), to convey both the geographical and the emotional impact that rage has on Satan, reveals.

The list of barriers that Satan has overcome, 'no bounds...nor yet the main abyss' (81–3), may have the side effect of advancing his heroic cause, but if that is how we react, then we ought to balance our reaction with the Father's immediate and matter of fact dismissal of such antics as 'desperate revenge, that shall redound/Upon his own rebellious head.' (85–6), the full stop midline emphasising the ultimate futility of Satan's activity. We should be in no doubt at all that, however energetic Satan's efforts, however dynamic his rage, he is always and eternally doomed to failure and damnation. To read the poem from here as though that were not the case, as though Satan were in some still undecided narrative battle with God, would be to ignore the Christian tenets on which the poem, and Milton, rely. Whatever drama we find in the poem, and there is no shortage of dramatic moments, cannot come from doubt about the outcome of this particular conflict.

Having dismissed any possibility of Satan's revenge, the Father quickly shifts attention towards the 'new created world' (89), since it is there that the real drama will be played out. The Father makes clear he is fully aware of Satan's intention to 'destroy' (91) man, but, more chillingly for Milton's Christian reader, he not only acknowledges Satan's intent to do 'worse' (91), by seducing him to his own side, 'by some false guile pervert' (92), but immediately predicts his success, 'and shall pervert' (91). In what sense is this a worse intent? Beëlzebub's earlier counsel in Book 2 provides the most eloquent response. There, speaking his master's words for him, Beëlzebub believed the best kind of revenge would be the successful seduction of mankind since the likely outcome would be God's destruction of the whole race and his discomfiture:

> Seduce them to our party, that their God
> May prove their foe, and with repenting hand
> Abolish his own works. (II, 368–70)

The 'joy' Beëlzebub anticipates in antithesis, in turning God into mankind's 'foe', offers an insight into Milton's understanding of the whole concept of evil, a concept that post-Darwinian, Western society finds hugely troublesome. Reversal of role or nature appears abhorrent to the Miltonic imagination.

In predicting Satan's successful seduction of mankind, 'and shall pervert' (92), God instantly opens himself to the charge of the atheist or agnostic sensibility that recoils at such indifference and apparently irresponsibility. Although one is obviously inviting contention to single out passages from this huge poem as more important than others, part of the job of a guide of this type is to focus attention and point students towards parts of the poem that they will gain most from. What follows is one of those passages.

The events concerned in this prediction take place in Book 9 (473–784) and the single fact God attributes to them here is easily overlooked, though the rhythm of the verse places a major emphasis on the final word, 'Man will hearken to his glozing lies' (93). One of the most valuable reasons for studying *Paradise Lost*, more than three centuries after the poet's death, is the frequency with which the poem clashes head on with modern cultural practice or theory, exposing or enlightening as it does so. Shakespeare's brilliant clown Touchstone divides lying[1] into seven 'degrees', but a contemporary taxonomy that embraces the political and commercial worlds might well run to many dozens more. When Milton is faced with the immense challenge of reproducing imaginatively the conversation between Eve and Satan in the Garden of Eden, he describes *how* Satan convinces the Mother of Mankind to break the 'sole command' (94) God has made. He does this by making Satan lie.

God's addition of the epithet 'glozing' (94) might cause some difficulty since the word is rarely in use today. Its root 'gloss' has a number of meanings, the most relevant here being 'false' or 'specious', although its elongated, sibilant sound might also have had much to recommend it. In considering Milton's treatment of God here, you may have found your attention drawn to the repetitious 'sole' (94–5) which at least hints at disapproval, if not downright criticism, a view bolstered by the unequivocal use of 'faithless' (96) to describe Adam and his entire race. If nothing more followed, we could be forgiven for thinking Beëlzebub's objective might well have been achieved, but God does not cease his reasoning here and poses the exigent question himself, 'whose fault?' (96), before immediately answering it with the rhetorical, 'Whose but his own?' (97), and describing Adam with some severity as an 'Ingrate' (97). The crucial idea Milton and God have been leading up to emerges as he reminds us that there was no flaw in Adam's creation, no fatal weakness, but quite the opposite. Not only was he made 'just and right' (98), he was also 'Sufficient to have stood' (99), the crucial idea being that man's flawlessness included the vital element of free will, a fact emphasised by the full stop after 'though free to fall.' (99) and the contextualisation that follows, linking man to the angels, since they too were created with free will. God's prediction culminates in the beautifully assertive statement, 'Freely they stood who stood, and fell who fell' (102), which has the brilliant effect of linking Satan with man while simultaneously confirming the latter's difference, since, as readers and *men*, not devils, we know that such choice is a constant feature of our lived experience, and not an isolated, unique, immutable event consigned to history or myth.

We might be forgiven for wishing God's prediction ended rather neatly and clinically here, but Milton lived in a post-Reformation Europe, where politics and religion were eager bedfellows, and the great opposing camps of Catholicism and Protestantism engulfed entire nations in their struggle for authority.[2] In the next few lines, Milton seeks to manage one of the most contentious territories in that struggle, Luther's wildcat amongst the pigeons of Saint Peter's Square: predestination.[3]

The first point is clearly and well made by God. Were man not free, what value could there have been in his entire relationship with God? How indeed could God have measured his sincerity, by 'faith or love' (104)? The second point too is quite accessible. Were man only capable of delivering according to need, not desire or wish, how could God in any meaningful sense praise him in return (105–6)? The third point is made through a longer, more complex sentence which should be less intransigent if we isolate the subject as 'will and reason' (108) and the main verb as 'had served' (110). God sees no sense in which there would be any 'pleasure' (107) to be gained in man's obedience, where he was merely serving necessity and not God himself. The logic which now follows is possibly easier to discern than the stages of thought that have led to it, since it is clearly signalled by the conjunction 'therefore' (111). Being made right in the first place 'as to right belonged' (111), man cannot accuse God of having made him badly or Fate of having dealt with him unfairly, since free will is not subject to predestination. This statement puts Milton at odds with conventional Protestant theology espoused by authors like Calvin, and allies him firmly with Arminian thought.[4] Milton's God does not condemn Eve or Adam to failure in advance by 'absolute decree' (115) 'Or high foreknowledge' (116).[5] They are both responsible for their own actions, and God's choice of the word 'revolt' (117) again links them to Satan in this respect before he closes up this complex line of argument with an emphatically decisive piece of logic that hints at just how brilliant a student Milton was himself:

> If I foreknew,
> Foreknowledge had no influence on their fault,
> Which had no less proved certain unforeknown. (117–19)

Indeed like a scholar delivering a particularly sophisticated academic paper, Milton's God now sums up for the reader all he has just said in lines 120–5, with the interesting addition of a subtle but highly significant change in tense. The surprising use of the present tense, 'They trespass' (122), through its immediacy and imprecision, again unites man with the fallen angels in revolt, reasserting that the fault lies with them and only them. God moves to his conclusion, declaring that, although in the act of creating them he had 'ordained' (127) them free, they had 'ordained their fall' (128) before finally distinguishing clearly between the fallen angels and mankind. The 'first sort' (129), Satan and his followers, chose their own downfall 'Self-tempted, self-depraved' (130), although you might be tempted yourself at this point to object that Satan tempted his followers just as he tempts Eve. The second, Adam and Eve, 'falls deceived/By the other first' (130), and that crucial distinction permits God to grant them mercy and the prospect eternally denied to the first of eventual salvation and joy in heaven, 'man therefore shall find grace' (131). That act of mercy God sees as just, and in justice and mercy he locates the greatest goodness of his reign 'so shall my glory excel' (133).

The Voice of the Son

In the continuing dialogue between Father and Son, the former explains how mankind, although initially betrayed into sinfulness by Adam and Eve, will ultimately find salvation. The convoluted theological nuances here might prove off-putting and there is a risk that, in seeking to ensure we have a strong grasp of the theology, we lose something of the poetry. A good illustration of this can be found in the first few lines God speaks in answer to the Son's series of questions. He calls him 'Son' no less than three times in the space of fourteen words (168–9) but perhaps more powerful poetically is the use of rhythm to evoke an emotional bond. Many critics find little in Milton's God to empathise with, but the praise heaped here on his only son seems to counter that, especially when we also reflect on the nouns God ascribes to the Son. He is 'My word, my wisdom, and effectual might' (170), the opening and ending of the line rhyming, not just internally, but with 'delight' in line 168, an effect which, while placing considerable emphasis on the emotional bond between Father and Son, also elucidates the paradox of the Holy Trinity. The statement which then follows reinforces this through the repetition of 'all' in the single line, 'All hast thou spoken as my thoughts are, all' (171), and in making it clear that the Son's words have matched God's purpose and decree 'As my eternal purpose hast decreed' (172).

Reassuring us that mankind shall be saved, the Father builds on all he has said about free will and makes it clear that it is not through free will alone that salvation will be gained, but through the essential gift of 'grace in me/Freely vouchsafed' (174–5). The concept of grace is an immensely complex one, with a bewildering theological history, and to have at the very least a firm understanding of Milton's thinking here you need to understand the fundamental difference between grace and mercy, the former having nothing to do with merit or individual effort. If you think of the word 'disgrace' and then apply your knowledge about that concept to the concept of 'grace' as you hear it in Milton, it will help you to follow his thought more confidently. You may have noticed that the Father uses a lot of repetition in his speech here, and not always merely for emphasis but as the result of the highly logical process Milton is putting him through, expounding, as it were, a clear line of argument. You can see the steps of this argument very clearly in the next few lines. Through the divine generosity of grace, God will once more 'renew' (175) mankind, even though original sin has corrupted them. Supported by God, 'Upheld by me' (178), he will once again be as he was before the Fall, fit to combat Satan 'On even ground against his mortal foe' (179). Using the same phrase from line 178, inverted, 'By me upheld' (180), God will bring mankind to understand his own frailty, the terrible precariousness of his fallen state and the knowledge that only through God can he find salvation. In this way, God concludes, he will ensure that mankind owes his hope of salvation only to God, 'to none but me.' (182): notice how the full stop and single syllable words resound forcefully.

Calvin believed in an absolute form of predestination. Each man's soul was saved or damned even before birth, a reality utterly beyond human control or influence. Milton is less implacable, although he does admit here that there are some 'chosen of peculiar grace' (183) by God, 'Elect above the rest' (184), and these are all men of Christian faith, whose way to salvation has been eased, if you like, though not at all secured. 'The rest' (185), God states, are not at all deserted by him, indeed they 'shall hear me call, and oft be warned' (185). Grace too will be granted to them and sufficient knowledge of right and wrong to 'clear their senses dark' (188) 'and soften stony hearts' (189) in order to encourage them to 'pray, repent, and bring obedience due' (190). The logical, precise way in which God's thought proceeds is rendered very visibly here by the slight modification and restating which follows, 'To prayer, repentance, and obedience due' (191), and this stark repetition is a forceful, spiritual reminder to any reader concerned about his or her own soul and salvation. The concept of grace is in a sense exemplified in the assurance God then gives, where 'sincere intent' (192) alone will always be enough to gain God's attention. And as a guide or 'umpire' (195) originally a legal term and not the sporting term familiar today, God gives all men the gift of conscience 'whom if they will hear' (195) will ensure their ultimate salvation.

But Milton was a Puritan, and it would hardly be fitting for him to leave the future looking so unashamedly rosy, and so God reminds us that those who ignore his grace, refuse or reject the ways he offers to salvation, shall inevitably find themselves more deeply embedded in sin, 'hard be hardened, blind be blinded more' (200), poignant words from the pen of a sightless poet. These, and only these, God assures us, 'from mercy I exclude' (202). Up to this point if you have been confidently following God's logic and aligning it with what you already know of Christian thought and practice, the shift he now makes into discussing man's disobedience (which should remind us of the poem's opening) may immediately lead you to pre-empt his thought and expect him to do exactly what he does, which is invite the Son to sacrifice himself in order that mankind may be saved.

The core of the argument that necessitates a sacrifice lies around this statement about man, 'Die he, or justice must' (210). It is not that death is God's punishment for sin, rather death is the result of treason, of disobedience. Knowing this, God calls for a volunteer amongst the heavenly host of angels, 'Say heavenly powers' (213), and does not direct his question solely to the Son. The wordplay and compression of meaning here is quite intense and, although it may be easy to notice the repetition of 'mortal' and 'just' in lines 214–15, it is less simple to account for it. Irony is one of the effects. It will require divinity to stoop to mortality in order to restore divinity to man and only a just figure can save and redeem the unjust, though perhaps more significant are the words that aren't toyed with. God asks far more than the simple question, who? He also asks the questions, 'Where shall we find such love' (213), the emphasis falling heavily on the final two syllables, and 'Dwells in all heaven charity so dear?' (216), where the rush of syllables in the first half of the line isolate and stress the word 'charity'. To treat this scene in a narrowly dramatic or narrative fashion is to miss the scale and ambition of Milton's project. 'For God so loved the world, that he gave his only begotten Son, that whosoever believeth in him should not perish, but have everlasting life'[6] are the words still spoken the world over today, in the sacrament of the Mass. It is through his love for man that God sacrifices his only Son, and therefore, of course, himself.

Whatever religious or secular beliefs you may hold as a student, you will come closer to a rich understanding of *Paradise Lost* if you dwell for a moment on the implications of this divine act. If, like Milton and the overwhelming majority of his seventeenth-century readers, you regard it as an absolute truth, there is clearly then so much that makes sense in what follows in *Paradise Lost*.

What is very striking when we start to look at the Son's selfless response (227–65) is how different the language used is to that employed by God in his address to the heavenly powers. It is as though we have moved from a logical, academic discourse straight back into the more familiar territory of dramatic narrative in a single breath.

Man's fate hangs in the air with the caesura after 'heaven' (218). There is no need, other than dramatic, to delay the Son's response but

Milton also uses the opportunity to extol the Son's virtues and courage by stating it as fact that 'none appeared,/Much less durst' (219–20) accept mortality and die for mankind. The same effects are achieved when Milton spells out clearly the danger for mankind, should no one answer God's call. The entire race of man would have been doomed to suffer death and then eternal damnation in hell, were it not for the intervention of the Son. The contrast with the way Satan manipulated the counsel in Book 2, such that he appeared to be volunteering, *and* in the best possible light, guides some of our response to the Son here. It is the Son's 'love' (225) which Milton chooses to single out as a quality before he answers his father's question with a clear and unequivocal affirmative. Within the first line of the Son's reply we can see not only his generosity, but also his obedience as a son to his father. 'Father, thy word is past' (227) acknowledges and embraces the will of the Father as immutable, while 'man shall find grace' accepts the duty offered him without doubt or qualification.

The account the Son then gives of grace as 'The speediest of thy wingèd messengers' (229) you may find syntactically difficult, but the key idea of grace preceding all else, independent of man's seeking it or prayer, 'Comes unprevented, unimplored, unsought' (231), is what really matters here. That is why man is 'happy' even though he can never seek grace 'once dead in sins and lost' (233). Grace is given freely and unconditionally. The dire circumstance mankind is in, highlighted by Milton at lines 222–4, is once more made chillingly clear through the idea that were he to seek 'Atonement' (234) or a suitable offering to placate the Father, an 'offering meet' (234), where 'meet' has the older meaning of suitable or appropriate, he would be categorically unable to find one. The terse negatives in line 235, the finality of the harsh sounding 'indebted' and 'undone', and the subtle assonance, 'undone' and 'none', combine to create an overall effect of absolute loss.

This grim acknowledgement is then immediately countered by the vitality and energy of the Son's 'Behold me then' (235) and the light, almost excited, rhythm of the following few lines, built up of short syllables and phrases, that give the Son's offer a dramatic impact. There is a beautiful simplicity, given the sophistication of the theological arguments which have led up to this point, in the Son's 'me for him' (236) and in the eagerness his voice seems to possess. The Son knows exactly what he is giving up and what he is accepting, so he talks of leaving 'Thy bosom' and the 'glory next to thee' (239), which he will 'Freely put off' (240), even be 'Well pleased' (241) that he is doing so, since he also knows that though 'Death wreak all his rage' (241) he is immortal and will ultimately 'rise victorious' (250). He gives the reader plenty to reflect on in his simple acceptance, 'by thee I live' (244), where Milton seems to be exhorting the reader to follow his example, the *sine qua non* of any Christian life.[7] The shift to the present tense is also significant and continued in the next line in 'I yield' (245) since the Son knows the mere act of answering has made his suffering and death on the cross inevitable, just as his resurrection and ultimate triumph over Death is inevitable. You might also have noticed here that the language of commerce and debt permeates this section. The Son says 'Account me man' (238) after talking of mankind being 'Indebted' (235) and speaks of his now being Death's 'due' (245) and 'that debt paid' (246).

In his description of his ultimate triumph, the Son asks no questions of the Father, since they are of one mind. Instead he makes clear statements, 'Thou wilt not leave me in the loathsome grave' (247) and 'I shall rise victorious' (250). He uses paradox and plays with words in the same way that the Father has, 'spoiled of his vaunted spoil' (251) and 'Death his death's wound shall them receive' (252), perhaps because on the simplest level such use of technique draws the reader's attention to an idea or an image, but perhaps also because, having personified Sin and Death in the detailed way Milton has, at this juncture it makes dramatic sense to mock and humiliate them. If you recall the encounter between Satan and Death, Milton made much of Death's 'mortal sting' (253) in Book 2 (672, 729) and here it ends a typically lengthy Miltonic sentence which has occupied twenty-seven lines. The Son then invites the reader to anticipate the Second Coming, which for many Protestants in Milton's age felt like a very real possibility and not some far distant, interstellar event. He draws for us a picture that we should find relatively easy to respond imaginatively to: Christ 'in triumph high' (254) leading 'hell captive maugre hell' (255), where 'maugre' simply means 'in spite of', and with Satan and all 'The powers of darkness bound' (256). The caesura here appears to be justified because the Son now defers to his father once more, 'Thou at the sight' (256), and depicts him 'Pleased' (257) and smiling, a very human detail which some of the Father's fiercest critics neglect. Paradox comes into play again in the succinctly witty 'While by thee raised, I ruin all my foes' (258) before, keeping strictly to the Bible's account, Death finally dies ingloriously, 'Death last, and with his carcass glut the grave' (259), the choice of 'glut' ironically recalling the terrible greed with which Death responded to Satan's promises in Book 2 (845–7).

The final few lines of his speech now describe, in terms far less exciting and dramatic than those used to describe the Son's triumph, the 'multitude of my redeemed' (260) entering heaven where, finally, the Father has been appeased, and 'peace' (263) and 'reconcilement' (264) combine such that 'wrath shall be no more' (264) and in God's presence there is eternally only 'joy entire' (265).

Hymns of Praise

The Son's acceptance of his Father's will causes all heaven to stand in admiration and to wonder 'what this might mean' (272), but they do not have long to wait before the Father tells them. What will almost certainly strike you first about this next section (344–415) is the return of complex syntax and the difficulty the reader faces simply trying to relate a large number of dependent clauses and phrases to each other coherently.

It is easy to appreciate that 'The multitude of angels' (345) is the subject of the first, lengthy and unwieldy sentence, but finding the main verb is less straightforward. You might regard 'uttering' (346) as the obvious candidate, but if 'uttering joy' is a phrase which qualifies the preceding simile, 'As from blest voices' (347), then perhaps 'rung' (347) is the main verb, an idea which becomes more tolerable if you invert 'heaven rung' (347) – but that would have been a simple option open to Milton. What is more straightforward is that until the caesura in line 349 after 'regions', the entire heavenly host excel themselves in expressing joy at what has really amounted to a complete plan for the entire universe to the end of time, an effect conveyed as much by hyperbole as anything else. The angels' shout is 'Loud as from numbers without number' (346) and the sound fills 'the eternal regions' (349).

Yet they are also deeply reverential, bowing to the thrones of both the Father and Son before casting their crowns of 'amaranth and gold' (352) to the ground in 'solemn adoration' (351). Milton digresses at the mention of amaranth to create his own mythical version of what his readers would have already known was a flower with a pedigree in Greek mythology and poetry, synonymous with unfading. How he does this is very typical of the way the poem weaves together classical and Christian literature, switching without hesitation or explanation from heaven to Elysium in his use of the 'Elisian flowers' (359) that the river of bliss waters. This whole passage seems intent on drawing a gorgeous, sensuous, colourful picture through the use of words like 'gold' (352), 'amber' (359), 'jasper' (363) and 'empurpled' (364) and through the very painterly, almost Pre-Raphaelite image of the angels binding their hair with the amaranth flowers and beams of light:

> With these that never fade the spirits elect
> Bind their resplendent locks enwreathed with beams, (360–1)

It is quite noticeably unpuritanical, the kind of imagery we would expect of the Catholic tradition, but not the ascetic Protestant palette Luther[8] had originated, and to which Milton subscribed. It is also the kind of luxurious decadence more likely to be associated with Royalists whom Milton often savaged in his prose writings. The end result of so many angels tossing aside their garlands of amaranth is a 'Pavement that like a sea of jasper shone/Empurpled with celestial roses smiled' (364), an image of quite startling beauty and luxury, purple being the colour of imperial Rome, and jasper a semi-precious stone of great beauty and variety that was hugely popular in the ancient world and often found in very Catholic religious artefacts such as reliquaries.[9]

The angelic voices then quickly proceed to express their praise of God in song, taking up again 'glittering' harps that are eternally in tune and which hung 'like quivers' (367). Whether Milton wishes us to connect the shape or the purpose isn't clear, though his angels are throughout the poem invested with a martial function and hierarchy. More obviously significant is the harmony that Milton conventionally associates with this heavenly music. This brief section typifies how alert you need to be, as students of Milton, to the historical nuances of the individual words he uses, or what might more generally be termed semantics. The angelic hymn begins with a 'preamble sweet' (367) where 'preamble' was a word more usually employed in the context of speech or writing, not music. And Milton appears to use the word 'symphony' (368) as much for its older meaning of 'harmonious' as to denote a musical piece without voice, while, in being also 'charming', we might hear first a highly qualitative judgement rather than the magical, spell-binding quality the word also conveys and which is much more appropriate here. The perfect nature of this music which 'wakens raptures high' (369) is reinforced by the assertion that all those present took part in the singing melodiously, since in heaven order and harmony is the natural state of affairs, 'such concord is in heaven' (371).

Their hymn opens with praise of the Father and next of the Son, and employs the kind of language familiar to readers of the Bible or possibly of later Anglican hymnals. The Father is given absolute superlatives, not only 'omnipotent' (372) but 'immutable, immortal, infinite' (373); he is the 'author of all being' (374) and 'Fountain of light' (375), the latter image providing the springboard to a complex interplay of images revolving around light and dark, all designed to convey the invisible, unknowable nature of God. The Father is imagined 'Throned inaccessible', (377) in 'glorious brightness' (376) of such magnitude that, even when he reduces the overwhelming power of that light and 'shad'st' (380) himself from view in a 'cloud' (378) encompassing him 'like a radiant shrine' (379), he retains sufficient light to dazzle the eyes of approaching angels. The climax of this image comes in line 380 where Milton uses a familiar oxymoron, 'Dark with excessive bright' to encourage us to feel the same sense of awe he himself seems to feel in contemplation of his God.

Secondly, the angels sing the praises of the Son, and again imagery of light and dark, brightness and cloud, is deployed to meet the require-ments of divine praise and duty as well as the theological difficulties inherent in the Holy Trinity. Milton's clever phrase, 'on thee/Impressed the effulgence of his glory abides' (387–8), is, for example, as eloquent an attempt to convey the nature of the Trinity as you are likely to find, where 'effulgence' is a synonym for 'radiance'. The angels now turn to events in their hymn, and specifically the events that will ulti-mately to the defeat of Satan outlined earlier. The past tense in 'threw down' (391) indicates that the event they refer to is the original con-flict in heaven, where it was the Son who led the forces of good against Satan, 'The aspiring dominations' (392), and defeated him, although the power he wielded was God's, 'Thy Father's dreadful thunder did not spare' (393). The final image of the Son's flaming chariot wheels, crush-ing the necks of 'warring angels' (396), gives us a foretaste of the more detailed account and description of this cataclysmic event to be found in Book 6 (746–866).

A third section of this hymn concerns man and reiterates the earlier statement made by the Father (90–134) that, knowing man's seduction to be by Satan, he will provide a mechanism to save man from the same fate again: the subsequent sacrifice made by the Son. You will come across a lot of debate and speculation in your critical reading on *Paradise Lost* that focuses on guilt and aims at describing precisely to what degree Adam and Eve are culpable. Mankind 'thou didst not doom/So strictly, but much more to pity incline (401–2) because, cru-cially, man has 'through their malice fallen' (400), where 'their' refers specifically to the earlier 'aspiring dominations' (392). The angels' hymn also lays considerable weight on the Son's immeasurable generosity, his willingness to sacrifice himself in order to save mankind. 'No sooner' (403) did he perceive the Father's intention to act less punitively against man, than he offered himself, 'Regardless of the bliss wherein he sat' (408). The power of this moment, once again signalled by use of a caesura, 'For man's offence' (410), is immediately followed by the hyperbolic exclamation, 'Oh unexampled love', and the assertion that such love supersedes anything man can muster, 'Love nowhere to be found less than divine!' (411).

The Power of Deceit

After a lengthy diversion to Limbo, a destination Milton relishes for the opportunity it provides him to ridicule Catholicism and those he saw as his intellectual enemies,[10] Satan settles on the sun and seeks directions to the earth from Uriel, but little else – yet this slight episode extends over almost 150 lines. We have seen Satan exert his influence over those who had followed him to hell and on the ignominious offspring of his rebellion, Sin and Death, but this is the first time Milton places him in an arena approaching the human. Though Uriel is an archangel, Milton treats him in a similar way to Adam and the conversation that takes place has many connections with Satan's later encounter with both Adam and Eve.

In stark contrast with the black and dark world from which he has escaped, this new world Satan enters is full of brilliance and light, his clarity of vision emphasised by the image of the shadowless sunlight created by the sun in its prelapsarian, untilted orbit. The physics of light was still in its infancy in Milton's era and so you may find yourself confused by the idea of light rays travelling from the eye to the object, as they do here. Unrestricted by shadow or obstacle, Satan's gaze lands on the figure of an angel, Uriel, who is also described in terms of light and brilliance, 'His back was turned, but not his brightness hid' (624); on his head he wears a crown, 'a golden tiar' (625) of 'beaming sunny rays'; and his hair shines 'Illustrious' (627), where the root of the word 'lustre' is privileged above the more immediate character sense of 'illustrious'. Milton's angel is conventionally still and impressive, as though standing guard over something of great import or deep in thought, the phrase 'or fixed in cogitation deep' (629) typical of the elevated, respectful tone Milton adopts of angels throughout the poem.

Satan is pleased at finding Uriel since he requires directions to Paradise, but Milton's description of him as the 'spirit impure' (630) is in itself interesting and points to how different in essence he is from Uriel and the other angels. Milton describes Paradise as the end of Satan's wandering journey but balances the line cleverly through the antithetical use of 'end' and 'beginning' (633). In telling this story, Milton faces the peculiar dilemma of all dramatists and storytellers who choose a well known tale as their source: how to maintain the listeners' attention when the outcome is already known. Part of the success of this complex and epic work lies in the way he achieves this, weaving intricate detail around the bare bones of the tale and drawing us into the world he creates as though we are simultaneously witnesses and victims. Slight asides, like the one contained within line 633, contribute to this effect because they draw us into the poet's confidence. When Milton says 'our woe' he is assuming his reader shares his own, deeply held, Christian faith.

The drama continues as Satan changes his shape to deceive Uriel. This characteristic ability of the devil to change form is one that would have not surprised Milton's readers in the least, and is indeed central to his deception of Eve in Genesis. It had, by Milton's era, become a commonplace indication of evil when manifest on earth. Throughout *Paradise Lost*, in most cases Satan chooses to change into an animal, but here he becomes 'a stripling cherub' (636) whose demeanour is so full of innocent admiration that Uriel is easily deceived. In Satan's new face, 'Youth smiled celestial' (638), and with heavy irony, Milton infuses his appearance with 'grace' (639), the one attribute eternally denied Satan. The physical description continues in the same, picturesque vein as the description of Uriel. He too wears a 'coronet' (640), his hair too is curled and 'flowing' (640), while the wings Milton gives him are especially gorgeous and ornate, 'Of many a coloured plume, sprinkled with gold' (641). Like many mythical messengers, he is made and dressed for speed, the sibilant combination 'speed succinct' (643) breaking the flow of the line abruptly, but adding to the image of his potential for swift movement.

As Uriel hears Satan's approach and turns to inspect him, the rhythm becomes more broken and shorter phrases help to create dramatic uncertainty about his reception by this, no ordinary, angel, but who is one of the seven principal angels who Milton reminds us 'are his eyes/That run through all the heavens' (650-1), which adds to the dramatic tension. When Satan speaks, Milton uses the present tense, again for dramatic effect, 'him Satan thus accosts' (653), and gives Satan an elaborately constructed, almost impenetrably lengthy, opening sentence which disarms Uriel as much as it demands our concentration. Try reading lines 654-67 not simply as a unit, but as also trying to give Satan's cherubic voice the kind of pace and tone you feel is appropriate. You are almost certain to make a hash of it at first, since the syntax Milton uses is so fundamentally different from contemporary speech, drama or verse. But if you try this simple shortcut, you may find it much less problematic. Start by reading only the single word of address, 'Uriel' (654), then immediately skip to lines 662–3, then again to line 666 and the end of the sentence which finishes midway through line 667. Turning this into prose for the moment, what you should hear is this: 'Uriel, unspeakable desire to see and know all these, his wondrous works, hath brought me from the choirs of cherubim alone thus wandering'. This is the core of this sentence and the brilliant excuse Satan's cherub uses to wheedle a way past the vigilant Uriel. He has left his companion cherubs in order to admire God's wonderful creations.

If you now try again to read the sentence as a whole, you should find it much easier to handle the digressions, the first, a lengthy and unctuous acknowledgement of Uriel's status, the second a much more cunningly delivered but vital reference to man as God's greatest creation. Satan's mission is to seduce man and to accomplish that he must logically locate him, but to ask directions to Paradise outright is hardly a tactic without risk, so Milton gives him this convoluted but skilful preamble to the question itself. A useful point to store for later use is the telling phrase the cherub uses to describe man, God's 'chief delight and favour' (664). Is it too fanciful to hear Satan's barely suppressed envy seeping through at this point, or is this an epithet Uriel would expect and acknowledge? In this respect, the cherub also makes clear his belief that all this newly created magnificence has been done for man's benefit and pleasure. A caesura marks out the preamble from the crucial question, and maintaining his deferential approach, 'Brightest seraph' (667), the cherub then asks Uriel directly where he can find man. The question is again contained within a lengthy sentence of difficult syntax, though less so than the previous one, and you may well find it straightforward to read this aloud and accurately, but, if you struggle at first, pick out the two uses of the 'that' as a conjunction. The basic structure used is 'tell (me)...that I may find him...that...we may praise...' (667–76).

Grasping the syntax is, as ever, only the start of a useful and intelligent analysis and this little piece of dialogue contains a wealth of critical material for the alert student. The first part of his question acknowledges the beauty of God's creation, 'these shining orbs' (668), while simultaneously testing to find out if God has set limits on man's realm, 'or fixèd seat hath none' (669), and you may even detect an oddly futuristic nuance to the notion that man might have been granted the freedom in 'all these shining orbs his choice to dwell' (670). The motive comes next, and it leaves Uriel no reason to doubt or challenge the cherub.

Satan's hypocrisy is ironically at its most visible to us, when it is invisible to Uriel, and his imputed desire to see man 'with secret gaze' (671) or 'in open admiration' (672) in order that 'The universal maker we may praise' (676) is of course the opposite of the truth. The subtlety of Milton's characterization and the skill of his dramatic writing is evident when, even at his best in terms of acuity and wit, Satan's coarse envy seems to seep through. We can hear it in the repetition and hyperbole:

> On whom the great creator hath bestowed
> Worlds, and on whom hath all these graces poured; (673–4)

Yet at the same time Milton is generating in us a sense of our own greatness and wonder. Man is, in Milton's philosophical view, a magnificent creation, genuinely made in the likeness of God. The key to the cherub's successful negotiation comes at this point where he not only asserts the correct, heavenly motive to his actions, but adds a few generous touches of his own. A key phrase is 'as is meet' (675), where 'meet' has the meaning of 'suitable' or 'appropriate'; but then the cherub suddenly makes a distinct and intriguing connection between man and hell which raises all sorts of critical issues for us.

Acknowledging God's just punishment of the rebel angels, 'Who justly hath driven out his rebel foes/To deepest hell' (677–8), he then states that the creation of man and this new universe was 'to repair that loss' (678). God, the cherub asserts, has created man directly – as a consequence of the war in heaven and the loss of the rebel angels to hell – 'to serve him better' (680), we must assume, than the rebels did. The final subtle flourish comes after this caesura, perhaps so we can admire the hypocrisy all the more: 'wise are all his ways' (680), where the roundness of the phrase created by what is in effect a half-rhyme between 'wise' and 'ways' sounds like a mock prayer or shared salutation.

The dialogue then shifts to the narrator and there may be a number of reasons why Milton felt the need to intervene here between his two characters. One of those is perhaps at the forefront of your own mind if you are relatively new to the poem, or to Milton, which is the issue about God's omnipotence. If God knows all, then why does he permit Satan to deceive Uriel in this manner? The answer rests in the crucially complex concept of free will. That appears to be what lies behind the explanation the narrator himself now offers the puzzled reader. He calls Satan a 'false dissembler, unperceived' (681) and asserts that 'neither man nor angel can discern/Hypocrisy' (682–3), since it is the 'only evil' (683) invisible to all but God, before the most important phrase, 'By his permissive will' (685). Milton ascribes to God the will to permit events as well as determine them, and into that permissive world he places man. If we are still bemused at Uriel's gullibility, then the poet rather than the philosopher in Milton comes to his rescue in the next few lines (686–9) where Uriel's state of mind is conveyed through an elegant combination of metaphor and alliteration. Like all good metaphors, it uses few words but is replete with meaning. Wisdom, suspicion and simplicity are all personified momentarily, perhaps even in stark contrast with Sin and Death. And to remove all doubt, Milton adds the kind of elegantly constructed phrase which can be easily overlooked or misread by the student unused to enjambment, 'while goodness thinks no ill/Where no ill seems' (688–9). All of this leads to Uriel's deception, even though he is 'The sharpest sighted spirit of all in heaven' (691), before the narrator gives way to Uriel's own voice.

That his deception is complete is rendered obvious by the ironic 'Fair angel' with which Uriel begins his reply to the cherubic Satan. Once again the syntax here can cause difficulty. Uriel uses a very logical, dialectic tone to argue that the cherub is blameless in straying alone from heaven to see God's latest creations in this unusual manner. The most difficult term is probably 'excess' (696–8), but on reflection you may agree that it is precisely the right word for the purpose since Uriel's point is that, in making this *excessive* journey alone, the cherub merits praise rather than blame since the motive, praising God, is without question good. It will also help to allow a sufficient pause at the end of line 701, after Uriel has recognized that the cherub is unusual in *not* being satisfied with report only, as is the rest of heaven, but must see God's latest creations for himself. The next few lines echo one of the most famous Psalms (111:2–4) and reiterate the positive motive behind admiration of God's creations before Uriel concludes the first part of his reply with his own divine eulogy which yet retains his logical tone. If all minds are created by God, then how can they, he argues, grasp either the scale or purpose of God's creations. Only God can know 'their causes deep' (777).

Many students of Milton find his metaphysics heavy going to say the least, and certainly the scholarly work that relates the Miltonic universe to the Ptolemaic one, to Virgil's *Aenied* or to Dante's *Divine Comedy* is something of an acquired taste; but if you read what Uriel now says about creation with a predominantly poetic rather than theological sensibility, then I think you may be pleasantly surprised. In one, long, rather beautiful sentence (708–21) Uriel describes what modern physics would term, with perhaps appropriately mundane understatement, The Big Bang,[11] although it is difficult to resist the temptation to compare Uriel's eloquent picture with the rather crassly alliterative marketing tone of the modern phrase. Uriel is the perfect witness: 'I saw,' he declares, 'when at his word the formless mass ... came to a heap' (708–9); and in trying to describe the indescribable, he resorts to both hyperbole and paradox, sometimes together:

> Confusion heard his voice, and wild uproar
> Stood ruled, stood vast infinitude confined: (710–11)

God's second action is the creation of light, 'at his second bidding, darkness fled' (712), and from this 'order from disorder sprung' (713). The four weighty 'cumbrous' (715) elements fly upwards with the ether, which forms the sun they are now both standing on, 'this ethereal quintessénce of heaven' (716), and combined with 'various forms,/That rolled orbicular' (717–8) and created the innumerable stars Uriel now indicates to the cherub. The listing of the single syllable elements creates a sense of urgency and impulsion before the ingeniously elided phrase 'Flew upward' (717) captures perfectly the instantaneous nature of the event. It is almost impossible to separate the two words and remain intelligible. There is also something equally attractive about the phrase 'rolled orbicular' (718), which Milton employs to describe the creation of the stars.

From their vantage point, Uriel now responds directly to the cherub's question and points out to him where the earth sits in the sky and where, on its surface, Paradise lies. This is in some ways a curious account, since at first sight we are given far more information about the moon, 'that opposite fair star' (727), than the earth. But a closer analysis produces some interesting things to consider. The picture Uriel gives us is of a planet where the hemisphere facing us reflects the light of the sun and is in daylight, while the other is in darkness, night. Perhaps the clue lies in the single word 'invade' (726) to describe earth's relationship with night. It is because the earth is threatened with invasion by the night, that the moon becomes so important, staving off complete darkness and the night's successful invasion, 'and in her pale dominion checks the night' (732). In contrast with Uriel's account of creation, this description is also distinctly lyrical:

> ... but there the neighbouring moon
> (So call that opposite fair star) her aid
> Timely interposes, (726–8)

This is a chunk of verse which could be pure Shakespeare. What this points to is Milton's dramatic control since, unlike Uriel, we know the cherub's intent and, like night, Satan is poised to invade the as yet innocently beautiful earth. There is something of an anticlimax in Uriel's parting assistance:

> That spot to which I point is Paradise,
> Adam's abode, those lofty shades his bower. (733–4)

Paradise becomes a 'spot' and its betrayal a simple physical gesture, although we might immediately think of Christ in the Garden of Gethsemane and Judas's own simple act of betrayal.[12] Possessed of the information he needs, Satan wastes no time on further conversation but maintains his cherubic disguise and leaves Uriel 'bowing low' (736), showing due deference and civility to the superior spirit. His eagerness is clear, 'sped with hoped success' (740) and 'Nor stayed' (742), but Milton adds to the irony by letting Satan indulge in a few aerobatics on his way down, 'with many an airy wheel' (741), all contributing to the suspenseful close to this book where Satan is left, ominously, on top of Mount Niphates, the perfect vantage point from which to survey Paradise.

Exercises

Lines 135–66. These few lines contain the Son's impassioned reply to his Father. Read it through yourself, or if possible listen to a recorded reading of it, and consider how the Son's tone contrasts with the Father's.

Lines 416–612. This section of the poem deals with Satan's arrival on the very edge of the earth, the region of the heavens Christian theologians would recognise as Limbo. As you read it, note and reflect on the extended similes and images he uses throughout and ask yourself why Milton might have expended so much energy and detail on this curious and little known location.

4

Paradise Perturbed

Summary

On the summit of Mount Niphates, Satan pauses, but, instead of joy or relief, he finds himself in a turmoil of doubt and despair, the living proof that, although he may have successfully escaped hell, left his companions and journeyed this far, hell is in fact a state of mind he brings with him. His inner debate over the acts that have led him here conclude in renewed enmity against God and his new favourite, man. In his passion, Satan betrays his true nature to Uriel who observes a physical change in his aspect from his place in the heavens. Satan avoids entering Eden by the gate and leaps over the high wall of trees unnoticed and alights on the Tree of Life where he freely admires the beauties and richness of Paradise. Amongst all the new creatures his regard finally settles on Adam and Eve. He notes their likeness to God and their obvious superiority to the rest of creation. Satan describes Adam and Eve admiringly, the viewpoint shifting uneasily from Milton to Satan, until Satan finally declares his overwhelming sense of envy at the sight of such grace and beauty and announces his determination to destroy them both, with all their children. Alighting from the Tree Satan adopts various animal disguises in order to get closer to Adam and Eve to spy on them.

Adam invites Eve to join him in praising God for all the rich beauty and pleasure he has granted them, adding the single condition that they do not eat the fruit of the Tree of Knowledge, dramatically providing Satan with the information he needs to seduce them into disobedience. Eve responds with words of love and she retells how she was brought to consciousness by God and how she learned that she was made from Adam's own body. Satan reacts angrily to their loving exchange and deduces that the price of disobeying God's sole command will be sin and death. He determines to engage them in conversation and deceive them into questioning God's sole command before leaving them alone to seek out more information he might be able to use against them.

Uriel flies down to meet the archangel Gabriel, where he sits on guard at the gates of Eden, and tells him of the spirit he directed towards earth and how he observed him change his aspect. Uriel concludes that one of the fallen angels has somehow escaped and is intent on evil. Gabriel promises Uriel that he will discover the intruder before dawn. Uriel flies back to his post.

Adam and Eve discuss what they know of the universe, all within the context of their love for each other and for God, before seeking rest in their bower which Milton describes as much in terms of their sexual relationship as a place of shelter. Gabriel sends two angels, Ithuriel and Zephon, to check Adam and Eve are safe but they find Satan whispering evil into Eve's sleeping ear. They escort Satan to Gabriel and he and Satan trade insults and re-enact something of the division which led to the war in heaven. It seems as though Satan might begin a new war as the gathered ranks of Gabriel's forces surround him and he grows more confidently angry; but God intervenes, creating a sign in the heavens which Gabriel draws Satan's attention to, and he flees.

Satan's Inner Hell

From the top of Mount Niphates, Satan has a truly spectacular view, but Milton delays our enjoyment of it to focus on Satan's state of mind. The opening to Book 4 contributes much to our understanding of Satan's motives, his psychological state and how both relate to Milton's understanding of hell and damnation, and therefore to mankind's own, inherited, moral vulnerability.

That narrator of *Paradise Lost* is never afraid to seek inspirational help, and Milton wishes he could summon the same terrible sense of impending disaster to be found in the book of the Apocalypse, since Satan's safe arrival on earth has such mortifying consequences for man, and therefore for us, the reader. He allows himself momentarily to wish that Adam and Eve had escaped Satan's 'mortal snare' (8), but it is a forlorn hope and quickly Milton takes the narrative back to Satan's here and now. Although at the end of Book 3 we left Satan wheeling through the air with hope of success, when he arrives his dominant emotion is unqualified 'rage' (9). He has already been likened to the apocalyptic dragon who 'Came furious down to be revenged on men' (4), and Milton is quick to focus on the cause of that rage. You would be perfectly justified in asking, what has man done to deserve this? After all, at this point Adam is living a completely innocent life with no connection of any kind to Satan. The connection is made by Milton through Satan, who 'inflamed with rage' (9) sees a pertinent connection between himself and man:

> To wreak on innocent frail man his loss
> Of that first battle, and his flight to hell: (11–12)

In Satan's envious mind, this new level of creation is God's reaction to his rebellion and the creation of hell, and therefore man has supplanted him directly. An idea first raised by Beëlzebub in Book 2 (345–77).

Sections of the poem, like this one, tempt some critics[1] to focus their attention on Satan at the expense of other key figures in the poem. Although Satan appears to have every right to feel 'bold' (13), since he has accomplished the perilous journey 'far off and fearless' (14) that he set himself at the counsel of the devils, even to 'boast' (14), quite another emotion fires him at the moment before he makes 'his dire attempt' (15). Milton captures this moment skilfully and provides us with a fascinating image to analyse. He selects birth as the central metaphor, 'which nigh the birth' (15), but then develops the image in a surprising way, 'Now rolling, boils in his tumultuous breast' (16). 'Rolling' is a very odd choice of word, even in Milton's era, to describe the subject it qualifies, which is 'his dire attempt' (15). The Oxford English Dictionary defines the word as meaning 'to revolve in one's mind, as of thoughts' as early as 1547, but this lies a little uncomfortably with the central birth metaphor. However, if you extract these few lines, you can begin to see right inside Milton's verse:

> ... which nigh the birth
> Now rolling, boils in his tumultuous breast,
> And like a devilish engine back recoils
> Upon himself; (15–18)

The major effect Milton appears to be seeking is the contrast between the gestation of the idea in Satan's mind and its surprising emotional effect on him; and he achieves this primarily through the contrast in sound as well as the 'devilish engine' image of the recoiling cannon. So 'Now rolling' is a lengthy, drawn out phrase, connected much more strongly to 'boils' by rhythm and sound than by meaning, as are both to 'tumultuous' (16). And this elongated line with its lengthy stresses is contrasted with the terse, stress pattern of the next line and the hard edginess of 'back recoils' with its clever internal repetition of the 'ck' sound, mimicking the effect of the back firing cannon, finally coming to an abrupt rest with the curt, natural cadence of 'himself' (18). There is also the witty internal rhyme Milton creates between 'boils' and 'recoils' that links the two lines together.

No longer the cherub who ended Book 3, Satan is confronted with the absolute consequences of his own, absolute actions. Milton gives us an intimate glimpse inside Satan's mind before turning to dramatic monologue at line 32 as the means to articulate it further. Satan's otherwise implacable intent is disturbed by 'horror and doubt' (18). Milton chooses this moment to replicate a conceit that would be well known to his contemporary readers, the idea that hell is not a place, but a state of mind. Its most famous appearance is perhaps in Marlowe's *Dr Faustus* where Mephistopheles answers the Doctor's question, 'How comes it then that thou art out of hell?', with chilling accuracy, 'Why this is hell, nor am I out of it'.[2] Here, the narrator refers to the 'hell within him' (20), adding that Satan not only carries hell inside, but 'round about him' (21) and ironically pointing out his failure to escape, through the image,

> . . . nor from hell
> One step no more than from himself can fly
> By change of place: (21–3)

This is all the more telling given the vast distance and perilous nature of his journey. After the caesura, Milton makes conscience the chief cause of Satan's uneasiness, allocating two objects to the one subject: 'despair' (23) and 'bitter memory' (24). Recalling what he once was causes Satan, surprisingly perhaps, to grieve, although the list and syntax used places greater weight on what is to come than on what was or is. It is a potent way to maintain the reader's empathy with the narrative, since it is Adam, and thus ourselves, who are the victims of what is to come. We may know this epic tale's ultimate outcome, but that doesn't necessarily mean we cannot respond to dramatic tension, and, when Satan's soliloquy begins, we undoubtedly listen with some care. In the few moments before his thoughts are given free rein, Satan looks sadly towards 'pleasant' (28) Eden and 'towards heaven and the full-blazing sun' (29) with the rich connotation of repentance that the pun on 'Son' gives rise to. There might be some confusion caused by 'revolving' (31) because of the recent mention of the sun, and editors usually translate this as 'pondering' to remove that confusion, but as we discovered earlier in the case of 'rolling' (16) Milton's choice of individual words can be instructive and 'revolving' conveys much more accurately Satan's indecisiveness.

Satan begins by addressing the watching sun, who, godlike, watches over 'this new world' (34) and whose brightness causes all the stars to 'hide their diminished heads' (35). It reminds Satan of his own former brilliance, 'how glorious once above thy sphere' (39), the pun on sun/Son (37) reminding us of the reasons for Satan's dramatic fall from grace. Satan chooses 'hate' (37) to describe his emotional reaction to the vision he now sees, and, in a moment of unusual honesty, ascribes his downfall unequivocally to 'pride and worse ambition' (40) in what was ultimately a futile contest since he chose to fight with 'heaven's matchless king' (41). Of all the epithets available to Milton to describe God here, 'matchless' is striking in that it comes from Satan's lips. The emotion Milton invests in Satan here is also evident in exclamations like 'Ah wherefore!' (42) and 'How due!' (48). Milton has gone to some pains to generate the irony in bringing Satan to this vantage point, where everything God has newly created for man is tantalizingly within sight but eternally beyond his grasp. As befits a dramatic monologue, Milton builds it around a series of questions, nine in all, some sounding highly rhetorical coming immediately after information that renders them almost nonsensical. So after reminding himself that God not only made him, but made him the glorious angel he once was, 'In that bright eminence' (44), and that God's essential goodness meant he was incapable of reproachful treatment of those who served him, 'Upbraided none' (45), 'nor was his service hard' (45), Satan is forced to conclude that paying him homage was 'The easiest recompense' (47). After the plaintive 'How due!' (48) comes one of the poem's most poignant statements, 'Yet all his good proved ill in me,/And wrought but malice' (48–9), the rhythm falling heavily on the final, powerful word.

Satan is undoubtedly an intellect to respect, if not admire, as he moves from raw emotion to more reasoned, agile argument. You can see this in the compressed way he conveys the complex idea that, having been raised to a position of great authority, he found praise and service beneath him, but, instead of a lengthy, drawn out process of undermining or challenging God, which might have been politically expedient, his reaction led to immediate rebellion. Satan's abandonment of goodness happened 'in a moment' (51). A good example is the unusual sounding 'I sdeigned subjection' (50), where choosing to contract the word 'disdained' and alliterate it with the first syllable of 'subjection' creates an audible sneer, before the logically neat progression of 'one step higher/Would set me highest' (50–1). His intellect is

equally clear in the currency image Satan uses to describe the consequences of the moment he abandoned goodness. The verb 'quit' (51)
introduces the image through indebtedness, but the nature of the debt is
more revealing if we are interested in exposing Satan's quick mind. 'The
debt immense of endless gratitude' (52) contains a number of lengthy
syllables, and the rhythm invites the reader to sustain the first syllable
of 'endless' to suit the sense as much as the sound. We gain a momentary insight into the motive behind Satan's fall when he articulates the
debt's eternal nature so well, 'still paying, still to owe' (53), but quickly
refutes his own feeling by asserting that he had forgotten the other side
of the debt, that which he had received eternally from God. The whole
image is then enriched by the paradoxical observation that 'a grateful
mind/By owing owes not' (55–6) since if it springs from genuine gratitude, it is simultaneously 'Indebted and discharged' (57). The debt image
culminates in the challenging rhetoric of 'What burden then?'.

Although there is clearly emotion in Satan's words here, perhaps
the most poignant appeal to the reader comes in his sad wish to have
been made not as he was, but as 'some inferior angel' (59) who 'had
stood/Then happy' (59–60) since he would never have been troubled by
his own personal seducer, 'Ambition' (61). The argument continues as
he challenges his own supposition, 'Yet why not?' (61), since how could
he know that some other leading angel would not have responded as he
did, seducing him to join a rebellion as he seduced others? The nimble
nature of his mind is clear as he immediately refutes this with the telling
acknowledgement that angels as great as he were not so tempted and
'stand unshaken' (64), if anything even stronger in resolve, 'to all temp-
tations armed' (65). His qualifying their loyal state with 'from within/Or
from without' (64–5) is another indication of just how redolent this
soliloquy is with self-knowledge, since he knows that his temptation
came from 'within'.

At this point Satan poses what might be regarded as the central question of the entire poem and of Milton's theodicy, to justify the ways
of God to men. 'Hadst thou the same free will and power to stand?'
(66). In this single line, Milton embeds his own Arminian belief in the
existence of free will, in direct contradiction to much contemporary
Protestant thought on predetermination, since Satan instantly responds
to his own question affirmatively, 'Thou hadst' (67), the simplicity and
the caesura sounding irrefutable. Logic leads Satan to another, significant, rhetorical question. Since he acted with free will, who can he
accuse or blame but himself? If you are deep into your study of this
poem, and have become familiar with it as a battleground for critical

debate, it is worth reflecting on Satan's recognition of God's goodness and love. The only thing there is for him to accuse, his argument tells him, is 'heaven's free love dealt equally to all?' (68).

Milton's Christian readership, and students who have had an education rooted in Christian thought and ethics, will fully appreciate that there is a relationship between penitence, mercy and salvation. So it is here that Satan, as it were in front of our very eyes, once again exercises his free will . . . and chooses evil. He does so in a single, noticeably short sentence, clearly separated out from the argument that has led to it. Yet ironically, there is a terrible logic to it:

> Be then his love accursed, since love or hate,
> To me alike, it deals eternal woe. (69–70)

But almost as soon as the dreadful words are uttered, and to Milton's readers these would have been dreadful words indeed, Satan feels doubt and instead curses himself, 'Nay, cursed be thou' (71), for using that free will God gave him to such catastrophic effect. Milton's syntactical skill is on show in the way he expresses Satan's regret, 'since against his thy will/Choose freely what it now so justly rues' (70–1). The two pronouns apply to the same noun 'will' and there is a near perfect balance achieved through the positioning of 'freely' and 'justly' while the single syllabled 'rues' brings the thought to a definitive close, inviting a new dramatic outburst of emotion, 'Me miserable!' (73), to follow. It is also worth noting that Satan uses the word 'justly' to describe his punishment. Milton has Satan writhe in an agony of doubt and remorse before our eyes. Relentlessly pursuing the logic of his own thought, with such beauty arrayed before him, Satan sees starkly the reality of his horizon, capturing the true nature of his dilemma in his inability to escape 'Infinite wrath, and infinite despair?' (74). If we were dealing with anyone else, this might be hyperbole, but for Satan and his followers this is literal truth and all the more terrible for that. 'Which way I fly is hell; myself am hell' (75) is equally a more powerful realization since it comes after such an epic journey.

Satan's metaphysical torment continues unabated as he resorts to hyperbole in the 'lower deep' that is lower than the 'lowest deep' (76) and which, compared to the hell he suffers now, 'seems a heaven' (77). Reminiscent of imagery Milton used to describe Death in Book 2 (666–79), this new horror 'Still threatening to devour me opens wide' (77), but it may not be immediately clear what this new misery consists of, until you remind yourself of the purpose of his journey. The consequence of any new assault on God's realm or divinity is further punishment, and Satan knows this is unavoidable. At this point his razor sharp logic has taken him to the only possible conclusion, 'Oh then at last relent' (79), where 'at last' sounds almost the product of exhaustion. The caesura leads to the most acutely pertinent question, which Milton's readers know is rhetorical, 'is there no place/Left for repentance, none for pardon left?' (79–80) since God is infinitely merciful. In a work of such magnitude and historical literary influence, it is difficult to recreate any kind of experience that could be described as a first reading, but, nonetheless, is it too fanciful here to imagine some of Milton's contemporaries holding their breath to see if Satan can find the humility necessary to save himself?

However strongly a reader is drawn into the drama, Satan's rejection of mercy is immediate and revealing. There can be no repentance without his 'submission' (81). Why, then, cannot Satan submit to God's greater goodness and mercy? The answer is twofold and highly significant. First, 'Disdain forbids me' (82) Satan states with neither qualification nor doubt, and it is worth reflecting on the strength of the noun he chooses because in essence he is committing a terrible sin every one of Milton's seventeenth-century readers would instantly recognise as pride. In an era where pride is almost a *sine qua non* of individuality,[3] you may find it difficult to appreciate how damning this decision is for Satan. In essence the disdain he refers to is a rather pitiful attempt to reassert his own angelic quality and status. Submission would be degrading. The second part of the answer is possibly more accessible. Satan dreads the 'shame' (82) he must endure from all those spirits he has drawn into hell with him, if he were to repent now. In the grip of an inner turmoil that renders his usual cunning and manipulative skills futile, he admits that he has 'seduced' (83) them with 'promises and other vaunts' (84), 'boasting I could subdue/The omnipotent' (85–6). The caesura allows a brief moment to reflect on the utter absurdity of that boast before he then voices a rare expression of self-pity in the most ironic terms, the 'Ay me', with which he begins this confession (86), indicative of emotion. This intricate though relatively brief sentence (86–92) is an excellent example of the economy of Milton's verse. If you read it through as a single sentence and focus your attention on how the pivotal phrase 'With diadem and sceptre high advanced' (90) fits into the structure, you should be able to see that it makes sense both forwards and backwards, in effect serving a dual purpose. In the backwards sense it qualifies his appearance 'on the throne of hell' (89) and going forwards it explains ironically how the higher he is raised in hell, the lower he actually falls until the ultimate irony, 'only supreme/In misery' (91–2). And the cause of all of this misery, Satan concludes, has been nothing more than his own 'ambition' (92). The rhythm isolates the single syllable 'joy' (92) and eloquently underpins the heavy irony. Even after reasoning his way to this clear expression of his dilemma, Satan postulates one last line of action. What if he could repent, he asks, and, more, actually recover 'By act of grace my former state' (94)? He knows that such a restoration of his position would inevitably lead to the same 'high thoughts' (95) which led him to rebel in the first place and that any submission would only ever be 'feigned' (96). As he writhes on the point of his own logic, Milton uses alliteration to give Satan the sibilant sounds to match his soon to be serpentine form:

> how soon unsay
> What feigned submission swore: ease would recant
> Vows made in pain as violent and void. (95–7)

Reminding himself of the hatred he feels, he can see no way to a 'true reconcilement' (98) and instead predicts such a return of enmity would inevitably lead to 'a worse relapse/And heavier fall' (100–1). Having taken Satan through this logical journey, Milton brings him to the close by tabling the central premise of his own theodicy: 'This knows my punisher' (103), Satan says. Since God knows all this, there is no possible escape for Satan; he is playing the role God has given him and peace between them is impossible. 'All hope excluded thus' (105), eternally exiled and cast out, Satan can now only admire the newly created world and God's 'new delight', man. To signal the close of this monologue, Milton repeats the idea that there is no hope left and lets Satan find some crumb of consolation in the knowledge that with the disappearance of hope, goes fear, 'So farewell hope, and with hope farewell fear' (108). To remove all doubt about Satan's reversal, Milton makes him dismiss forever 'remorse' (109), abandoning doubts and regret about past actions, freeing him completely to indulge future ones. Knowing now that 'all good to me is lost' (109), Satan can make the ultimate paradox sound entirely plausible, 'Evil be thou my good' (110). Reiterating the view expressed at the council of the devils, that at least this way they can divide the universe (II, 330–40), Satan finally declares war not just on God, but on man, 'As man ere long, and this new world shall know' (113), and prepares the way for the most dramatic encounter of the poem, his meeting with Eve.

Adam and Eve

Amidst the novel beauty and rich variety of Eden's landscape, from his predatory, tree top vantage point (194–6), Satan identifies man by his godlike appearance. The physical distinction is in their standing on two, not four, feet, 'Godlike erect' (289), but it is really their superior bearing and demeanour which catches Satan's attention. Milton uses a difficult phrase, 'with native honour clad' (289), to indicate this apparent authority. A modern sensibility might read 'native' as synonymous with natural, but in Milton's era literature on the differences between native and civilised cultures was popular and linked to the expansion of the map by explorers who were frequently encountering previously undiscovered native cultures in Africa and the Americas, which makes the phrase a highly conscious oxymoron. He is also exploiting the myth of the golden age[4] in which man lives a natural, rural, bucolic life in a kind of innocent bliss untainted by civilisation.

Satan recognises 'majesty' and acknowledges them as 'lords of all' (290) because he also sees their divine inheritance, 'for in their looks divine/The image of their glorious maker shone, (291–2). The divine qualities Milton ascribes to both Adam and Eve are 'Truth, wisdom, sanctitude severe and pure' (293), the last noun meaning saintliness, and in this little list you can see Milton's Puritan background. Never the most conventional of Puritans, he senses the need to qualify that very severity which the Puritan mind would most admire by repeating the word and adding an Arminian refinement, 'but in true filial freedom placed' (294). It is this freedom which will become so significant when temptation is put before both Adam and Eve, the freedom that a wise father bequeaths to his children as their birthright. From this original source, Milton then asserts, all 'true authority in men' (295) derives.

Paradise Lost is a favourite text for feminist literary criticism,[5] and one of the reasons why is because of the way Milton distinguishes between Adam and Eve. A crude analysis would emphasise the statement 'though both/Not equal' (295–6), but the way Milton goes on to describe *how* they differ, and how they behave together, should give you plenty of scope for discussion on gender equality. His starting point is that, as their sexual characteristics make self-evident, they are not equal, but he goes on to attempt to explain just how they differ. The first difference is that Adam has been made for 'contemplation' and 'valour' (297) while Eve, for 'softness' and 'sweet attractive grace' (298). It is easy to see why feminist critics find rich pickings here, when such an apparent intellectual hierarchy is implied, and, added to that, 'attractive graces' (II, 762) is the phrase Sin uses to describe how she won over all heaven and, chiefly, Satan. Milton's choice of 'softness' too creates real difficulties since it has a number of meanings, perhaps the most relevant being gentle or conciliatory, even complimentary. There is more difficulty as Milton next makes clear that a hierarchy exists in Adam and Eve's relationship with God, 'He for God only, she for God in him' (299). The operant verb is still 'formed' and so, following biblical precedent, Milton believes God created Eve not only *after* Adam and from his flesh but in a sense one step removed from communication with him, seeking God in Adam. Any theological position that treats women's relationship with God as somehow mediated by men is going to encounter resistance today. Of course this was not the case in the seventeenth century, but that does not entirely remove the difficulty modern students encounter. And this one-step-removed relationship with God is how Milton continues to portray Eve throughout the poem.

We are in the middle of a typically convoluted and lengthy Miltonic sentence here which began at line 268 and ends at 311, and consists of a number of sections, the third section (300–11) consisting of what might first seem a frivolous digression on hairstyles in paradise. But if you invest a little energy into the analysis of these lines, you should see that, though of minimal interest to a hairstylist, they are immensely interesting to any student of Milton. Adam is firstly given a 'fair large front' (300), where Milton is almost certainly specifying forehead, and 'fair' means attractive rather than pale or blonde. Combined with an 'eye sublime' (300), this aspect gives Adam 'Absolute rule' (301) over Eden, and simultaneously puts Eve in her place. But then his hair comes into view and all kinds of questions clamour for attention. Adam's hair is 'hyacinthine' like the well known flower in that it hangs in clusters, 'locks' (301), and is parted in the middle. As some critics have pointed out this is just like Milton's own or Oliver Cromwell's. It is also long, but not shoulder length, 'not beneath his shoulders broad' (303).

In a post-1960s Western culture, it's worth asking how you react to Milton's assertion that this hairstyle is 'manly' (302). It clearly was to him. We also tend to think of the Royalists of Milton's period as the champions of long, curling hair,[6] not the Puritans, whose entire aesthetic was one of austerity. Milton was steeped in classical literature and he had seen some of the Renaissance's greatest art works on his European travels, so it would be difficult for him to embark on physical descriptions of the first human forms that weren't influenced by these factors. This influence continues as he turns to Eve's own coiffure, which she wears much longer, as a 'veil down to her slender waist' (304). Eve's hair is 'unadornèd' and 'golden' (305), though 'Dishevelled' (306), and, most intriguingly of all, waves in 'wanton ringlets' (306) 'As the vine curls her tendrils' (307). Vines tend to cling to things in order to grow, and Milton sees Adam as the firm stake around which

Eve grows and indeed bears fruit. Why does Milton seem eager to stress Eve's hair is 'unadornèd', and does 'wanton' imply anything more than 'untied'? Is 'golden' just poetic shorthand for blonde? Anticipating the debate, Milton uses this comparison to point towards the quintessential differences between the sexes.

Milton acknowledges that Eve's vine-like hair 'implied/Subjection' (307–8) but he is quick to qualify that in a way guaranteed to provoke feminist critical interest. Any subjection, Milton insists, is only the result of 'gentle sway' (308) by Adam, where 'sway' carries the meaning of persuasion or rule. His concern to balance their relationship is evident in the next, beautifully concise line, 'And by her yielded, by him best received' (309), as though once Eve has succumbed to Adam's 'gentle sway', the onus is on him to respond with equal generosity and love. Milton concludes this introduction to primal sexual politics with a number of provocative paradoxes that invite our imaginations to work quite hard. So although we might find 'coy submission' quite conventional in some respects, 'modest pride' (310) is more of a struggle, and the concluding 'sweet reluctant amorous delay' (311) is fraught with difficulty.

In keeping with Genesis, Milton presents Adam and Eve as naked but unashamed, although he sounds rather coy himself when referring to their 'mysterious parts' (312), and you might detect a note of anger in the repetition of 'shame' (313), the paradoxical 'honour dishonourable' (314), and the heavy emphasis placed on the second use of 'shows' (316), all which he neatly ascribes to the personified Sin, a figure he has been at pains to place in the narrative such that his overall project, to 'justify the ways of God to men' (26), succeeds. Milton's golden age, a prelapsarian idyll where mankind was at his happiest, 'banished from man's life his happiest life' (317), is possibly a less than attractive prospect for contemporary students, but its 'Simplicity' (318) is tempered by what every Christian soul yearns for, the 'spotless innocence' that preceded Eve's temptation and their consequent inheritance of original sin.

Untroubled, Milton pictures Adam and Eve walking hand in hand, a symbolic image of harmony and trust, naked through the garden undisturbed by the sight of God or angel. Dramatically, he has been concerned to foreground their innocent happiness since this shifting viewpoint is strictly speaking Satan's 'where the fiend/Saw undelighted all delight'(285–6). The idyllic scene we find appealing, or even touching, is agony to Satan, and fuels his envy. Milton captures brilliantly the sense of impending tragedy where he calls them 'the loveliest pair/That ever since in love's embraces met' (322). The open invitation to feminist criticism this section of the poem offers is given an unconscious boost in the final comparison Milton makes between the pair. Adam may be 'the goodliest man' who has ever lived, but Eve is merely 'the fairest' (323–4), the line's rhythm placing an almost plaintive cadence on the final 'Eve'.

Satan's Response to Love

In the second soliloquy of the poem (358–92), Satan is again shown engaged in an intense, internal struggle between good and evil. There is obvious dramatic benefit in employing this technique to develop Satan's character, but there are also some awkward side effects. The exclamation that begins this soliloquy echoes Satan's earlier grim discovery (75) that, however hard he strives, however vast the distances he traverses, hell will always be his ultimate destination. But hell here is also precisely related to his recognition that he and his fellow rebels have been supplanted. 'Into our room of bliss' (359) God has placed a new race, 'Creatures of other mould' (360), the midline rhyme of 'mould' with 'behold' (358) reinforcing the impact both of the caesura and of the shock. What shocks Satan is how moved to admire Adam and Eve he finds himself. It was not what he expected when he proposed his grand project at the council in Pandaemonium. Satan finds himself drawn to Adam and Eve, and in that reaction lies one of the chief, awkward side effects. If you look closely at what stimulates this reaction, it is clearly man's 'resemblance' (364) to God, something Milton's theodicy cannot avoid, but which may strike readers as awkward on the lips of Satan. So strongly do they resemble God, that Satan feels 'wonder' and is even moved to consider the possibility of 'love' (363). Some of this awkwardness is diluted by the irony Milton employs towards the close of Satan's little eulogy. The characteristic that impresses Satan most profoundly is the 'grace' (364) that God's 'hand' (365) has imbued both Adam and Eve with. A characteristic that he has 'poured' (365) on them, and which implies much more than a merely physical indication of elegance or charm, and points towards their intimate relationship with God, their loving Father.

Satan's interior monologue now slithers from wonder and admiration into foreboding and enmity. Milton avoids too dramatic a shift in tone and opts instead to use the same exclamatory voice Satan began with, 'Ah gentle pair' (366), before shifting the reader's stance from objective observer to empathetic victim. Satan uses 'ye' and 'you' repeatedly in this second half of his soliloquy, as though he were addressing the pair directly, but the effect is to address us and to remind us that this is as much our tragic story as it is Adam and Eve's. Satan's confidence is another potentially awkward side effect. He speaks of their innocence and coming 'woe' (368–9) as though he possesses the same foreknowledge as God, but amidst his 'pity' (374) he seems to relish the thought that their coming woe will equal their current happiness, 'More woe, the more your taste is now of joy' (369). The literary term for this anticipation of events is prolepsis, and from Milton, or Milton's God, the use of prolepsis in relationship to Adam and Eve is understandable, but in Satan's hands it smacks of arrogance. We might also detect arrogance in his quick wittedness. In the single clause, 'and this high seat your heaven/Ill fenced for heaven to keep out such a foe' (371–2), he shifts the meaning of the same word 'heaven' from referring to the place, to an epithet for God.

Another awkward side effect of Satan's warring sides arises out of his attempt to express pity for Adam and Eve, 'To you whom I could pity thus forlorn' (374), even as he himself claims to be 'unpitied' (375). The problem accrues around his claim *not* to be plotting evil towards Adam and Eve, 'yet no purposed foe' (373), as though it were possible to distinguish inimical action aimed at God from that aimed at man. Milton's contemporaries would perhaps have been more alert to this kind of Machiavellian rationalising than we are. Satan pursues it relentlessly, describing his anticipated relationship with Adam and Eve in almost loving terms, 'league with you I seek' (375) is closely followed by the intimacy of 'and mutual amity so strait, so close' (376) and the disturbing image of his and Man's fates being forever intertwined. He uses the verb 'dwell' (377) to describe this closeness, which reminds us of our inherent capacity for good or evil, as well as the ultimate consequences of the latter, the antithesis of this, or any other, Paradise. The tendency to abstraction is countered succinctly by the word 'sense' (379) which contrasts the sensual luxury of Eden with the vivid description of the burning lake where we discovered Satan in Book 1, lines 59–74.

Satan exploits this contrast for his own Machiavellian purposes, petulantly suggesting that man receive the gift of hell from him gratefully, in a parody of St Matthew's gospel (10:8) 'freely ye have received, freely give', as though it were a kindness for him to pass on to man the eternal punishment God has given him. In another biblical echo, he predicts a future where hell is replete, even with kings. The heavy irony of 'entertain', combined with the intimacy of 'you two' (382), would have stirred something akin to fear in Milton's fervently religious contemporaries.

He dismisses all the rich expanse of Eden as 'these narrow limits' (384) and appears eager to 'entertain' Adam and Eve's 'numerous offspring' (385), continuing his perverse logic by claiming to be reluctant 'loth' in his revenge and suggesting Adam and Eve thank God instead for their future entertainment. Casting himself as the victim, 'On you who wrong me not for him who wronged' (387), is the kind of strategy which lures some readers into regarding Satan as the poem's hero. The final sentence (388–92) is especially valuable in this respect.

There is a marked shift of tone which separates the first, poignant, almost plaintive image of Satan being moved by the sight of Adam and Eve's 'harmless innocence' (388) from the image of his righteous courage in the face of tyranny, which is cleverly determined by the rhythmic shift at 'Melt, as I do' (389). The series of first stressed syllables in

> ... yet public reason just,
> Honour and empire with revenge enlarged, (389–90)

differs markedly from the gentler stresses and longer vowel sounds which precede it, as though he has had to pull himself together, shake off the weakness that accompanies pity, and all for the 'public' (389) good. A number of questions compete for attention at this point. How do you find yourself responding to the notion of Satan melting at the sight of Adam and Eve's 'harmless innocence'? In what sense is Satan really compelled and would he genuinely 'abhor' (392) his actions if he had not been damned? How do you react to his appeal to 'Honour and empire' as good reasons for his action? Milton's educated, post-civil-war readers would have had a very political, Machiavellian context from which to work and which is most easily discernible in the two lines that follow the soliloquy (393–4) where Milton, the republican polemicist and regicide, reminds us that tyrants always plead necessity to justify their most tyrannical acts.

God's Only Command

The next section under scrutiny (393–535) contains the first words spoken between Adam and Eve, and, besides detailing the fundamental laws that govern Eden, is full of interest because it establishes the relationship between the two of them. But before we are treated to this uniquely significant human event, Milton manoeuvres Satan into position to listen and observe.

From his tree top vantage point, Satan now drops to the ground and mingles with the animals in order to get closer to Adam and Eve.

Before he eventually commandeers the serpent's shape as a disguise, Milton gives Satan quite a talent for metamorphosis as he changes shape into first a lion, then a tiger, in both instances stalking Adam and Eve in a completely inappropriate way for a prelapsarian predator conventionally depicted as gentle or tame.

The caesura in line 408 stops Satan's tiger in its metaphorical tracks as, overhearing Adam speak to Eve, he is suddenly and ironically captivated, 'Turned him all ear to hear new utterance flow' (410). Adam's first sentence (411–39) is a hefty 168 words long, and begins with an unequivocal declaration of love for Eve. Milton is not especially renowned for his wit, but the economy of 'Sole partner and sole part of all these joys' (411) compresses a number of possible meanings arising either from a pun on sole/soul or from the less obvious toying with 'partner' and 'part'. The subsequent endearment, 'Dearer thyself than all' (412), is touchingly simple in comparison. You might find the frequent use of ellipsis here confusing, but a clearer understanding is possible by resupplying the words or phrases Milton omitted. The expression 'needs must' (412) is itself elliptical, meaning 'God cannot help but be...', but the completion of the verb is delayed until line 414 where we discover what it is the Almighty cannot avoid *being*, which is 'infinitely good' (414).

It is easy to lose sight of Adam's argument inside the compressed language and unfamiliar syntax, but his choice of 'dust' (416) as the word to describe both their origins can help. What Adam is eager to stress to Eve is his belief in their creator's immense generosity, and contrasting 'dust' with 'all this happiness' (417) makes that point for him, especially when against that is added the reality that Adam and Eve have neither merited such a reward, nor can they carry out any action their creator needs or desires. The sole 'service' (420) God has commanded of them is, in Adam's words an 'easy charge' (421), forgoing the pleasure of eating the fruit of the one tree, but it is dramatically important for him to replay it to Eve because Milton requires Satan to overhear it. In his referring to the close proximity of the Tree of Knowledge and the Tree of Life, Adam reveals his complete ignorance of death, 'what'er death is' (425), and, because we may be very familiar with the account in Genesis, this point may be easily overlooked. Milton treated us to a vivid and horrifying picture of Death in Book 2, lines 666–74, but Adam and Eve have no concept of Death at all. They are, as God made them, immortal until they disobey the 'easy charge'. The minor nature of the one restriction God has placed on them is contrasted with his immense generosity in giving them 'power and rule' (429) over the rest of his creation, 'all other creatures that possess/Earth, air and sea' (431–2), a contrast made overt through Adam's use of 'easy' and 'hard' in his advice to Eve for them to maintain a proper perspective.

Adam's closing few lines here, reminding Eve that they should 'praise' God 'and extol/His bounty' (436–7), shouldn't be undervalued. It is God's immeasurable generosity that Adam is eager to value, a feeling made clear by his use of 'bounty' (437) but also by the more unusual idea that their stewardship of Eden, 'To prune these growing plants and tend these flowers' (438), is for him a 'delightful task' (437) which, even were it arduous, is 'sweet' (339) since he shares it with Eve.

Eve's reply is likely to stimulate ardent debate in any post-feminist, co-educational classroom since superficially she appears so submissive and even servile. Examining the biblical references[7] here will fuel that debate, so it is more productive to analyse thoughtfully what Milton actually makes her say and how she speaks. Her first sentence is very formal in structure and tone, echoing the biblical language Milton's readers would have known so well, 'O thou for whom/And from whom I was formed flesh of thy flesh' (440–1). She accepts without question the truth that, without Adam, her existence is meaningless, 'without whom am to no end' (442), and describes him most significantly for the choices they both make later in the poem as 'my guide/And head' (442–3). Considering the compliment Adam has just paid her, there seems to be nothing tender or intimate in her words, but it's important to follow her sentence to its conclusion because that is where her key point lies. What Eve wants to do is agree with what Adam has just said. She wants him to know that his words were (in her words) 'just and right' (443) and she does this because, like Adam, she is motivated by love. This becomes clear as she goes on to select, from all the multitude of things she could select from, reason to praise and give 'daily thanks' (445) to God for her possession of Adam. Eve says hers is 'the happier lot, enjoying thee' (446). And is it servility that makes her add that just as she enjoys Adam, 'Pre-eminent by so much odds' (447), he 'Like consort to thyself canst nowhere find' (448)?

The account Eve now gives of her first waking into consciousness is also likely to stimulate a lot of subjective debate. Milton conveys the depth of her naivety with a list of questions (451–2) and describes the pool of water she lies beside in lyrical, languid terms. As Eve hears the distant sound of running water, 'from thence a murmuring sound' (453), Milton shifts the rhythm from languid, muted consonants to the more urgent, sharply sibilant sounds 'Of waters issued from a cave' (454) before ending with the wonderfully limpid image of the 'unmoved'

(455) glassy surface of the pool, 'Pure as the expanse of heaven' (456). As Eve contemplates her reflection in the lake's still surface, there is a clear echo of the classical myth of Narcissus,[8] the beautiful youth who epitomises vanity, but Milton's account of Eve's actions offer much more to the alert student. There is a hint of comedy as she starts back at the sight of herself... starting back, and at the 'answering looks' (464) she gives herself; but superseding any humour is the notion of 'sympathy and love' (465) so powerful that, if God's voice had not intervened, Eve says she would have remained entranced 'and pined with vain desire' (466).

Some of the questions you might find yourself asking are: why does Milton introduce the idea of the reflection at all? What does he gain by describing Eve in this way? If you consider this from a different viewpoint, you could ask yourself how you would choose to describe Eve, the mother of mankind, were *you* to be writing about her. I suspect you will immediately encounter some of the same issues Milton faced. Is she beautiful? What is the best way to convey beauty? By physical description, which runs the risk of being led by taste, and guides rather than stimulates the readers' imagination, or allusion to an archetype? It's equally valuable to reflect on the level of understanding Eve is given here. God's invitation to her is a very specific one. Observing her futile enrapture, he lures her away by offering her the satisfaction she craves, 'him thou shall enjoy' (472). But when she first sees Adam, what she first notices is that he seems a poor substitute for the figure she saw in the pool's surface, 'less winning soft, less amiably mild' (479), and promptly turns on her heel before Adam's voice grabs her attention.

The paradox Adam employs, 'Whom thou fly'st, of him thou art' (482), that Eve is in fact running away from herself since it is from his very flesh 'His flesh, his bone' (483) that she has been formed, originates in Genesis, but the more intriguing appeal comes after this, where Adam's words are more reminiscent of love poetry than anything else: 'Part of my soul, I seek thee' (487). The caesura in line 488 dramatises the hugely significant moment when Adam's 'gentle hand' (488) 'Seized mine' (499) and it is no accident that the epic ends with the image of them walking out of Eden, hand in hand (XI, 648–9). Given what God said to Eve to lure her from the pool, the almost incidental 'I yielded' (489) implies a great deal more, and is linked by Milton to a statement many modern students cannot help but find contentious. According to Eve, it is from the moment of her sexual union with Adam that she learned to put beauty, the beauty she saw reflected in the pool, in its proper place and appreciate her own inferior nature:

... and from that time see
How beauty is excelled by manly grace
And wisdom, which alone is truly fair. (489–91)

Eve's inferiority is reinforced in the subsequent lines where Adam admires her 'submissive charms' (498) and smiles with 'superior love' (499), but any discussion of what Milton intends by this needs also to take into account the classical partnership between Jupiter and Juno[9] within which it is framed. You will also find it valuable to interrogate the sensual, visual imagery Milton employs to describe Eve's 'half embracing' (494) Adam and their exchange of kisses, which is all contained within a legitimate, marital context and all very powerfully acted out in front of Satan.

Satan's character is caught in the headlights when Milton describes how he first reacts to Adam and Eve's 'kisses pure' (502). Milton has Satan turn aside 'For envy' but immediately qualifies this with a different adjective, 'jealous' (503). Commonly used interchangeably and in error today, it is worth your reviewing the etymological history of both jealousy and envy before coming to some conclusions about why Milton makes this qualification, 'jealous leer malign' (503), and depicts Satan watching the couple in what is clearly a voyeuristic manner, 'Eye'd them askance' (504).

If you link that thinking to the first few lines of his monologue, the discussion becomes even more fruitful. It is not the physical Eden, Satan envies, but the paradise he sees the couple share 'in one another's arms' (506), a place he calls 'The happier Eden' (507). On page 32 we noted that eternal separation from God's love and grace was a punishment far worse than banishment to hell, and that notion is reinforced here where Satan tells us that, without joy or love, the 'fierce desire' (509) the devils still feel is 'Among our other torments not the least' (510).

But Satan brings himself out of this jealous fit in order to focus on the business in hand, Adam and Eve's ruin, and he is impressively quick not just to see the rich potential of what he has overheard, but to understand precisely how to use it to devastating effect. He calls the Tree of Knowledge 'fatal' (514) and in a series of rapid questions reasons that the consequence of their eating from the Tree is sin and death. With scintillating irony, Satan latches onto this 'fair foundation' (521) on which he will 'build/Their ruin!' (521–2). The linear reasoning in his argument is conveyed through the syntax of the next sentence where, having first excited them to question and to reject God's command, he reasons it is inevitable that they will taste the fruit and so die. A caesura after

'They taste and die' emphasises the rhetorical question, 'what likelier can ensure?' (527), as though Satan reaches this conclusion joyfully, if not triumphantly. It is also worth spending some time looking at the motives and psychology Satan ascribes to God in this monologue. One of the questions he poses himself is, 'Why should their lord/Envy them that?' (516–7), and a little later he imagines how he will persuade Adam and Eve to 'reject/Envious commands' (523–4). These are difficult issues for the pro-Satan, critical lobbiest. To ascribe envy to God in *Paradise Lost* is either wilfully to misread the poem or to fall into the trap of reading it entirely as a dramatic epic, devoid of theodicy.

The monologue concludes with more dramatic business, as Satan delays his revenge in order to survey the garden fully, in case he encounters 'Some wandering spirit of heaven' (531) from whom he might gain more intelligence. This shows considerable confidence if we compare it with his discussions with his compatriots in Pandaemonium. It is as though his success thus far has wrought an even greater degree of arrogance than that which led to his original fall from grace. This is succinctly conveyed in his final, unvoiced promise to Adam and Eve that their happiness is short lived and is only to be enjoyed for the interim:

> ... enjoy, till I return,
> Short pleasures, for long woes are to succeed. (534–5)

Life and Love in Eden

The section of the poem that describes Adam and Eve enjoying the interim Satan granted them while he searches the garden more closely (598–775) is a justifiably well known section of the poem, not least because it deals with the idyllic life of the first humans on earth and because golden age mythology has always attracted an adult readership seeking inspiration, philosophy or merely escape. Sexual politics also figures prominently.

Your studies of Shakespeare or other dramatists predating Milton has probably alerted you to their imaginative use of language to set a scene. Here Milton devotes twelve lines to describe the change from evening to night, from twilight to moonlight, as the light of the evening star, Hesperus, and other stars, 'living sapphires' (605), is gradually replaced by the 'peerless light' (608) of the moon. Only the 'wakeful nightingale' (603) breaks the silence, 'She all night long her amorous descant sung' (603), preparing the way for the lovers. Among the numerous poetic descriptions of moonlight any student of English literature is likely to come across, Milton's has to be one of the most elegant and evocative. Instead of replacing or competing with the night, his moonlight is cast like a cloak, 'her silver mantle' (609) on the dark.

The first thing to note when Adam addresses Eve is the formality of the title he gives her, 'Fair consort' (610). When Eve replies she calls him, 'My author and disposer' (635). This grandeur is lost after the Fall when their usual form of address is simply by name. Your initial reaction might well be that, as a lover, Adam's approach is hardly the most seductive. His reminder that the night time is their appointed rest is much more to do with their relationship with God than with each other. The central point to appreciate is the statement that closes Adam's first sentence, that of the animals' doing, 'God takes no account' (622). Adam differentiates man from the animals by their activity and purpose, 'his daily work of body or mind' (618), activity which links them both completely to God since it wins man 'the regard of heaven on all his ways' (620). Adam then reminds Eve of how early they need to rise to carry out the work necessary just to maintain the fertile garden. Though there may be nothing the least seductive in Adam's kibbutz-like instruction, it is richly laced with images of fertility through words like 'overgrown' (627), 'wanton' (629) and 'unsightly and unsmooth' (631). With a glance towards the future generations of mankind, he adds that such work needs far 'more hands than ours' (629).

Eve replies 'with perfect beauty adorned' (634), keeping to the account in Genesis that links nudity to shame only after the Fall, as though beauty is all the clothing she requires. The twenty-three lines of her response (635–58) are well worth your rereading as a single unit since they contain a wealth of rhetorical technique. She begins with a hierarchical statement of obedience and subservience, God–Adam–Eve, that is bound to provoke debate. Without pre-empting that debate, I would urge you to note that it is Eve who says her praise and happiness is predicated on one very significant phrase, 'to know no more' (637). From there Eve moves into language more recognisable as that of a lover, losing all sense of time as long as she is talking to Adam, while so engrossed is she that the seasons 'all please alike' (640). The next sentence begins and ends with the same, neatly inverted phrase 'Sweet is … is sweet' (641–56) and is full of rhetorical flourish and skill. Eve's imagery builds on Adam's own words as she expresses her own delight in 'the breath of morn' (641) and the 'Glistering' (645) dew she sees 'on herb, tree, fruit and flower' (644). The alliterative sounds of fruit and flower are picked up in 'fragrant the fertile earth' (645) and then embellished by the long stresses and 's' sounds of 'After soft showers' (646), all combining to convey a sense of gentle freshness which seems to suit the simple cyclical nature of their life in Eden. The central theme of her reply, sweetness, is now applied to the arrival of 'evening mild, then silent night' (647) and the same romantic elements that Milton used to set this scene: the nightingale, the stars and the moon are brought into play in what begins to add up to a highly lyrical expression of her own love.

Eve's rhetorical agility all turns on the phrase 'But neither' (650) since what she now does is relist all the images she has used, in the same order and with almost identical phrasing, in order to build up to the powerful statement of love she wishes to make. None of these beautiful, delightful things, she says, are after all sweet 'without thee' (656). Then, as though in spontaneous contemplation of the very objects she has been describing, Eve asks Adam why such immense beauty as the moon and stars is on show at night, when there are no eyes to see it. The question avoids Adam having to respond to her expression of love, and instead gives him an opportunity to demonstrate his greater knowledge and closeness to their creator.

As before, the titles used are highly formal and respectful, 'our general ancestor' (659) and 'Daughter of God and Man' (660), and Adam adds the compliment 'accomplished' (660) which acknowledges not her physical beauty, but the sophistication of her recent speech. In contrast with Eve's lyrical praise, Adam's speech is almost coldly rational and his answer to her question is obscure and dense. He first explains that the stars have a nightly course to run, visiting each part of the earth in turn, places he calls 'nations yet unborn' (663), and in so doing they prevent the return of darkness which would mean the extinction of all life, since God called light and life into being. What you are likely to find less accessible than the stars and moon as bulwarks against darkness is the notion that they have a positive influence on earthly affairs, something Adam conveys through 'soft fires' (667) and 'kindly heat' (668), phrases which counter the expected dangerous nature of fire. Not only does he say the stars bathe 'all kinds that grow' (671) with a quality he calls their 'stellar virtue' (671) but they prepare the world for the healthy, life giving power of the sun, making everything 'hereby apter/To receive perfection from the sun's more potent ray' (672–3).

As though aware that his answer has been convoluted, he restates the question for Eve, reminding her that, therefore, the stars 'Shine not in vain' (675) before adding a new and highly significant concept. He tells Eve not to think that were man not to exist that either the heavens would lack 'spectators' (676) or that God would lack praise. 'Millions of spiritual creatures' (677) inhabit the earth not just free to admire its rich beauty, but engaged in 'ceaseless praise' (679) of God, its creator. As proof he reminds Eve of how often 'Both day and night' (680) they have heard these spirits hymning God's praise, 'Sole, or responsive to each other's note' (683), engaged in perfect harmony. But most importantly of all, he adds that their songs and music 'lift our thoughts to heaven' (688).

However strongly we find ourselves captivated by Milton's characterisation of Adam and Eve, we misread the poem if we fail to appreciate the nature of their relationship, not with each other, but with God. There is nothing peripheral or occasional about their worshipping their creator: it is the *focus* of their life and existence in Eden.

As the couple enter the 'blissful bower' (690) chosen for them by God, they are hand in hand, the same poignant motif Milton will use for their expulsion from Paradise at the epic's close. Before commencing a detailed description of the bower, shot through with flower imagery and classical allusion which all points towards the sexual climax of this scene, Milton reminds us that this entire world was created by God for 'man's delightful use' (692), a view that would have surprised none in his day but which may surprise many educated via a school curriculum clumsily tinged by green politics.

Architectural or decorative parallels – 'roof' (692), 'Mosaic' (700), 'Broidered' and 'stone' (702) – enrich what might otherwise seem a rather temporary, natural environment, as does the complete absence of any other living creature, 'Beast, bird, insect or worm durst enter none' (704). A caesura introduces classical allusions to Pan, Silvanus, Faunus and the generic 'nymph' (707). All three named deities have a strong sexual aspect to their character, particularly seduction, although the two significant adjectives Milton employs to connect these mythological haunts with Adam and Eve's bower are 'sacred and sequestered' (706). The private, intimate nature of the sexual act is reinforced by the 'close recess' of line 708 and set firmly within the context of marriage by a brief flashback to when Eve prepared for her own first wedding night by decorating her bed with 'flowers, garlands and sweet smelling herbs' (709), accompanied by 'heavenly choirs' who sing the wedding hymn or 'hymenean' (711). Milton wants us to read this most private and personal of events as a central aspect of marriage.

A parallel made between Eve and Pandora dramatically disturbs the gentle, amorous nature of this scene. The image of Eve, led by an unnamed 'genial angel' (712) 'in naked beauty more adorned' (713) than Pandora, is at first consistent with earlier images of Eve where her nakedness is seen as a beautiful garment in itself (634); but Pandora[10] is the mythological purveyor of all misery on earth and immediately we are invited to see Eve in the same light. Milton says Eve is 'More lovely than Pandora' (714) and makes the parallel overtly clear through an unusual narratorial exclamation, 'and oh too like/In sad event' (715–16).

In something approaching a ritual, the two then turn and 'under open sky' (721) praise and worship their maker in terms that convey gratitude and appreciation of the richness of the world he has created for them. The moon becomes a 'resplendent globe' (723) and Eden a 'delicious place' (729) where God's generosity 'thy abundance' (730) is such that they are too few to harvest it all and much 'uncropped falls to the ground' (731). But central to their prayer is their acknowledgement of what they call 'the crown of all our bliss' which is their 'mutual love' (728), a love 'Ordained' (729) by God himself. Milton also slides almost imperceptibly from narrative to their direct speech in line 724, which has the effect of enjoining the reader with their prayer.

Similarly, as they remind us that God has promised them that they will father a race of men 'To fill the earth' (733), Milton links the reader to them and to our inherited Christian duty as sons and daughters of Adam and Eve. With no further 'rites' (736) – 'rites' being a word Milton would have associated with Catholicism and corruption, he asserts his belief that 'adoration pure' (737), by which he means spontaneous, heartfelt prayer, is what 'God likes best' (738) – Adam and Eve proceed to their bed. With no clothes or 'troublesome disguises' (741) to remove, they 'Straight side by side were laid' (741), at which point Milton grants his hero and heroine the privacy he has so carefully orchestrated, but not without making it very clear that sex forms the climax to their day. The archaic word 'ween' (741) might cause you some difficulty, but it merely means 'believe' or 'suppose', as will the choice of 'Mysterious' (743) to describe sex in an age where popular culture finds little else to discuss – but you need to appreciate just how sincere Milton is; and 'mysterious' is here linked to the concept of divine mystery.

With true Protestant zeal he then leaves the couple to their love making and launches into a diatribe against catholic 'hypocrites' (744) for approving celibacy in its priests and denouncing, 'Defaming', sex 'as impure' (746) when God has declared it not just pure, but indeed a command 'to some' and even 'free to all' (747). The rhetorical question which follows, who but Satan would bid us abstain when God has commanded us to populate the earth?, 'Our maker bids increase' (748), is very helpful since it alerts us to the connection Milton assumes between sex and life, between love and birth.

From this ideological platform, Milton launches into a robust defence of marriage, 'Hail wedded love' (750), declaring it the 'true source/Of human offspring' (751–2) and the only form of proprietorship in Eden where everything else is shared, 'of all things common else' (752). Again twenty-first-century students are likely to find ample elbow room for disagreement as he argues that it is marriage which has not only rendered 'adulterous lust' (753) bestial, but it is the fountainhead of all filial or familial affection. A place fit for 'saints and patriarchs' (762), Milton calls marriage the 'Perpetual fountain of domestic sweets' (760), not a phrase you are likely to hear on a modern political platform. Getting into his stride, on what biographers suggest[11] may have been something of a raw nerve for Milton, he next turns his criticism against the Royalists, his lifelong political opponents. The colourful images he chooses – Love's 'Golden shafts' (763), a 'constant lamp' (764) and Cupid's 'purple wings' (764) – connote passion, fidelity and constancy and are instantly contrasted with the feigned colour of the world of courtly romance. The latter he condemns unreservedly as prostitution, 'the bought smile/Of harlots, loveless, joyless, unendeared' (765–6), the opposite of the vital fertility of Eden through the rather ugly phrase 'Casual fruition', (767) and which he links to the courtly pastimes of dancing and love poetry, 'wanton masque' (768) and 'serenade' (769). The courtly poet Milton mocks savagely as a 'starved lover' (769) 'best quitted with disdain', while his mistress is the shallow, 'proud fair' (770).

Milton returns us to the present and the sleeping forms of Adam and Eve with the immediacy of a simple pronoun, 'These' (771), as though they are there in front of us, for our contemplation. Unlike the shallow lovers of the court, their sleep is 'lulled by nightingales' (771) and roses are 'Showered' (773) on their embracing, naked bodies as the morning approaches. This entire episode allows us to see Adam and Eve vitally active in their Paradise, in complete harmony with it, with each other and with their creator, but Milton reminds us poignantly that this is only a temporary state and concludes this section of the poem with half a desire that their fall from grace could be avoided. 'Sleep on/Blest pair' (773–4), he pleads, before returning to the weakness which will lead to their ruin with a sententious play on words, 'and know to know no more' (775).

Exercises

Lines 114–287. Uriel's detection of Satan quickly turns to a highly detailed and ornate description of Eden which weaves typically in and out of biblical and classical allusion to create a strong sense of magnificence and beauty. In this instance, rather than exploring the relevance of the various allusions, focus your attention on Milton's use of sensual imagery to convey awe and beauty. How effective is this technique?

Lines 325–57. The biblical significance of this passage is very overt, but in other, less purely literary respects, how convincing in human and natural terms do you find the picture Milton paints of Adam and Eve, surrounded by the flora and fauna of Eden?

Lines 536–97. Although this short section might be of special interest to students of Milton's cosmology and astronomical knowledge, the conversation between Uriel and Gabriel, in which it becomes clear Uriel has seen through Satan's disguise, dominates it. Considering the confidence and assurance Satan displayed at the close of the previous monologue, ask yourself what purpose this exchange between the angels serves.

Lines 776–1015. Book 4 ends with a dramatic encounter between those angels set to guard earth and Satan, who they find poisoning Eve's dreams. The exchanges between Satan and Gabriel are tense and hark back to a time before his rebellion. Look carefully at the characterisation of both figures here and particularly at how they respond to each others' words and to the intervention from God that precipitates Satan's flight. How successfully does Milton manage to juxtapose good and evil inside the constraints of what are clearly the military, heroic conventions of epic poetry?

5
Wilful Transgression

Summary

Eve is woken by Adam and tells him of the disturbed night's sleep she has had, the first such experience, and then shares with him the detail of the dream, which we know has been induced by Satan. In that dream she wakes to find herself alone and looking for Adam. She finds herself at the Tree of Knowledge where an angel greets her. She watches as the angel praises the Tree, openly desiring its fruit as a means of deification before he takes the fruit and eats it, offering Eve some to taste in turn and become, as he says he has, godlike. The angel presses the fruit right up to Eve's lips and, although she resists, she finds herself flying up to the heavens with the angel before the dream ends abruptly and she wakes to find Adam beside her.

Adam tells Eve that, however ominous her dream, it is merely the product of imagination and not reason. He reassures her that although she may have dreamed an evil action, the eating of the fruit, that does not necessitate her doing evil in reality, nor does it mean she is culpable. Adam's words cheer Eve and before setting out to their day's labours, they pray together.

God sees them and calls Raphael to him, instructing him to speak with Adam and to warn him about Satan and his intent to ruin mankind. When Adam sees Raphael approaching, he asks Eve to gather suitable food for their heavenly guest, which she does willingly. Raphael accepts Adam's invitation to eat with them and Eve serves them both. Adam questions Raphael about the nature of angels and Raphael uses the opportunity to warn Adam to remain obedient and to understand the nature of the free will God has given him, telling him of those who have fallen and are already damned.

Adam asks to know more and Raphael begins to relate the history of the war in heaven, how God proclaimed the Son his heir, demanding subservience from all in heaven, and how this provoked Satan to envy and to convince his legions to support him in rebellion. Only the angel Abdiel speaks out against Satan, and although Satan refutes his warnings, and he stands alone, Abdiel boldly predicts their downfall and damnation, before departing unharmed.

God's Instructions to Raphael

The comparatively short passage containing God's instructions to Raphael (224–45) is one of the most vital passages in the entire poem. Any discussion of Milton's theodicy or of Adam and Eve's relative culpability is of limited value without reference to the instructions God gives Raphael here.

After their prayers, Adam and Eve return to their labours and it's useful to note that the word Milton chooses to motivate God before he speaks to Raphael is 'pity' (220). Clearly and unemotionally, God summarises the knowledge shared with Raphael and the other angels who have encountered Satan. The 'stir' (224) he has created an earth is not just of Eve in her sleep, but of both Adam and Eve, since God relates 'disturbed' (226) to 'the human pair' (227). There is no doubt about Satan's intent. It is, 'In them at once to ruin all mankind' (228), an image which dramatically reminds the reader of the personal relevance of these events.

Raphael is instructed to find Adam, where he has chosen to rest 'from the heat of noon' (231) or eat, and speak to him 'as friend with friend' (229). The latter detail is important since it reminds us of the superior spiritual state Adam and Eve existed in before the Fall, friends to angels and even to God himself. Raphael is told to remind Adam of the happy state he enjoys with Eve, a happiness inextricably linked to his free will, 'Happiness in his power left free to will' (235), a phrase reshaped immediately for emphasis and clarity, 'Left to his own free will' (236), and then refined, 'though free/Yet mutable' (236–7). Milton's Arminianism, the belief that mankind has the free will to either embrace or reject God's grace through faith, is evident here.

God instructs Raphael to warn Adam. The key word 'beware' (237) implies both caution and alertness, while 'He swerve not too secure' (238) implies failure through naivety or over-confidence. Raphael is to spell out the nature of the danger and identify its perpetrator: 'tell him withal/His danger, and from whom' (238–9). What could be more clear?

God's intent is to leave no room for excuses. Adam must be in a position to appreciate the danger if he is to exercise free will. God even goes so far as to reassure Adam that he will not allow Satan to use violence, but that 'deceit and lies' (243) will be his chosen method. With the benefit of omnipotence, God is even able to state the outcome. 'Lest wilfully transgressing' (244), and the last two, multisyllable words, 'unadmonished, unforewarned' (245), emphasise the gravity of this warning through an abrupt change in rhythm.

God's speech over, there is one final indication of how crucial this passage is to Milton's project as a whole. 'So spake the eternal father' (246), he adds with biblical intonation and gravitas; 'and fulfilled/All justice' (246–7), the caesura closing off the idea from Raphael's immediately obedient flight. In Milton's view, neither Adam and Eve, nor their numerous descendants, have grounds for complaint.

Raphael Delivers God's Warning

After sharing their meal with Raphael, so impressed is Adam with the superiority of Raphael to his own form and capability, 'whose excellence he saw/Transcend his own so far' (456–7), he seizes the opportunity to learn more about angels and heaven. He compliments Raphael for deigning to dine with them on earthly food when his more usual fare is divine, 'Food not of angels, yet accepted so' (465), and is sensitive or intelligent enough to intuit that Raphael has displayed not the least sign of dissatisfaction. God instructed Raphael to speak to Adam 'as friend with friend' (229) and Adam's curt question, 'yet what compare?' (467), could almost be humorous. But Raphael's reply retains a highly formal, measured tone, as though acutely aware of having a message to deliver and a duty to fulfil. He avoids Adam's question and instead delivers a mini-lecture on the structure of the natural world including man and the angels' hierarchical relationship to God. His account is uniquely Miltonic in that Milton sees God as having created the world out of pre-existing materials, 'one first matter all' (472) he shaped to their uniformly good ends. He also sees those creatures closest to God as superior, 'more refined, more spirituous, and pure' (475), drawing an analogy with the plant world in which all growth stems from the root, culminating in the perfume of 'the bright, consummate flower' (481). Raphael's 'flowers and their fruit' (482) aspire to higher things, 'to both life *and* sense' (485), as well as 'fancy *and* understanding' (my italics; 486), seeing reason as the soul's key attribute. For Raphael, there are two different forms that reason takes, 'Discursive, or intuitive' (488), the former chiefly human, the latter angelic, although 'Differing but in degree, of kind the same' (490). If this explication leaves you confused then skip ahead to Adam's reply at lines 509–12 where you will find the clarification you need in Adam's own summary of what he has understood Raphael to have said.

Having reasoned thus far, Raphael turns at last to Adam's question and tells him not to be surprised that the food God saw fit for man is also fit for him and that he is able to turn it to proper use or 'substance' (493). Cleverly, he turns his answer to God's purpose by implying that, in time, Adam too might be able to 'turn all to spirit' (497) under the one crucial condition:

> If ye be found obedient, and retain
> Unalterably firm his love entire
> Whose progeny you are. (501–3)

Raphael concludes by advising Adam to enjoy and indeed relish the happy state he and Eve share and understand 'Your fill' (504) without striving for a spiritual advance they can't yet understand, 'incapable of more' (505).

When Adam replies, you might immediately notice the grandeur of the title Milton gives him. He isn't Adam, but 'the patriarch of mankind' (506). Summarising what he has understood Raphael to have said in teaching them how to get closer to God through 'contemplation of created things' (511), Adam latches onto the warning, just as God intended, and asks Raphael to clarify 'What meant that caution joined' (513). Since he has never been disobedient, Adam cannot contemplate what form such behaviour takes and is logically puzzled, even more so by the consequence Raphael put on their disobedience that it will cost them God's love. If there is any moment in the poem where the gentle naivety of Adam and Eve, uncorrupted by society or the pressures of man as complex, political animal, is most obvious, it is in the question Adam now asks. How, he asks, can he who made us from dust to enjoy such bliss and plenitude ever reach a state of not loving us? When you understand why Adam asks this question, you begin to come closer to a responsive and informed understanding of Milton's theodicy.

Obedient Free Will

Raphael's response to Adam's question (519–60) echoes precisely the message God commanded him to deliver. It is worth dwelling on because so many of the questions critics have been exercised by over the centuries depend on an understanding not just what Raphael says, but what Adam *understands* him to say.

Raphael retains a highly formal term of address, 'Son of heaven and earth' (519), before the curt imperative, 'Attend' (520), a clear signal to take heed of what is coming. This time the syntax is transparent, Raphael making his point through a series of highly logical, brief but tightly linked, statements whose import far outweighs the space they occupy. Firstly, it is to God that Adam owes his current happiness. Secondly, that happiness can only be sustained by Adam himself, and only through one means, obedience. The expression is laconic, following a long tradition inherited from Latin and Greek writers steeped in rhetoric, that combines clarity with brevity to invest a statement with authority and significance. Only the final, end stopped phrase lends itself to any kind of speculation, 'therein stand' (522). It reminds us of God's words to the Son in Book 3, 'Freely they stood who stood: and fell who fell' (102), and the verb appears throughout the poem, especially when Milton is seeking an image to convey either a moment of vital choice or courage. Here Raphael uses it to convey to Adam how important it is that he listens to this advice and understands that obedience, far from being a burden, is in fact the foundation upon which he is free to enjoy 'bliss' (517).

Faithful to his master and God, Raphael connects his statement unequivocally to Adam's question, 'What meant that caution joined' (513), by adding, 'This was that caution giv'n thee; be advised' (523). Milton was a precocious scholar and his scholarly acuity is evident in the developing argument Raphael now expounds for Adam. 'God made thee perfect, not immutable' (524), he says, placing responsibility firmly on Adam's shoulders before continuing by adding that although perfection of course means 'good' (525) it does not mean permanently so:

> ... but to persevere
> he left it in thy power, ordained thy will
> By nature free, (525–7)

Adam has the power to remain good and perfect. A power which is his and his entirely. Neither 'fate' (527) nor 'strict necessity' (528) have power over Man, a sentiment which distinguishes the poem markedly from its classical models. And there is good reason for this, Raphael asserts. God 'requires' their 'voluntary service' (529) since any other kind is neither desired nor, much more crucially, valued. The rhetorical question Raphael poses here is invaluable in any critical attempt to relate the poem to Milton's goal to 'justify the ways of God to men' (I, 26).

In essence he asks how it could be possible for Adam, or the angels, to worship God, 'Can hearts, not free, be tried' (532), if they are not free to choose to do so, but are constrained to do so by 'destiny' (534).

As commanded, Raphael now begins to shift his message from the theoretical, towards a more concrete warning about Satan and temptation. Like Adam, he acknowledges that even he and all the angels retain 'our happy state' (536) only as long as they retain their obedience. The key word 'hold' encompasses the single line 537 and echoes the earlier image 'stand' (522) as well as a whole wealth of imagery in the poem relating to warfare and the heavenly conflict. In the repeated adverb '...freely we serve/Because we freely love' (538–9) and in 'in this we stand or fall' (540) we can hear an implicit echo of God's accounting for Satan's fall (III, 102), before Raphael makes that connection explicit by telling Adam that 'some are fallen, to disobedience fallen' (541), his final exclamation serving as part of the warning he has come to issue, 'From what high state of bliss into what woe!' (543).

It is one thing to issue a warning, another to heed it; and in his reply Adam displays the childlike naivety and innocence that singles him out from his ancestors. Like a good pupil, he assures Raphael, his 'Divine instructor' (545), that he has been listening not just with interest, but with greater pleasure than that he experiences listening to the cherubs' 'Aërial music' (548). That God was of course right in sending Raphael with this warning becomes clear where Adam admits his own former ignorance, 'nor knew I not/To be both will and deed created free' (548–90). In spite of that lack of understanding, Adam asserts that his 'constant thoughts' (552) 'Assured me and still assure' (553) that neither he nor Eve will fail in loving and obeying their creator since his 'Single' claim on their obedience 'is yet so just' (552). A caesura midway through line 553 marks the childish way he eagerly leaps to what is really interesting him, Raphael's hint at discord in heaven. That part of Raphael's account, Adam admits, moved him to some degree of doubt, a comment which is easily lost amidst so much intense argument but which is not at all without critical value. If Adam had not shown some sign of doubt, how could he have proved he had understood? His momentary admission of doubt is crucial *because* it confirms his free will. But the innocent in him gallops on to the more exciting matter, and he asks Raphael, while almost half the day remains to them, 'for scarce the sun/Hath finished half his journey' (558–9), to tell him more, 'The full relation' (556), of what occurred in heaven. Throughout this section of the poem, Milton succeeds in contrasting Raphael's lucidly precise philosophical discourse with the eager, innocent conversation of Adam which of course begs the question, where, all this while, was Eve?

Abdiel Confronts Satan

After choosing rebellion, when Satan addresses 'the third part of heaven's host' (710), we are treated to some of the most subtle, difficult dialectics in the whole epic. One thing to keep firmly in mind when looking at the surprising counter-rebellion by Abdiel (772–848) is Milton's ardent republicanism.[1] Satan begins by using the same form of address used earlier by God (601) when he declares his newly begotten son, his heir, 'Thrones, dominations, princedoms, virtues, powers' (772); but, by doing so, he immediately renders himself a potential usurper on a level with his own maker. Unlike God, who follows his address with a clear and unequivocal decree, Satan sounds like the Master of Ceremonies at some heavenly banquet, so convoluted and ornate is the rhetoric that follows and we have to wait some time before we hear a verb that relates directly to his grand guest list. It comes at line 787, 'Will ye submit your necks', after Satan has questioned the very value of the titles he employed, hinting that the declaration making the Messiah 'vicegerent' (609) has neutered all their power and authority. Until the 'ye' (787), throughout the first part of this speech, Satan empathises with his listeners, using 'us' and 'we' repeatedly, a subtle means to align their feelings with his. The envy is palpable, reverberating through words like 'engrossed' (775), 'eclipsed' (776) and 'prostration vile' (782), and in the irritation Satan expresses at their having to assemble in such 'haste' (777) merely to devise 'honours new' (781) for the Son, a word Satan avoids using since to do so would, in his eyes, signal acceptance.

Intent on rebellion, Satan declares any form of subjugation to the newly begotten Son unendurable through a subtle use of hyperbole that has clear connections with republican sentiments of seventeenth-century England. Such 'Knee-tribute' (782) to God, he states was even 'Too much to one' (783), so how much more offensive is it to also be made to revere 'his image' (784) logically, a 'double' (783) humiliation. Warming to his theme of oppression and freedom, Satan invites his listeners to 'erect/Our minds' (785–6) – the third person again uniting them unconsciously – and 'to cast off this yoke?' (786), a conventional symbol of servitude. He reaches a minor climax at 'The supple knee?'

(878), pausing to supply the answer to the question he has asked himself on the basis that he knows them as well as they know themselves. And in case there is any misunderstanding that might lead to future dispute about authority, he carefully qualifies his line of reasoning to ensure no-one listening makes the mistake of thinking themselves his equal. In Satan's view, all are 'Equally free' (792) but not equal. It is easy to imagine what he means by 'orders and degrees' (792) but quite how they 'Jar not with liberty' in the world he is inventing, 'but well consist' (793), is much more problematic. He puts forward no evidence for this supposition, relying it seems on a kind of public acceptance of the hierarchical picture he is painting, where it is wrong for God to command free spirits, but not for some free spirits to command others.

Marshalling two immensely potent words to reinforce his argument, 'reason' and 'right' (794), he rejects the concept of monarchy itself, using the *might does not mean right* line of argument, 'if in power and splendour less' (796), to suggest what God has done is an example of pure tyranny, since they are all 'In freedom equal?' (797). It is difficult to imagine what Royalist readers, familiar with *Eikonoklastes* and other of Milton's prose writings, must have made of these lines in the troubled years following the accession of Charles II when the poem was first published.[2] The parallel with seventeenth-century politics is even more overt when Satan turns his attention from tyranny to law, adding that God's decree is imposing 'Law and edíct' (798) on those who 'Err not' (799). Charles I had been adamant in his dealings with Parliament before the civil war, about his divine right to govern by rule of law. It's not clear whether Satan uses the demonstrative in '*this* to be our lord' (my italics; 799) as a deliberate insult aimed at the Son or as shorthand for the decree God has made. Whichever it is, we are given an insight into the true nature of his sense of grievance in a final complaint that assumes, before God's late decree, all had been 'Our ordained to govern, not to serve?' (802), in which the use of the third person sounds remarkably regal.

Until this moment, Satan's burgeoning sense of outrage has gone unchallenged, but Milton introduces a new and significant character here, Abdiel, a figure he quickly asserts as the model servant of God, 'none with more zeal adored/The Deity' (805–6). It's no surprise that his first act of defiance is to stand and that his zeal is conveyed 'in a flame' (807), a symbol for ardent faith and spiritual purity with a long history in literature and the visual arts. Abdiel's first words are targeted well. Satan has indeed uttered blasphemy, lies, but above all attempts to make a virtue of the deadly sin of pride.[3] Abdiel calls attention to Satan's exalted rank, 'thyself so high above thy peers' (812), to emphasise the severity of his betrayal which he condemns fervently as 'impious obloquy' (813), the very sound of the phrase conveying something of his disgust. Abdiel also uses a rhetorical question (813–18) to counter Satan's argument, but his use of the third person is far more limited. Instead he repeatedly uses 'thy', 'thee' or 'thou' which directs his speech more at Satan and less to the assembly. You will find plenty to discuss about the basis upon which he refutes Satan. Does he, for example, assume a connection between the 'just decree of God, pronounced and sworn' (814) and the Messiah's adoption of kingship, his 'regal sceptre' (816), or the requirement for 'every soul in heaven' (816) to 'bend the knee' (817) and 'Confess him rightful king?' (818)? It is easy to see why, in this case, many academic critics are drawn to psychoanalytical theory as a critical tool. Milton's had been one of the most articulate, ardent and unwavering voices calling for the execution of Charles I, and here he is, in the bloody and tumultuous political aftermath, apparently using divine right as a defence against individual freedom.

The next step in Abdiel's defence of God addresses freedom and equality head on. He seizes on the idea of injustice, implied but not actually stated by Satan, and relates it to the concept of equality and the role of law, summarising Satan's case that, as they are all free and equal, no-one has the right to exercise power eternally over them. Once stated, Abdiel immediately refutes it with more rhetorical questions. The first is an entirely logical interpretation of the facts. Satan is himself the one making laws, 'Shalt thou give law to God' (822). By his act of defiance he is shaping law and has reversed the natural law of the universe. The second is more complex, as though Abdiel really were trying to convince Satan, since, when he reaches the end of this first speech, he gives Satan the chance to save himself and seek forgiveness:

> hasten to appease
> The incensèd Father, and the incensed Son,
> While pardon may be found in time besought. (846–8)

Abdiel's second question mirrors Satan's actions to his face, pointing out the absurdity of Satan's questioning the will of his creator, the God who not only created him, but all beings 'Such as he pleased, and circumscribed their being?' (825). The way Abdiel then refines this point is easy to overlook and undervalue, yet it is crucial to a strong understanding of Milton's theodicy. Experience has taught Abdiel, and here he does resort to the rhetorical third person, that God's purpose is entirely to their benefit and good. Far from acting as Satan asserts, to reduce or belittle them, God is 'bent rather to exalt/Our happy state' (829–30) and his aim in decreeing the Messiah his heir is to unite them even more closely, 'under one head more near/United' (831–2).

Abdiel's next question is difficult because of the way Milton makes words work so hard for him and because two subjects are linked to the principle verb 'count' (833). Milton's instinctive gift for compression does seem to hinder meaning here and a more colloquial prose version of Abdiel's question is helpful. Essentially Abdiel says, let's say, for the sake of argument that we do agree God has been unjust and allowed our equal to reign over us as monarch, do you really count yourself, great and glorious though you are, or the entire angelic host combined, the equal to God's son? Abdiel's sense of outrage at this notion is then compounded as he reminds Satan of the central part in the creation of all things Christ has played, and of the 'honour' (844) they receive as a result of his being 'reduced' and becoming 'One of our number' (843).

The caesura (845) marks the point at which Abdiel feels he has made his point unequivocally, and so he turns to what, as an angel and servant of God, he is bound to do, seek a means for forgiveness and reconciliation. To his sincere plea to Satan to seek forgiveness from God, before it is too late, he adds the poignant image, 'And tempt not these' (846), emphasising that throughout his complaint has been with Satan, not with the weaker spirits he seduces, mirroring the way he is physically to confront Satan on the battlefield in Book 6, lines 111–93.

Finally, to provide just a taste of Milton's real world politics, here is a brief extract from *Eikonoklastes*, his attack on Charles I's influential posthumous defence, *Eikon Basilike*, for you to compare with the angry exchanges between Satan and Abdiel:

> That people that should seek a king claiming what this man claims, would show themselves to be by nature slaves and arrant beasts – not fit for that liberty which they cried out and bellowed for, but fitter to be led back again into their old servitude like a sort of clamouring and fighting brutes, broke loose from their copyholds, that know not how to use or possess the liberty which they fought for, but with the fair words and promises of an old exasperated foe are ready to be stroked and tamed again into the wonted and well-pleasing state of their true Norman villeinage, to them best agreeable.[4]

Milton gives Abdiel the last word in this book (877–907) and his final departure from the assembly of fallen angels is one of the most well known sections of the poem, partly because it deals with courage in the face of adversity and partly because it has no precise antecedents in the literary landscape Milton plundered for inspiration.

Although he is surrounded on all sides by a vast host of enemies, in the white heat of rebellion, Abdiel finds the courage not merely to defy them, but denounce them and predict their inevitable ruin. He replies to Satan's ignoble warning to 'fly, ere evil intercept thy flight' (871) in three distinct sentences, brimming with the confidence that comes from an unassailable faith. The first begins with an exclamation, and with epithets that expose starkly the consequences of Satan's actions. He is a 'spirit accursed', now 'alienate from God' (877), the latter conveying the terrifying consequences of disobedience, as much to the Christian reader as to Adam. Abdiel pronounces their fate as unequivocally as any last judge, telling Satan and his 'hapless crew' (879) they have forsaken good itself and, in keeping with Milton's theme of standing or falling, he predicts their imminent punishment, 'I see thy fall/Determined' (878–9). In an image which reminds us that Sin and Death are lurking hungrily in the background waiting for Satan to deliver on his promise that 'all things shall be your prey' (II, 844), Abdiel predicts the infectious nature of evil, 'contagion spread/Both of thy crime and punishment' (880–1), but stops almost mid-thought to deliver a devastatingly ironic warning.

Satan need not worry any longer about trying to escape Christ's tyranny, 'No more be troubled how to quit the yoke' (882), a fantasy of oppression Abdiel corrects as 'indulgent' (883) since the Messiah's indulgence has forever been withdrawn and other, immutable 'decrees' (884) have already started the process of his destruction and damnation. He ends this first sentence with the powerful antithesis of God's 'golden sceptre' (886), the symbol of his authority and love, being transformed into 'an iron rod' (887) which will 'bruise and break/Thy disobedience' (887–8), the alliteration conveying a sense of repeated blows. In naming Satan's crime, Abdiel also takes us right back to the poem's immense opening line, and, since his words form part of the advice Raphael is giving Adam, at God's behest *before* the Fall, the reader finds him- or herself woven into the theological argument not as an academic participant, but as a living, breathing, fallible human linked ineluctably to all other living, breathing, human beings by this original sin. Disobedience is, for Milton, the first crime of all, that principle sin from which all others have grown and spread.

Abdiel's second sentence bristles with confidence and disdain, again using heavy irony to great effect. He thanks Satan for his advice to 'fly' (889) not because he fears their 'threats' (889) but in case the punishment soon to be inflicted on them, the 'wrath/Impendent' (890–1), sweeps him up too in its 'sudden flame' (891). In what is a typically elided sentence, supplying the missing conjunction 'but' in line 890 helps make the sense clearer. Milton is using the formula 'Yet not...*but* lest' (889–90). The third sentence is sententiously brief and consequently potent. Abdiel's confidence is evident in the way he plays with words, using inversion to end each line emphatically with a main verb, 'learn' (894) and 'know' (895), the latter gaining in meaning from its contrast with the former. He also uses the euphemism 'uncreate' (895) to replace Death, but, in Milton's narrative, at this point Death remains unknown in the world and it is therefore entirely sensible and literal of Abdiel to use 'uncreate'. There is also the haunting sound of 'lamenting learn' (894) which forces the reader to linger on the longer first syllable and which reverberates with tragic undertones.

Alliteration is used liberally in the words Raphael chooses to eulogise Abdiel, and the antithetical 'Among the faithless, faithful only he' (897) is the kind of economical, intense expression of a far weightier concept that invites quotation. The list of negatives which follows is a favourite rhetorical technique of Milton's, which works through a combination of rhythm and emphasis, created by repeating the heavily stressed 'un-' prefix. If you dwell on the meanings of the negatives rather than on their poetic effects, you also see a figure of martyr-like courage, able through faith to resist every manner of temptation or threat. Sound and meaning are tightly woven in this closing passage, the single syllables 'His loyalty he kept, his love, his zeal' (900) appear to recommend the ideas themselves to Adam as advice, as though God is speaking directly through Raphael. Milton finally grants Abdiel the most dramatic of exits, walking not only unruffled 'Long way through hostile scorn' (904) but exuding the very qualities which enabled him to resist, 'which he sustained/Superior' (904–5) and returning scorn for scorn on the entire edifice of rebellion and malice that Satan's sinful pride has created.

Exercises

Lines 1–233. In this section, the dream Satan induced in Eve is described in detail and the anxiety she experiences as a result is clearly unfamiliar and deeply disturbing for Adam too. Look closely at both the honesty with which Eve details the dream and the reasoning Adam employs to allay her anxiety. Both these aspects of their dialogue will help you understand how Milton develops their relationship and prepares us for the more critical dialogue between them which takes place once Eve has eaten the forbidden fruit in Book 9.

Lines 246–450. Raphael's rapid descent to earth is shot through with classical allusion, signifying his benign relationship with mankind, and when he locates Adam and Eve the three sit down to a meal prepared by Eve. The whole section resonates with exotic, sensual imagery. You could select from the passage a number of these images and ask yourself what effect they have on you and on your ability to imagine the scene as Milton dramatises it.

Lines 561–771. Raphael's account of Satan's rebellion forms an integral part of God's warning to Adam, but it is also a major contributor to the poem's epic ambitions. Read this section selecting from it those characteristics which advance the poem's epic quality and then ask yourself how you respond to the scale and detail of the language, imagery and political machinations which fuel the entire passage.

Lines 849–76. Encouraged by the complete absence of support for Abdiel from the assembled angels, Satan rejects Abdiel's arguments, and even attempts to employ him as his subordinate messenger to declare war on the Messiah. Look at the stance Satan finally adopts before Abdiel's departure, at the arguments he musters to convince himself and his supporters. What do they imply about his motives and his character?

6
War in Heaven

Summary

Abdiel returns to the throne of God, thinking he is the bearer of dire news, only to be welcomed by vast armies of faithful angels already prepared for battle. God approves of Abdiel's faithfulness then instructs the archangels Michael and Gabriel to lead the forces of good against the rebel angels and expel them from heaven to the place he has prepared for them, hell. As the two vast armies advance on each other, Abdiel steps from the ranks of God's side to confront Satan face-to-face, predicting his ultimate ruin. Satan mocks Abdiel in return, as a mere servant of God, before Abdiel begins the battle by striking Satan a blow of such magnitude that he is for a moment felled and severely wounded. Michael then signals the attack and the war begins on a scale fit for warring angels.

In the midst of the battle, Satan sees Michael wreaking havoc amongst his legions and confronts him. Michael accuses Satan of being the cause of all the chaos and destruction but Satan remains unrepentant and full of confidence, noting that, in spite of all Michael's efforts, his fallen troops simply rise again and return to the fight. The angels make room for the two commanders to fight and, with one slash of his sword, Michael cuts through Satan's sword and on into his body, almost cutting off his right side, but, being an angel, Satan's body reforms itself. Nonetheless, his supporters are so dismayed by this first sign of weakness, they rush to his aid and carry him on their shields to safety.

Elsewhere on the battlefield, Gabriel likewise wounds Moloch and Uriel, and Raphael defeats Adramelec and Asmadai, while Abdiel defeats Ariel, Arioc and Ramiel. As Satan's armies begin to retreat and show signs of losing, they are pursued by an emboldened force for good, before night intervenes and enforces a truce. While Michael's forces rest and keep watch, Satan rallies his troops by telling them they are invincible, as the battle has proven, since none can die but, however badly wounded, are quickly restored. In response, Nisroc complains bitterly of their new experience, pain, and calls for more powerful weapons so that they can at least inflict some pain and damage on their enemies.

Satan responds by instructing his forces to build artillery from the raw materials around them and they quickly go to work mining the minerals from the earth to create gunpowder and smelting metal to cast cannons. When the two armies meet again, Satan issues a series of ironic commands aimed at hiding their new weaponry until he is ready to use it to best advantage. Satan's forces stand aside to reveal their new weapons and begin bombarding their enemies, who are momentarily forced to retreat in the face of a power they cannot resist. Satan mocks them to encourage his own troops and Belial joins him in laughing at the forces of good, but this advantage does not last long. Michael's forces throw away their armour, which is useless against the artillery, and gather up the hills, woods and mountains, which they hurl down onto the artillery and evil angels.

On this third day, where the worst of the fighting is happening amidst an unimaginable backdrop of natural chaos, God fulfils his promise and instructs the Son to drive Satan and his forces out of heaven and into hell. Accepting the charge readily, and praising his Father, the Son then mounts his chariot and leads a further host of angels into the battle. Seeing his ensign in the air, Michael's forces take heart and retire to allow the Son free rein. The Satanic host, although sorely pressed, prepare to face the Son with renewed hatred and determination. The Son commands all the forces of good to stand still and rest while he alone faces the enemy, since he alone was the focus of their envy and rebellion. Roused with God's anger and power, the Son then rushes down on Satan's force and reduces them instantly to weakness and despair. As the Son drives them before him like goats, heaven's wall opens and he forces them all through the gap and down into the hell God has prepared for them. Terrified at what they see opening up before them, but even more terrified of the Son's fury behind them, they throw themselves into hell to escape punishment. For nine days they fall while the broken wall of heaven is resealed and the Son returns to the throne of God, victorious.

Finally, Raphael tells Adam he has recounted all this history of the war in heaven to warn him that Satan is now plotting how to trick him into disobedience and that the same consequences will follow were he

or Eve to disobey. Raphael makes it clear that it is Adam's duty to warn
Eve too.

The First Blows

Book 6 begins with Raphael continuing his account of the war in
heaven, that Adam requested, and he describes how, when God greets
Abdiel with delight for his fidelity and obedience, in his words of
approval we can hear clear warnings for Adam. For God, the harder fight
for Abdiel has already been fought when alone, surrounded by temptation and evil, he maintained his sense of right and confronted the
legions of fallen angels without fear or doubt. The battle to come is easy
in comparison. There is something of a spiritual contradiction about
angels going to war and Milton relies heavily on his classical models to
manage this.

With the two armies drawn up against one another ready for battle,
Milton gives Abdiel a soliloquy in the same way Shakespeare delivers the
intimate thoughts of some of his most famous characters.[1] He begins
with an exclamatory 'O heaven!' (114), prompted by the blasphemous
sight of a triumphant Satan in 'his sun-bright chariot' (100), and asks
himself how Satan can retain his impressive, angelic appearance and yet
lack all 'virtue' (117). In Abdiel's thinking, both 'strength and might'
(116) should inevitably desert those who have abandoned faith and
reality ('realty'; 115). To look at, Satan appears 'unconquerable?' (118),
but Abdiel's expectation is that in practice Satan will prove as weak as
he appears bold. Putting his faith in God, 'trusting in the almighty's
aid' (119), Abdiel determines to fight Satan. Having defeated Satan in
debate, and exposed his argument as 'Unsound and false' (121), Abdiel
asserts that it is only justice that now he should also 'win in arms' (123),
turning his hatred of violence, 'though brutish that contést and foul'
(124), into a greater good. The final wordplay around 'reason' (125–6) is
very elliptical but the argument is one only too familiar to students of
history, that where 'reason hath to deal with force' (125) all the more
reason for sense and balanced thought to defeat irrational anger or violence. Armed in this hermetic way, Abdiel steps out of the ranks of the
army as a free thinking, courageous defender of the truth and confronts
his enemy directly, infuriating Satan at the same time that he makes
sure he cannot avoid fighting him, 'Incensed, and thus securely him
defied' (130).

The way he now addresses Satan, dropping soliloquy for direct
speech, is, as before, brimful of a confidence born out of knowing the

ultimate outcome of this encounter. Abdiel now abandons any pretence of respect, calling Satan what he is, 'Proud' (131), and reminding us of the essence of his sin. Several centuries of use have rendered what to Milton's readers was a deadly sin, plain and simple, into something almost approaching a quality to be admired. Overlaying modern meanings onto early English text is a very understandable mistake for modern students to make, but it is a serious mistake because it can send you off on entirely unprofitable critical byways.

Abdiel's terse greeting is followed by a typically lengthy Miltonic sentence whose determining feature of its developing sense is not the full stop or comma, but the caesura. The first section ends with the phrase 'Or potent tongue' (l 135) and mocks Satan for assuming that he could have defeated God 'unopposed' (132), the rest of heaven's force having 'Abandoned' (134) God, terrified of Satan's power or, most pointedly when we recall his meeting with Eve to come, his 'potent tongue' (135). A heavy caesura and the long vowel sound gives weight to the insult 'fool', an effect made even stronger by the staccato burst of single syllable words, 'not to think how vain' (135), that follow.

The antithesis Abdiel uses is striking, affording to God the power to raise 'incessant armies' (138) from the 'smallest things' (137), not, as we might imagine, to destroy the vast force Satan has managed to assemble, but his diminutive 'folly' (149). Again a caesura hardens the insult. Milton's God is often criticised as an Old Testament tyrant, and, in the vast sway and power Abdiel gives him, it is easy to see why. With his 'solitary hand' (139) able paradoxically to reach 'beyond all limit' (140), God 'Unaided could have finished thee' (141) and Satan's 'legions' (142). Yet another caesura separates the imagined destruction of Satan's legions from the reality: war with the pious, faithful angels. With obvious relish, Abdiel reminds Satan of their last encounter, and his final talk of error and the multitude seems to reverberate with the contemporary politics of Milton's own era.[2] The last caesura in Abdiel's speech invites Satan to view the opposition he has raised, 'my sect thou seest' (147), before his sententious conclusion, 'How few sometimes may know, when thousands err' (148).

Satan's reply is full of the arrogance we have come to expect, evident in the way he toys with the word 'first', repeating it three times in a few lines to assert his pleasure at finding Abdiel so keen to confront him, and in his elevating himself and his followers to 'gods' (156). In Satan's view, Abdiel's 'contradiction' (155) requires 'revenge' (151) and he is eager to fight, not the view he expressed at the time (V, 869–71). His description of the feeling he ascribes to his followers is a wholly unverifiable extension of his own motivation, and oozes pride. He tells Abdiel 'Vigour divine' (158) inspires them and drives them to 'allow/Omnipotence to none' (158–9) then mocks him. With heavy irony he states how glad he is that Abdiel has stepped forward since his 'Destruction' (162) will serve as an example to the rest. The irony rebounds on Satan because what we hear is more of the same overweening pride and selfishness, since he credits Abdiel with his own motives. Abdiel has said nothing at all to indicate he is driven by ambition, but that is the motive Satan gives him.

The word 'first' (164) crops up again, suspiciously, as Satan now turns his attention to the rest of his enemies and insults them as indolent servants, 'the minstrelsy of heaven' (168). The puritan mind always had a bit of a problem with religious music. Satan tries to create an antithesis between freedom, 'liberty' (164) and servility, 'sloth' (166), implying that the only reason his enemies did not join him was because they were servile and lazy. It is an insult with some rich literary precedents.[3] For Satan, this antithesis will prove the determining factor of the imminent battle, 'As both their deeds compared this day shall prove' (170). But Abdiel is beyond insult and rhetoric, and makes one final speech before striking the first, immense, physical blow of the war in heaven.

This time the belittling form of address is 'Apostate' (172), a word which in seventeenth-century terms describes Satan perfectly. He has abandoned both his faith and his religious duty, and has consequently condemned himself. Abdiel rejects Satan's argument stating that natural law and God's law are the same, that it is right that the 'worthiest' (177) both 'governs' (178) and 'excels' (177) those inferior to him by nature. He throws Satan's insult back in the face of all his followers telling them it is 'servitude' (178) 'To serve the unwise' or whoever rebels 'Against his worthier' (180) as they currently do by believing and following Satan, and adds a piercing insight by telling Satan that he is in reality enslaved to himself, his own ego and ambition, 'Thyself not free, but to thyself enthralled' (181). But perhaps the most valuable point Abdiel makes in rejecting Satan's charge is the one most easily passed over in the first few lines. He tells Satan 'still thou errst' (172), adding the terrible notion that his erring will be eternal, his existence always 'from the path of truth remote' (173). Satan is the archetypal liar. It is his rejection of truth that sets him apart and germinates both Sin and Death, the twin destroyers of Paradise. In a closing, angry outburst, Abdiel expresses his amazement that, given all this, it is Satan who remonstrates with the faithful angels, using the adverb 'lewdly' (182), not as it is most commonly used today in connection with sex, but more politically, indicating unprincipled or vulgar behaviour.

The chronology of *Paradise Lost* is complex but Milton always seems in control, so when, in the few moments before he strikes him, Abdiel urges Satan to 'Reign thou in hell thy kingdom, let me serve/In heaven God ever blest' (183–4) we can see a very conscious reminder of Satan's earlier rhetorical claim that it will be far better to rule in hell than serve in heaven (I, 263). Abdiel's final few words owe much to heroic antecedents as he uses heavy irony to turn his 'greeting' (188) into an immensely powerful stroke of his sword. There may even be a hint of wit in his use of 'erst' (187) which on one level simply means 'first' but is so close to his repeated 'errst' that he may be refuting the accuracy of Satan's choice of the word 'flight' (187) to describe his earlier departure.

Satan's Duel with Michael

In the midst of the raging battle, Satan sees Michael destroying 'squadrons' (251) and seeks him out, in the tradition of Homeric heroes, as though drawn to an individual to match his own power and strength. Michael breaks off from his 'warlike toil' (257) hoping to put an end to the fighting by defeating and capturing Satan.

Satan is addressed by Michael as the 'Author of evil' (262), an image he eagerly elaborates. The irreversibility of events is conveyed through the repeated negatives, 'unknown' (262) and 'Unnamed' (263), each word carrying a heavy stress on the rhyme created by the first two syllables. Michael's insistence that evil is not only new, but 'plenteous' (263), adds to the sense of tragedy and to his just anger. He makes it clear that this violence is 'hateful to all' (264), even though Satan and his followers are suffering the worst of it 'by just measure' (265). 'Heaven's blessèd peace' (267) has been destroyed and the natural world infected with 'Misery' (268), a new concept *created* by Satan's rebellious act, although again Milton opts for the negative 'uncreated' (268) to carry more weight.

Michael constructs his first assault on Satan around the same, rhetorical question, 'How hast thou' (266 and 269), which is more a statement of disbelief and blame than enquiry. Lengthy, dialectic sentences sit uncomfortably with the savagery and scale of the underlying dramatic action, so Milton gives Michael some short warnings to deliver. Michael affords Satan not the slightest hope of success. Without mentioning God, it is 'heaven' that 'casts thee out' (272) and later 'Heaven the seat of bliss' (273) that rejects Satan, banishing him forever 'From all her confines' (273), depersonalising the conflict as though nature itself has turned against him for the disturbance he has brought. In a second terse sentence Milton's acute sense of the sounds of English, of poetry as an aural art form, is exemplified perfectly:

> Heaven the seat of bliss
> Brooks not the works of violence and war. (273–4)

Besides the alliteration linking 'bliss' and 'Brooks' and 'works' and 'war' is a subtle shift in sound from 'Brooks' to 'works' which is not quite assonance, and not quite the half or sprung rhyme of later poets like Gerard Manley Hopkins or W. B. Yeats. The combined effect is to invest Michael's statement with a degree of gravitas. Michael finally urges Satan to depart for hell and to take all that is evil with him, 'Thy offspring' (276), before either himself or God 'begin they doom' (278). The image he chooses, 'Precipitate thee with augmented pain' (280), harks back to the opening of the poem in which Satan and his followers are discovered in hell (I, 44–9).

We have noted how careful Milton is about terms of address and so the contrast between Michael as 'prince of angels' (281) and Satan 'The adversary' (282) is stark. The word 'adversary' has the specific meaning 'Satan' when preceded by the definite article, so this is not a generic cognomen but a literal one. Like Michael, Satan avoids lengthy dispute in favour of angry, shorter sentences. He accuses Michael of making empty, 'airy threats' (283), that he is incapable of following up with force, and as evidence indicates his entire army who remain unharmed, 'Unvanquished' (286). None have fled nor fallen, because they are, of course, immortal and simply return to the fight unharmed. Satan mocks Michael further implying that his 'imperious . . . threats' (287) are a futile substitute for his failure in arms. Matching warning for warning, he tells Michael not to make the mistake of thinking that there is a possibility of ending the conflict through any means except force. But he himself makes a more obvious mistake, denying that the concept of evil even exists, renaming 'The strife which thou callst evil' (289) euphemistically 'The strife of glory' (290). With equal confidence he denies the existence of hell, promising to 'turn this heaven itself into the hell/Thou fablest' (291–2), apparently unaware of the contradiction inherent in the promise, and more concerned to position himself as a liberator, 'to dwell free' (292), even if victory eludes them, 'If not to reign' (293). Earlier in this study we examined how critics through the centuries have had differing reactions to Satan, many finding themselves drawn to him, and certainly in his advice to Michael to call on Christ for help, 'join him named Almighty to thy aid' (294), there is something of Macbeth's desperate courage in the face of inevitable destruction, 'Yet I will try the last'[4] and of the Homeric hero striding the battlefield in Satan's claim to 'have sought thee far and nigh' (295).

When Michael and Satan cease talking, 'They ended parle' (296), Raphael digresses from the action for a moment to prepare the listener for the unimaginable. It is as though Milton is suddenly confronted with the results of his own poetic ambition and sees before him the descriptive mountain he has set himself to climb. The word Raphael settles on to convey the immensity of their imminent fight is 'Unspeakable' (297). It is literally beyond the imaginative capacity of man, even though Raphael speaks 'with the tongue/Of angels' (297–8) to convey to Adam the reality. Neither are there earthly objects which he can use to draw comparisons with, 'or to what things/Liken on earth conspicuous' (298–9). 'Human imagination' (300) lacks the 'godlike power' (301) necessary to appreciate this momentous battle. Of course the tactic Milton uses is to disarm criticism in advance, and you can decide for yourself how successful this tactic is once you have reached the end of Raphael's dramatic account. What Milton certainly does not do, is what Raphael's preamble implies, is eschew hyperbole.

Although they are only angels, and of a lower order than God, Raphael likens both Michael and Satan to gods, 'for likest gods they seemed' (301), whether they stand or move, and to the spectators it seems that on their one-to-one combat rests the fate of heaven, 'Fit to decide the empire of great heaven' (303). The initial hyperbole is not difficult. Their swords are 'fiery' (304) and make 'horrid circles' (305) in the air as they prepare to fight, and their shields become 'two broad suns' (306) blazing in opposition; but as Milton warms to his task, the imagery and syntax become complex and dense. The long vowel sounds of 'Blazed opposite' force a natural pause before the harsher consonants of 'expectation stood/In horror' (306–7) in imitation of the action. The throng of spectators on both sides are frozen momentarily as they realise what is about to happen, before rushing back to make space for the principal combatants, 'and left large field' (309), their own safety at risk from the sheer violence of Michael and Satan's movements. At this point, and using a conventional formula popularised by Virgil of comparing great things with small, the hyperbole takes off and Milton compares the two figures to two planets colliding. The dense syntax unravels if you simply put 'as' before 'if nature's concord broke' (311) and locate the subject of the main verb 'Should combat' (315) which is 'Two planets' (313). But to appreciate the image fully you also need to bring into play astrology and the concept that planets can be aligned in harmony or opposition. The force of the planetary impact is also evoked through what is almost an internal rhyme, 'combat...confound' (315).

Milton has built the dramatic tension to the point where we feel, even though we know Satan's fate from our reading of the earlier books, that the outcome of the entire battle now hangs on this moment. Simultaneously, 'Together both' Michael and Satan raise swords with a strength almost matching God's, 'next to almighty arm' (316), with the same intent. That is to deal a single, fatal blow 'That might determine, and not need repeat' (318). A blow so strong, neither could repeat it instantly, and to the observers' eyes equal in force and speed, 'nor odds appeared/In might or swift prevention' (319–20). This tension is broken by the slightest of words, 'but' (320). When Raphael uses that 'but' he exposes the crucial difference between the combatants. It is Michael who has been armed by God and whose sword is 'tempered so' (322) that nothing can resist its blade, 'neither keen/Nor solid might resist that edge' (322–3). The word 'edge' has an awkward, truncated sound that makes it difficult to link it smoothly with anything else, and its use here creates a significant pause before we discover its dire effects. Alliteration helps to evoke the savagery and speed of the blow, 'The sword of Satan with steep force to smite' (324), where even the odd word out visually, 'force', is actually phonetically alliterative.

Such is the power of Michael's sword, it cuts Satan's own sword in two and continues on into his body, cutting off his entire right side. The verb 'shared' (326) is a variant spelling of the more conventional 'sheared', although both have their root in a physical object, the 'share' or blade of a plough. The effect is dramatic, causing Satan to writhe in agony, anticipating his adoption of the serpent's shape to seduce Eve (IX, 510–18), 'And writhed him to and fro convolved' (328), the last, near onomatopoeic word specifically describing the action of coiling or twisting in folds. The subtle contribution sound can make to meaning is clearly audible in the clash Milton creates between the dominant sibilant sounds which have accompanied the speed and descent of Michael's sword, and the throaty, percussive harshness of 'griding' (329). This unusual word carries a lot of poetic weight, implying a cut which is the opposite of clinically precise or neat, and rather one that tears the flesh in a savage, agonising fashion, an effect compounded by the idea that it may also be 'discontinuous' (329), requiring renewed strength and effort from Michael to continue the sword's progress, rather than a single, clean slice.

But Michael's hope to end Satan and the rebellion with this single blow is disappointed. Immortal, Satan's 'ethereal' (330) form repairs itself in the same way that he described his followers returning to the fight, 'unvanquished', earlier in this meeting with Michael (285–6). The image he presents us with here, of a horribly wounded, bleeding Satan, is one that would have been much more accessible to his first readers than it is to today's students. Many educated readers in Milton's age would have had personal experience of battlefield horrors. Their reading too would have made the wounds and deaths played out before the walls of Troy and in imperial Rome very familiar, so the image drawn here of Satan with 'all his armour stained' (334) with 'nectarous humour' (333), which is made as close to blood as possible by the adjective 'Sanguine' (332), would have resonated a lot more powerfully than it might today, three centuries later and with millions of hours of film and television violence to dilute it.

Satan is carried off the battlefield on shields by his aides, while others rush in to cover his retreat. This intervention of Satan's aides, in true epic fashion, selflessly risking harm to rescue their commander, may raise some challenging questions. If, for example, we were to imagine that these few lines describe not Satan's followers, but Michael's or Abdiel's, would our reaction to them be any different? By electing to deal with the war in heaven in heroic, but nonetheless essentially human terms, and relying largely on hyperbole to inspire awe, Milton lands his reader with a peculiarly painful moral dilemma. To feel the full impact of this dilemma one need only remember Christ's advice to his disciples, 'Greater love hath no man than this, that a man lay down his life for his friends'.[5]

Removed from the battle, Milton has no such problem dealing with Satan who he now describes tormented, not so much by the wound to his physical form, but that inflicted on his image of himself. Milton's talent for linking sound to meaning is again audible in the single line 'Gnashing for anguish and despite and shame' (340), where the alliteration may be quite noticeable, as is the use of 'and' for stress, but the intense closeness in sound between the words 'Gnashing' and 'anguish' may not be. Once more the sin that Milton's intellect hones in on is 'pride' (341) and it is the tragic discovery that, in spite of all his posturing and oratory, he is in reality 'so far beneath ... God in power' (342–3) that causes Satan such anguish.

Milton uses this lull in the battle to digress for a moment. Returning to the topic of the angels' immortality, he asserts that, unlike 'frail man' (345) whose entire being is a complex chain of interdependent organs, 'entrails, heart or head, liver or reins'[6] (346), the angels exist 'Vital in every part' (345) and 'Cannot but by annihilating die' (347). It is a fascinatingly fine distinction. Annihilation, for Milton, implies utter and complete non-existence, a total and complete reversal of being and, by this definition, is something only God can bring about.

Satan Regroups

When Satan speaks to his exhausted troops during the night, he is addressing a host of individuals who have all experienced pain for the first time. Yet their immortality means they simply heal and return to the fray. There is already something hellish about this. However, Satan launches immediately into the rhetorical mode we have come to expect from him when acting in command. He turns their near rout into a reason for celebration, his strategy being one of flattery. He carefully avoids any reference to himself as leader, instead aligning himself with his troops as 'companions dear' (419) and tells them they have all been tested in arms but have not been defeated and therefore shown themselves 'worthy' of more than mere 'liberty' (420). He lists the prizes that await, 'Honour, dominion, glory and renown' (422), which in themselves sound apparently worthy, although on closer scrutiny all reflect his own ambition. Having survived 'one day in doubtful fight' (423) Satan poses the rhetorical question: Is there any reason why they cannot 'survive eternal days?' (424). If that piece of logic seems strained, then the next step in his argument is even more audacious. Since they have survived the worst 'heaven's lord' (425) could throw at them (note Satan diminishes God's title), God must therefore be 'fallible' (428). But the reasoning relies on a simple false assumption. Satan assumes God has sent his most powerful force to 'subdue us to his will' (427). Whether Satan's denial of God's omniscience is a genuine mistake or another rhetorical strategy is a critical quagmire since, if Satan believed God to be omniscient, any rebellion would be doomed before it began. There is potentially a rich philosophical argument worth pursuing which sets Satan's understanding of free will against God's.

A caesura makes this issue even less clear since it signals not just a new line of argument, but a degree of self-doubt. 'True is' (430) gives the impression that Satan himself has doubts about the accuracy of his earlier thinking, as though he were saying 'what we *do* know is that we were less well armed than the enemy'. Given the ferocity of the fighting immediately preceding the lull, Satan's summarising the day's outcome as 'Some disadvantage' (431) is almost comically euphemistic and he works hard to minimise the damage caused by his followers' novel experience of pain. He admits pain was previously beyond their experience, 'Till now not known', but dismisses it as trivial, 'but known as soon contemned' (432), because it has taught them the meaning of their own immortality. The repetition of the negatives 'Incapable' (434) and 'Imperishable' (435) bolsters his argument, as does his appeal to their own, self-generating power in the phrase 'by native vigour healed' (436). This, of all Satan's many arguments employed to manage, inspire or deceive his followers, is perhaps the most revealing. Presented with a reality where pain can be inflicted at will by God or his representatives, on him and his followers, combined with an infinite capacity to endure it, Satan finds not just more reason to continue their struggle, but reason to expect victory. He dismisses pain as 'evil then so small' (437) before arriving at his answer to their problem, 'more valid arms' (438), which crudely translated means greater force, and which he himself qualifies as 'Weapons more violent' (439).

The obscure angel Nisroc continues the debate, his appearance and demeanour contrasting starkly with Satan's account of their status. 'Sore toiled, his riven arms to havoc hewn' (449) conveys fatigue and despair not just through the visual image of his ruined armour, but through the long vowel sounds of 'Sore toiled' and the forceful, alliterative use of 'r' and 'h' sounds throughout the whole line. His pessimism and exhaustion appear in his face, 'And cloudy in aspéct' (450), even before he speaks, but he is careful to show respect and praises Satan as 'Deliverer' and 'leader' (451). Nisroc accepts that Satan has shown them how to enjoy their freedom and 'right as gods' (452) but exhibits a stronger grip on reality by suggesting there is little advantage in being godlike when their enemy is so superior and able to fight free of the debilitating pain that weakens their every effort, 'and makes remiss the hands/Of mightiest' (458–9). 'Valour or strength', Nisroc argues, are of little use 'though matchless' when 'quelled with pain' (457). By introducing pain's antonym, pleasure, he is able to pursue the debate and counter Satan's rhetoric, without overtly being seen to deny anything Satan has said. Nisroc imagines a life lived without pleasure as possible and even 'content' (461), but he cannot imagine an existence subject to constant pain, calling it 'the worst/Of evils' (462–3), which is able in excess to usurp 'All patience' (464). Unwittingly, he glimpses the future for himself and his companions. If there is any direct challenge to Satan in his stance, he hides it well in the way he concludes his statement, returning to Satan's own point about their need for better weaponry. Whoever can design the arms 'more forcible' (465) with which to wound

'Our yet unwounded enemies' (466), or which can equal their defence, Nisroc states, deserves the same reward as Satan for delivering them from slavery.

Picking up Nisroc's own verb 'invent', Satan assures him that what he asks for is already available, 'Not uninvented' (470), and he wastes no words on promising delivery with the assertive, present tense, 'I bring' (471). Returning to the rhetorical question as his main strategy, he then invites his listeners to contemplate the richness and variety of their world, 'this ethereous mould whereon we stand' (473), a 'spacious heav'n' (474) replete 'With plant, fruit, flower ambrosial, gems and gold' (475). He asks who can witness all this variety without also contemplating its source and origin, 'Deep under ground', where 'materials dark and crude' (478) lie waiting for 'heaven's ray' (480) to ignite them and transform them into the 'beauteous' (481) forms they take on the surface. The imagery of fire and ignition, and a diction associated with artillery, anticipates the making of gunpowder and artillery, which is the practical action Satan now outlines. He describes the crude essentials of a canon, 'hollow engines long and round' (484), which are 'Thick-rammed' (485) with 'Such implements of mischief' (488) that once they are ignited 'with touch of fire' (485) will 'Dilated and infuriate' (486) rival heaven's thunder in sheer noise, and 'o'erwhelm whatever stands/Adverse' (489–90). Satan ends his suggestion with the tempting prospect of their striking such fear into the enemy from surprise and sheer noise that they will believe he has stolen God's 'only dreaded thunder bolt' (491).[7]

Satan promises them that only a few hours labour under darkness will suffice to deliver what he has promised by dawn, 'Effect shall end our wish' (493), and then turns to rallying them for the effort required with far less rhetoric than he began with. A series of terse imperatives – 'revive' (493), 'Abandon fear' (494) and 'Think nothing hard' (495) – bring about the necessary change such that they set about the task with renewed energy and determination. But before Raphael recounts their covert mining operations, he digresses to connect the devilish invention of gunpowder and artillery with Adam's descendants, predicting its invention at some future date by 'Someone intent on mischief' or else 'inspired' (503) by 'devilish machination' (504).

At first, the plan works exactly as Satan predicted and the newly created artillery pieces cut the enemy down in their thousands, forcing them to retreat in ranks. But soon the forces of good overcome the new weapons with even greater force, burying them under entire mountains.

God as Military Commander

As the fighting between the two sides escalates, God steps in to this prelapsarian arms race. In an effort to keep up with the escalating violence he has set in motion, Milton now uses understatement, suggesting that in comparison with this ferocity 'war seemed a civil game' (667). Repeating the word 'confusion' he creates a sense of burgeoning lack of control, 'horrid confusion heaped/Upon confusion rose' (668–9), where the noun carries far greater weight than it might today. The section of his narrative in which Raphael explains why God intervenes (667–718) is critical to any informed understanding of Milton's theodicy. To prevent the complete 'wreck' and 'ruin' (670) of heaven, God simply speaks to his 'Son beloved' (680). But Raphael is careful to outline in detail the reasons behind the timing and the action, and it is one of those rare examples in the poem where a rather pedestrian approach to the text is helpful.

One way to begin this approach is to list the operative verbs Raphael assigns to God, because there are quite a few. Firstly he has God sitting 'Shrined' (672) and removed from the conflict and then, in quite quick succession, there are these relevant verbs: 'Consulting' and 'foreseen' (673), 'permitted' and 'advised' (674), 'fulfil' (675), 'honour' (676), 'declare' (677) and finally 'began' (679). With careful re-reading you should be able to connect the phrase 'Had not the almighty Father' with the verb which completes it, 'foreseen' (673), and then see how the next verb in the list moves the idea of his foresight forwards to a greater act of granting permission, 'permitted' (674). In mundane language the meaning runs, 'Heaven would have been destroyed had God not only foreseen this chaos, but allowed it'. And in-between this meaning Milton inserts the concept of omniscience through the wonderfully simple but apt phrase, 'Consulting on the sum of things' (673). No-one else possesses, to use a very modern phrase more usually employed for far less significant purposes, *the single version of the truth* that God owns. Some of the difficulty with the syntax here comes from the immediate addition of what looks like yet another verb, another action, 'advised' (674). But the word is actually being used as an adverb to qualify the preceding verb, 'permitted'. If you emphasise the pause after 'all' (674) you should be able to hear the effect more easily, the last word in the line rhythmically as well as etymologically encapsulating the magnificence and absolute nature of God's consultation.

The next section moves away from God's consultation to his purpose, and that purpose is more plainly stated: 'To honour his anointed

Son' (676), that is to enable him to avenge the wrong done to him by his enemies and finally to declare the transference of all power to him. Partly because the poem is so lengthy, students frequently only study certain books, two and nine being amongst the most popular. But if we are to understand *Paradise Lost*, and by that I mean at least engage with the complete poem intelligently and critically as readers and students, we need to place the entire history of Adam and Eve and their relationship inside this overarching divine will. Put in the crudest of terms, God knows what he is doing.

Immediately he addresses the Son we can see the contrast with the forms of address used earlier when Abdiel or Michael spoke to Satan. The Son is 'Effulgence of my glory, Son beloved' (680), the first phrase plundering the Bible for its inspiration where Christ the Son is often the bright and visible presence of God, the second a poignantly simple, human contrast.

God reminds the Son of the events of the past two, heavenly days. Two days in which Michael's fight with Satan has been 'sore' (687), by which he means strained and painful, while the balance between the two sides has been unshaken since 'Equal in their creation they were formed' (690) and 'to themselves I left them' (689). But God does qualify their equality a little, adding that sin has made a difference, 'Save what sin hath impaired' (691), although as yet too small a difference to be perceived, 'Insensibly' (692), because he has withheld their final punishment. With admirable logic he concludes that they will continue this marginally unequal battle for eternity, 'and no solution will be found' (694). Some of the sense of this dismal prospect is conveyed through the heavy stress that falls on 'last' (683) and then is carried over to the next line into 'Endless' (694). War has done what war can do, and God does not seem all that impressed by the outcome. The metaphorically loosened 'reins' (696) implies all the reckless danger of the out of control horse, while 'mountains as with weapons armed' (697) adds the scale. The outcome is that the universe itself is now in danger, 'and dangerous to the main' (698).

As with Christ's resurrection, the third day is the significant one, and God now gives that day over to his Son, 'the third day is thine' (699), for him to put an end to the war in heaven, 'that the glory may be thine' (701), because only the Son can end it. The biblical second person, 'thy' or possessive pronoun 'thine', is used repeatedly throughout this speech, underscoring that this is the word of God. The next sentence (703–9) is packed with significance in any discussion on Milton's theodicy. As previously, it helps to read it with the express intention of grasping a clear understanding of the syntax, and what might seem at first to be a bit of a drudge really does repay the careful student. The structure pivots around the phrase 'that all may know' (704) because the sentence has a fundamentally 'I have done a and b so that x, y and z will be understood' formula, and once you have seen that it is relatively easy to fill in the missing factors. The first factors are 'virtue and grace' (703) and God has given the Son such 'Immense' (704) quantities of these divine qualities – transfused, literally poured out from himself into his Son – that all 'heaven and hell' will acknowledge 'thy power above compare' (705). But before he adds the y and z factors to the other side of the equation, God links the act of giving grace and virtue to the Son's unique power to end this war, 'And this perverse commotion governed thus' (706). Only this way, God insists, can order be restored.

Milton now adds to the equation by stating that the consequence will be that the Son is manifestly 'worthiest to be heir' and, intriguingly for a regicide, 'king' (707) 'Of all things' (708). The most valuable word here is 'manifest' (707) because it leaves no room for doubt about God's intention. It usually means to make obvious, plain and clear to either the mind or eye by action or intent and here Milton exploits that meaning very cleverly. It is not enough for God to make the Son his heir: the Son has to be seen by all to *merit* that inheritance. This emphasis is in many ways quite understandable from such a vehement anti-monarchist as Milton. Having reached this point, Milton completes this important equation with the final factor. All this will be done with due religious rite and ceremony, 'By sacred unction', confirming for all the Son's right to this inheritance, 'thy deservèd right' (709).

That announcement made, God sends his Son to war with words that foreshadow the terrible outcome. In a conflict where scale and extremes have already figured highly, the repetitious 'mightiest in thy father's might' (710) ramps things up even more as does the list of tools God provides for the Son to complete the job. God's own chariot is brought to the field, with wheels 'That shake heaven's basis' (712), and the Son is given the freedom to deploy everything in the Father's power, 'bring forth all my war' (712), where war is a synecdoche for weaponry and a series of heavy stresses carries as much force as the image itself. The list continues with 'bow and thunder' and 'almighty arms' (713) and finally God's own sword is given to the Son.

The final instructions spoken by God to the Son reverberate with biblical authority. The Son is told to 'Pursue these sons of darkness' (715) – where, if we focus on the obvious 'darkness', it is easy to miss the irony implied in 'sons' – out of heaven completely and into hell, 'the utter

deep' (716). There, God predicts ominously, they will truly know what
it is to 'despise' (717) both himself and his Son. The concluding phrase
'anointed king' (718), being a literal translation of the name preceding
it, Messiah, adds more weight to the crucial concept that this entire
event is necessary to prove the Son's right to the throne of heaven.

Exercises

Lines 189–261. It is at least interesting that Milton has the faithful
angels strike the first blow and, if you read this section describing the
war in heaven before Michael's great speech interrupts the flow of battle,
you will find many examples of where Milton works hard to describe
action which by its very nature is indescribable and beyond human
experience. How effective do you find his choice of imagery to convey
the scale and significance of this immense conflict? Can you find any
common techniques or stylistic details that he uses to place his epic on
a higher level than its literary predecessors?

Lines 354–417. After digressing to discuss the immortality of the angels
and to prepare us for Satan's changing shape in Book 8, Milton returns to
the battle, listing other victories and one-to-one combats before allowing night to bring a halt to the fighting. You might find it valuable to
examine the behaviour of the fallen angels here and compare it with
earlier descriptions of their demeanour. You could also remind yourself
of what God asked Raphael to do when speaking to Adam (V, 224–45)
and then read this section looking for evidence of narrative consistency.

Lines 719–912. In choosing to describe war in heaven, Milton took on
an immense poetic challenge and so far we have seen a number of ways
in which he tries to meet it. In the final section of Book 6 he describes
the Son's arrival on the battlefield and how he fulfils God's command to
pursue Satan and his followers out of heaven and into hell. When you
read this section, look at how well Milton succeeds in reaching above the
descriptive heights already attained in describing Abdiel and Michael's
encounters with Satan. Given that this is the final battle of the war in
heaven, what strategies does Milton employ to meet the challenge he
set himself?

7
Genesis

Summary

Milton again invokes his muse, this time the goddess, Urania, and then relates how Adam seeks to learn more from Raphael. Adam asks Raphael how and when the known universe came into being, giving as a reason his desire to praise God more fully. Raphael explains that God has instructed him to answer Adam's questions, within reason, as there are some things which are known to God alone and it is not for Adam to seek to know them.

He tells Adam how, after Satan's fall, God then announced to the heavens his intention, in part to repair the loss, to create a new world and a race of men who by degrees can work themselves worthy of a place in heaven and finally bring about the unification of heaven and earth. God then instructs the Son to create heaven and earth. Then Raphael describes how the Son left heaven to carry out this command. God then creates light, day and night before adding the sky, oceans and the land itself. At the end of the third day, God covers the dry land with vegetation of all kinds before creating rain to nurture its growth. The next day God creates the sun and the moon and all other celestial bodies, linking them to the changing seasons and to the fortunes of men. On the fifth day he populates the sky with birds, the oceans with fish and reptiles; and on the sixth he adds all other land dwelling creatures. God finally makes man in his own image, to rule over all other life on earth and to sing his praises and worship him throughout eternity. Breathing life into Adam, God adds his sole command that he does not eat from the Tree of Knowledge, telling him that death is the penalty.

Returning to his throne on the seventh day to admire the goodness of his creations, God receives praise from all the angels and is joined by the Son. Raphael ends his account with more description of how the heavenly host sing God's praises and approve all his great works, the last of which is man.

Raphael's Warning

Book 7 begins with an authorial preamble (1–69) in the same vein as Books 1, 3 and later 9. After the immensity of the violence of the war in heaven, it seems sensible in terms of dramatic narrative to instil some calm but there are a number of undercurrents in the preamble, which seem unconnected with any narrative imperative. Milton's choice of muse[1] stresses his interest in 'wisdom' (9) and her ancient, heavenly pedigree, but juxtaposed against this not unsurprising desire for intellectual credibility we also find Milton unusually slipping into what sound like deeply personal comments on his blindness and political isolation (25–39). What links these together is his signalling that halfway through his story, events have now moved from the divine to the earthly, and it is chiefly in dealing with Adam and with Eve that he now seeks inspiration.

Adam's curiosity to know more of the universe and man's place in it is fuelled rather than sated by the angel's lengthy account, even before Raphael begins to speak again (70). But it's worth recalling why Raphael is here. He has been sent by God to warn Adam of the danger he faces from Satan. Otherwise it is tempting to see Adam's entire dialogue with Raphael as one driven by natural, rather naïve curiosity. The risk of looking at it in this way is that when we face the vital questions that arise after the Fall, about Adam and Eve's relative culpability, we may fail to give Raphael's warnings their due weight.

Adam is full of gratitude, because so much of what Raphael has related has been, not just beyond the reach of human knowledge, 'which human knowledge could not reach' (75), but beyond Adam's imagination, 'full of wonder' (70). As before, Adam is deeply respectful of Raphael, calling him 'Divine interpreter' (72), but this time the term of address also contains an open acknowledgement of Raphael's role. He is literally interpreting the word of God. Milton wants there to be no doubt at all that Adam understands Raphael's role and message. He acknowledges the purpose of the visit was to 'forewarn' (73) them in case the fate of the fallen angels becomes theirs. He knows that this has been done in advance of the danger, 'timely' (74). He thanks God, via Raphael, for this, in terms that reflect perfectly the relationship described to date between man and his creator, one of imperturbable faith and worship. Adam offers 'Immortal thanks' (77) to a God he calls 'infinitely good' (76) for 'his admonishment' (77), and it is important that the specific meaning of the noun is appreciated since so much rests on it. To admonish means to warn, urge action on, or advise someone *in advance*. It is not that Adam or Eve have already done anything to merit reproof or a reprimand from God, it is what they *might* do that merits Raphael's visitation. So when Adam now reaffirms on behalf of himself and Eve total submission to God's will, describing it with true Protestant zeal as 'the end/Of what we are' (79–80), he is showing that he has understood and assimilated everything Raphael came to tell him. So significant is this moment for the poem as a whole, it merits repeating here, Adam agreeing fully:

> ... with solemn purpose to observe
> Immutably his sovereign will, the end
> Of what we are. (78–80)

Adam now uses Raphael's first account as a reason to hear more, suggesting to him that, since he has already revealed to them heavenly matters that God believed concerned them, 'as to highest wisdom seemed' (83), he might reveal more to them that might prove equally valuable, 'What may no less perhaps avail us known' (85).

Adam has a number of closely connected metaphysical questions which he crams together, so it may help to unravel them, even though to do so risks making them seem naïve. The first two employ the same phrase, 'How first began' (86), which seems to elide two questions into one: how and when? So how and when did heaven come about? Adam asks. And by heaven he means specifically the sky and stars, 'this heaven which we behold' (86), which is filled at night 'with moving fires' (87). The second is how and when did the air come about that fills the entire space that surrounds them, 'Embracing round this florid earth' (90). Some of his childlike wonder is evoked in the diction he uses. Stars are 'moving fires' and the heaven is 'Distant so high' (87), but there is also an almost scientific register in 'Innumerable' (88), 'interfused' (89) and 'florid' (90). The two combined make Adam seem innocent, yet intellectually keen. Adam's third question sounds like a *what* but is really a *why* as he asks: why did God create the universe at all? He understands that God is eternal, and that, at some recent point 'so late' (92) on eternity's timeline, he chose to build the known universe out of chaos, but he doesn't understand why God should have broken 'his holy rest' (91) to do so. The final question, like the preceding ones, is one that displays a fascination with time. In asking 'how soon/Absolved' (93–4), Adam means simply: how long did it take?

In case his enthusiasm has taken him too far, Adam reins his curiosity in a little and assures Raphael he has no desire to know anything he shouldn't, 'not to explore the secrets' (95), and cites an appropriate reason for his desire to learn: 'the more we know' the more they can 'magnify his works' (97) and praise God. In what is both a beautiful and lyrical conclusion to his appeal, Adam brings the twin faces of the natural world itself to bear in order to persuade Raphael to stay and talk. He begins by pointing out that plenty of daylight remains, personifying the sun as 'the great light of day' (98) who has yet to run 'Much of his race' (99), but then eloquently imagines the sun delaying his setting at the sound of Raphael's 'potent voice' (100) because he is eager to hear Raphael describe his own birth, 'His generation' (102) and the origin of all nature 'from the unapparent deep' (103). On Satan's lips such words would smack of flattery but Milton affords Adam a gentle caution, which sounds eloquent and lyrical. Adam then imagines the evening star and the moon hurrying to listen to Raphael's alluring account, night bringing 'Silence' and 'sleep' (106), the latter willing to watch over them as they talk, or, if Raphael prefers, Adam suggests they postpone sleep, 'bid his absence', until Raphael has concluded his 'song' (107) before the dawn, 'ere the morning shine' (108). Milton works hard in *Paradise Lost* to evoke a Paradise worthy of loss, yet one which we can also imagine and admire. In the carefully orchestrated and managed depiction of the growing friendship between Adam and Raphael, we can see a little of how he does this. Adam displays deference and courtesy in other terms he chooses. So Raphael is his 'illustrious guest' (109) and Adam's questions were 'besought', the past tense form of the highly deferential verb, 'to beseech'. Raphael's 'mild' (110) response complements Adam's respectful tone, and Raphael himself notes that Adam's request has been 'with caution asked' (111) as he grants it.

Before embarking on the creation account, Raphael whets Adam's appetite, and so ours, by denying his own or any other angels' ability to describe such a wondrous event. 'What words or tongue of seraph can suffice' (113) includes both the language and the delivery, while on the receiving end he also denies man's ability to understand. We are entitled to ask at this point, why then continue with your story? But Raphael forestalls that criticism himself with an explanation that clearly reaffirms his overall message of obedience. What Adam and Eve can understand, 'attain' (115), which enriches their capacity to 'glorify the maker' (116) and increases their own happiness, he has been instructed by God to tell, his 'commission from above' (118). He makes it clear that there are limits as well as a purpose to what he is able to tell and warns Adam not to go too far, 'beyond abstain/To ask' (120–1), and provocatively adds a new warning, 'nor let thine own inventions hope/Things not revealed' (121–2), which implies a restriction on Adam's, and therefore mankind's, imagination that may be difficult for modern readers to accept. But we should remember that, in Milton's era, astronomical scientific inquiry brought some very eminent figures into conflict with religion, Galileo[2] being possibly the most famous. Such is the dominance of technology today and the promise of progress it brings with it, modern students can find Milton's acceptance of the unknown frustrating, but the concept of divine mystery goes hand in hand with the concept of omniscience, something Raphael himself makes clear here, 'the invisible king,/Only omniscient' (122–3) having 'suppressed in night' (123) some things which are 'To none communicable in earth or heaven' (124).

Similarly, modern students might find Raphael's concluding simile, 'But knowledge is as food' (126), quite surprising. Although there is ample knowledge left for man to 'search and know' (125), like food, he argues that the appetite for knowledge should be tempered and we should know 'In measure what the mind may well contain' (128). If not, and we gorge ourselves on information as it were, then the result is, like overeating, discomfort, 'Oppresses else with surfeit' (129) and, more significantly, ignorance. 'Wisdom' becomes 'folly' (130) in precisely the same way that overeating results in wind. It is difficult to know how Milton intended Raphael's final point to be received. Angels chatting about flatulence is not common in epic poetry.

A Role for Man

Raphael picks up his story exactly where he left it with Satan's defeat by the Son of God. Adam's questions have been about the heavens and so it is appropriate that Raphael kicks off with an image of Lucifer (not Satan) as a star once brighter than the brightest stars in heaven, falling in flames with his 'flaming legions' (134) into hell. Christ having returned 'Victorious with his saints' (136), God now speaks again to his Son.

The syntax here is difficult (139–61) but if you reread specifically with the purpose of understanding the structure and locating the main verbs and their subjects, you should be able to make swift progress. It helps to break this lengthy sentence into two parts at line 144, which divides God's account of Satan's plotting from his plans for creation.

The principal subject of the first part is 'our envious foe', who God says has 'failed' (139) before elaborating on that failure as a plot to dispossess him of his throne, 'the seat/Of deity supreme' (141–2), which drew to it 'many, whom their place knows here no more' (144). Once again Satan's sin is unequivocally named as envy. However many were lured 'into fraud' (143) by Satan, 'far the greater part' (145) remain in heaven, to 'possess her realms' (147) and carry out the 'ministeries due and solemn rites' that God, their creator, requires of them. The connection made by God between the loss of Satan and his followers, and the creation of the earth and man, provides plenty of scope for debate. A good starting point is to disentangle the formula used from the ideas expressed, so once you appreciate that Milton here uses a simple 'But lest …' (150) such and such happen, 'I can …' (152) do such and such, where 'can' really means *will*, you will find it much easier to connect the ideas and enjoy the metaphysical debate. That 'lest' (150) is crucial, as its meaning is an unambiguous *in order to prevent* Satan from preening himself – 'his heart exalt him' (150) for having 'dispeopled heaven' (151) – or for believing he has undermined or harmed God, 'My damage fondly deemed' (152).[3] The second part of the formula now comes into play as God states his intention, 'I can repair' (152) any 'detriment' (153). Milton then gives God what seems a rare moment of doubt for an omniscient being, as he qualifies any 'detriment' caused by the loss of the fallen angels with an important correction, 'if such it be to lose' (153). But the correction is entirely rhetorical. They were 'Self-lost' (154), God notes, a point he made unequivocally clear in Book 3, line 102 when he described free will.

God's 'repair' (153) will comprise the creation of 'Another world' (155) which he can do 'in a moment' (154), where speed and not delay is the intended meaning. That world, he will populate with 'men innumerable' (156), created 'out of one man' (155), and make that world rather than heaven to be their dwelling place. For Adam, and for Milton's religious readership, this is a critical moment since it is here that God explains the purpose of life. His intention is that through 'long obedience tried' (159) man will raise himself 'by degrees of merit' (157) and, in doing so, open for himself a path to heaven so that ultimately 'earth be changed to heaven, and heaven to earth' (160). This lengthy sentence finally closes with words reminiscent of much Christian prayer: 'One kingdom, joy and union without end' (161). One cannot fault Raphael for delivering his master's message. At the core of the vision God has here for Adam and for the whole of mankind is obedience.

Next God instructs the 'powers of heaven' to spread out into the space left by the fallen, 'inhabit lax' (162), while he sets the Son to work on the business of creation. God addresses the Son both as 'begotten Son' and 'my Word' (163), echoing the association made between divinity, language and creation in the New Testament.[4] In separating action from word – 'speak thou' while 'This I perform' (164) and summoning God's 'overshadowing spirit' (165) to accompany the Son – Milton depicts the holy trinity in action. God mobilises his own divine power for the Son, 'and might with thee/I send along' (165–6), instructing him to create heaven and earth from the 'Boundless... deep' (168). This idea is fraught with chronological difficulty since it appears to imply heaven does not yet exist as the Son is to 'bid the deep... be heaven and earth' (166–7). It is equally difficult to extract clarity from God's description of the 'deep' here as 'Boundless' (166), but if you think of the deep as 'chaos', uncontrolled potential in every sense, then God's description of himself as 'I am who fill/Infinitude' (168–9) makes good sense as the antithesis of chaos. This meaning is reinforced in the next few lines where God states that he is 'uncircumscribed' (170) and unaffected in any way by 'necessity and chance' (172) since what he wills *is* 'fate' (173).

Milton makes some words work extremely hard considering the small space they often occupy. One such example occurs here where Raphael describes God's speech as 'His Word' (175) while simultaneously using the same phrase to refer to the Son, the phrase ending one clause and beginning another. The effect is to bring to life Raphael's concept of 'knowledge within bounds' (120), some of Raphael's ideas stretching Adam's (and the readers') human capacity to comprehend them. Raphael himself now hints as much when he attempts to describe the speed of creation, 'Immediate are the acts of God' (176), and set a limit on Adam's understanding that semioticians[5] would admire, since it is language and its limitations that determine the means and the meaning of all human communication.

Heaven then rejoices at the new creation in terms that stress the underlying theme of Raphael's conversations with Adam – obedience – and the justice of what God has ordained. God's 'avenging ire' is 'just' (184) and he has expelled 'the ungodly' (185) from 'the habitations of the just' (186), that is those who remained faithful and, more importantly, obedient. There is more room for argument about the idea that man has been made to occupy the space left by the ungodly, and even about the description here of mankind as 'a better race' (189). But the end purpose is perhaps the one Milton wishes his readers to contemplate most carefully because it returns us to the powerful concept of grace. The new creation of earth and man allows God to 'diffuse' (190) his goodness into 'worlds and ages infinite' (191).

As Raphael implied, the creation story then proceeds in a very similar narrative vein to that he used to recount the war in heaven, evoking mythical precedents but holding to the chronological account in the book of Genesis throughout. Milton lists a wide range of creatures as an introduction to the beauty and harmony of Eden before introducing its chief glory, man.

The Creation of Adam

With the earth complete and teeming with animal life, all that remains for God to do is to add humanity in the form of Adam and Eve. At this point, Raphael's account sets the entire heavens in motion (499–500), as though with one movement of his hand God provided sufficient force to impel the stars and planets on their eternal orbits in complete harmony with each other.

Milton makes beauty a principal feature of this moment in the history of the universe, where the heavens and earth radiate 'glory' (499) and a richly attired earth 'Consummate lovely smiled' (502). 'Consummate' suggests completion but within a few lines we learn that is only partially true as 'There wanted yet the master-work' (505). The lists which then follow imply fertility, a combination that Milton has already used in describing Eve (V, 492–504). Fire is unsurprisingly absent from the list of elements, 'air, water, earth' (502), while there is an exact parallel between the 'fowl, fish, beast' (503) and their subsequent actions before we are reminded that there yet remains a sixth day. The remaining part of the lengthy sentence (499–516) pertains to man, his nature and God's plan for him. The syntax is typically complex but as usual yields to a little structural analysis.

The first structural feature is another list, which this time describes the same subject. The 'master-work' (505) is also the culmination of all creation so far, 'the end/Of all yet done' (505–6), and a creature unlike all others in natural intelligence and upright stance, 'not prone/And brute as other creatures' (506–7).

The second structural feature to note is the relationship between 'who' (506) and both verbs, 'might erect' (508) and 'Govern' (510). Raphael's vision, of as yet unformed mankind, is of a being destined for power over all others on earth through his divinely ordained reason,

'His stature...upright with front serene' (509), the outward symbol of his difference to all other creatures on earth. If you apply the conditional 'might' (508) to 'Govern' (510) as well as to 'erect' (508) then the sense is of man first standing and distinguishing himself and *then* governing through his superior intellect. Another significant distinguishing feature is man's 'self-knowing' (510). This is significant because it repeats Milton's central belief in free will, the lynch pin of his theodicy. On earth, only man possesses self-knowledge and thus the power of independent action, which in turn generates the complex tension between responsibility and culpability.

The final structural element is signalled by the phrase 'from thence' (510), which makes an overt link between man's independence and his obedience. God creates man virtuous, that is 'Magnanimous' (511) and inextricably connected to heaven, but that magnanimity is equally visible in his gratitude since he also knows it is a gift from God. Man knows the source of his own best qualities, 'whence his good/Descends' (512–3), and consequently worships his creator 'with heart and voice and eyes' (513). The extreme terms Milton chooses to describe man's essential relationship with his creator, 'devotion' (514) and 'worship' (515), make absolute sense when put in the context, as they are here, of man as 'the master-work' (505). Milton brings this section of the Genesis account to a close by returning to that crucial concept, man as 'chief/Of all his works' (515–16). A caesura marks the end of man in theory, from man as physical being, because God now instructs the Son to proceed with what he has outlined, 'thus to his Son audibly spake' (518).

God's words now have all the formal force of an Old Testament imperative, placed in a single, short and unequivocal statement. The two things to note are simply that man is created in God's image, 'our similitude', and that he is to 'rule' (520) over all life on earth. Raphael's distinctive voice returns directly to address Adam, although the words are closely linked to those in Genesis, and Raphael repeats twice more the message that man is made in God's image. The moment of creation is captured in the definitive statement which ends the sentence, 'and thou becam'st a living soul' (528), where considerable dramatic weight falls on the final word. The soul being the one thing which encapsulates man's duality: born on earth but destined for heaven.

One reason *Paradise Lost* is such a rich text for contemporary study is that a post-feminism culture has plenty to say about Eve, even before she figures as an active agent in Eden and in Adam's fate. Raphael spells out the conventional wisdom that Adam was created first and Eve created as his 'consórt' (529) and to populate the earth, 'Female for race' (530). He wastes little time on her creation, preferring to dwell on their dual role as the parents of an entire race, 'blessed mankind' (530), through God's command 'Be fruitful, multiply, and fill the earth' (531). That command alone is bound to cause some students consternation, never mind the subsequent command to 'subdue it' (532), which under the shadow of global warming sounds more like a death knell than a joyful invitation. At the time of writing, most of the planet had yet to be measured, charted or in any sense quantified.

Raphael continues to personalise the narrative for Adam, reminding him how God brought him to 'this delicious grove,/This garden' (536–7) and of the rich variety, beauty and plenitude he found there. God's trees are 'Delectable both to behold and taste' (539). This single line is one of those excellent examples of Milton's brand of lyricism. The elongated first word seems to savour the imagined fruits, while the whole line has a balance and roundedness of sound, created by the assonance of the central 'both to behold' phrase and the strong 't' sounds at either end. This lyricism continues on until the caesura at 'without end' (542).

Raphael's accounts of the war in heaven and of creation are so dramatic and indeed plain long that it is easy to forget his chief purpose. Here he reiterates the warning God commanded him to deliver in the clearest of terms. 'Thou mayst not', Raphael states, of the one tree forbidden them to taste. The consequences of disobedience too are spelt out, 'in the day thou eatst, thou di'st' (544). The punishment could not be clearer: 'Death is the penalty imposed, beware' (545). But Raphael does not rely solely on the threat of death and, as God instructed him, he issues the warning to Adam to be on his guard and to 'govern well thy appetite' (546) in case he is caught unawares by 'Sin . . . and her black attendant Death' (546–7).

Raphael concludes Book 7 with an account of the Son's triumphant return to heaven, his resting with God and of the rejoicing and celebrations there that formed the basis for the Sabbath day. The picture he creates is one of complete triumph, God having turned the evil of Satan's rebellion to inestimable good, and man as the ultimate beneficiary. It is a poignant reminder to Adam of all he stands in trust of, and a dramatic staging for the temptation to come.

Exercises

Lines 192–498. As Raphael implied, the creation story then proceeds in a very similar narrative vein to that he used to recount the war in heaven, evoking mythical precedents but holding to the chronological account in the book of Genesis throughout. Milton chooses to list a wide range of creatures in this section of the poem. How do you react to his handling of them as individual species, and their combination as an introduction to the beauty and harmony of Eden?

Lines 548–640. Read Raphael's account of the Son's triumphant return to heaven and of the celebrations that form the basis for the Sabbath day. How does Milton use this closing section of Book 7 to reinforce his map of the universe?

8

Divine Love and Love Divine

Summary

Charmed by Raphael's account and presence, Adam wishes to learn more and asks him to explain why a body as small as the earth is yet so central to the entire universe? At this, Eve quietly removes herself from the conversation with Raphael, not because their conversation is too sophisticated for her, but because she prefers to enjoy Adam alone, and his didactic conversations with her are a key part of that experience. Raphael answers Adam's question at some length but entirely tangentially, insisting that God reserves some knowledge to himself and predicting various, often foolish efforts of mankind to understand the workings of the universe through science, astronomy and maths. He advises Adam to concentrate on the world God has given him to rule, on Eve and on their duty together as God's creations to praise and worship him.

Adam expresses his gratitude and satisfaction at Raphael's account, restating Raphael's warning not to think of things beyond his proper sphere and, as proof, offers to tell Raphael his own story of how he came into being and discovered himself to be God's creation. Raphael approves of Adam's speech and manner and accepts the invitation to listen to Adam's story since he was not present at Adam's creation.

Adam tells how he woke to find himself in a landscape and surrounded by all the delights of creation which gave him great joy. He walked and ran, exploring his own form and strength, as well as the place in which he found himself, and, when he attempted to speak, found he could name everything around him. He tells how he then asked the animals and the land itself to tell him who had made him so that he could straight away express his thanks and adoration. When they do not answer, he rests and sleeps on a flowery bank, for a moment thinking sleep is returning him to his former, insensible state. Immediately he dreams that he is named Adam, first man of many, and is led by a divine spirit to a mountain top. There he sees Paradise stretched out before him and such is its beauty and richness it makes what he has seen up to now seem drab in comparison. At which point he wakes to find himself in Paradise and God approaching him. He falls to his knees in adoration but God raises him and, speaking mildly, tells Adam that Paradise is his realm, provided he restrain from eating the fruit of the Tree of Knowledge. God then explains, more sternly, that should Adam disobey this sole command and eat the fruit, he will inevitably die. Adam acknowledges his freedom to choose before God returns to his more gracious demeanour, telling Adam that not only is Paradise his, but everything that lives and moves in it is his too, to enjoy and rule over. In pairs, each living thing is then paraded before Adam for him to name and recognise.

Adam then complains, in the mildest and most deferential of terms, of his solitude, asking God how he can enjoy all the richness and beauty he has been granted when he is all alone. God gently rebukes him, asking whether all the living creatures are not enough company and whether he has not given him enough. But Adam persists, arguing that there is a hierarchical gulf between himself and the beasts, that he is God's substitute on earth and as such is unable to find companionship with the animals. Without anger, God replies by suggesting that if he applies Adam's argument to himself, then he, God, must also have to endure solitude amongst so many living things that are his inferior, since there is only one God. Adam's reply shows he has learned the lesson Raphael taught him and he says he is not seeking knowledge beyond his being, that God is infinite and perfect, and as such is not subject to the same weaknesses as man. Man, Adam insists, must reproduce and he cannot envisage this without a companion.

God voices his satisfaction with Adam, linking his determined argument to the free will he has given him, and tells Adam that he has already considered and prepared a suitable companion for him. He promises to bring Adam what he has wished for and, as though the intensity and magnitude of the discussion has proved too great for him, Adam sinks into a trance-like sleep, nonetheless able to see and understand what God then does. He describes how God then opens up his side and, from one of his ribs, fashions another human form, but of different sex and so lovely that Adam instantly feels bound to her. The female form disappears and Adam wakes, instantly missing her but immediately perceives her being led towards him by God, although God remains invisible to Eve. Adam praises and thanks God for this, his best and greatest gift, and names her Eve. Adam then leads Eve to their nuptial bower and nature celebrates their union.

Adam then confides to Raphael his sense of being in Eve's power, even though he knows her his inferior. His account of passion and love alarm Raphael enough for him to warn Adam about retaining rationality and his free will. He distinguishes between passion and love, the former a dangerous leaning that tends towards the bestial rather than the angelic. Adam defends his love for Eve and asks Raphael whether angels feel love too, at which Raphael blushes and implies that they do and even that they enjoy sex before finally reminding Adam again to beware letting his passions affect his judgement and so the fate of all mankind. Raphael then departs on gracious terms, assuring Adam of his continuing goodwill while Adam thanks him for his words and kindness before returning to his bower and to Eve.

Eve's Deferential Departure

When Raphael finally comes to end his account of the war in heaven and creation, Adam's response is not just to thank him, but to pursue even further his thirst for knowledge and he asks Raphael to explain why, amidst such a vast universe, it is the earth, a small and insignificant body in comparison, that is its centre. Eve treats this metaphysical conversation Adam initiates as her cue to depart and, given the contemporary critical interest in gender issues and Eve, this passage (39–62) is of obvious interest, but it also provides us with an insight into the kind of relationship Milton prescribes for Adam and Eve. Milton treats us to Eve's point of view and it is through her eyes that we see Adam's face betray the depth of thought his question has provoked, 'which Eve/Perceiving' (40–1), and that causes her to depart silently. It is easy to see why this idea causes feminist critics such consternation. Adam's face reveals the 'studious thoughts abstruse' (40) that are troubling him and it does indeed seem as though Eve withdraws because such matters are too difficult for her, in the time honoured fashion of downtrodden womenfolk throughout history. But this is a very premature criticism to make since a few lines further on we come across the phrase 'Yet went she not' (48) and a very clear description by Milton of why Eve, freely, chose to leave at this point in their conversations with Raphael. Before he does this, Milton also paints for us a brief picture of Eve which is every bit as interesting as the fact that she quietly departs. She is, for example, sitting 'retired in sight' (41), which implies she has kept a backseat throughout Raphael's entire narrative, while Milton's choice of 'Perceiving' (41) implies no such thing, suggesting that she is in fact so alert and attentive that she immediately notices the change in Adam's 'countenance' (39).

Eve is given two qualities when she leaves. The first is the oxymoronic 'lowliness majestic' (42) and the second is 'grace that won who saw to wish her stay' (43). Specifically, the oxymoron describes the way she 'Rose' (44) 'from her seat' (43) but the paradox it toys with begs some questions. However majestic she may appear, she is still lowly, and is this because she is inferior to Adam and Raphael, or is Milton trying to convey a kind of shy beauty? Similarly, there is a paradoxical quality to the 'grace' she exhibits. The word of course has great religious significance, raising Eve's stature dramatically, but at the same time it is so visually impressive that anyone witnessing it is moved to plead for her to stay. Which implies neither Adam nor Raphael see her depart, since, if they had, they would have urged her not to. On the face of it that seems at least logical, but are we really happy to accept that the two male figures in this tableau are so unaware of the single female that they fail to notice when she gets up and leaves? This ambiguity reappears a little later in lines 60–3.

Eve's goddess-like fertility is evident both in the action she now pursues and in the lyrical way Milton handles it. She leaves to attend 'her fruits and flowers' (44), and the alliterative line ending is echoed immediately in the subsequent line by 'bud and bloom' (45) and a little later by 'gladlier grew' (47). Her maternal nature is implied in both 'prospered' (45) and 'nursery' (46). But how are we meant to respond to the way that her plants respond to her? As she enters her nursery 'they at her coming sprung' (46) and burgeon as she caresses them, 'And touched by her fair tendance gladlier grew' (47). The sexual connotations cannot be ignored and although it is highly unlikely that Milton was even aware of any indecent meaning of the verb 'to come', since its origins are about this time in bawdy poetry of the period, Eve's sexuality and her comparison with classical goddesses is undoubtedly on show.

After digressing to exhibit his goddess in this way, Milton returns to counter any charge that she is Adam's inferior with the key phrase already noted, 'Yet went she not' (48). It isn't difficult to understand the reasons Milton now gives for her departure, but whether we choose to accept them or not is far less straightforward. Eve is every bit as 'Delighted' (49) by Raphael and his 'discourse' (48) as Adam, nor is her comprehension inferior to his, 'or not capable her ear/Of what was high'

(49–50). Eve prefers to hear such things from Adam when they are alone together, 'Adam relating, she sole auditress' (51). For her it is a 'pleasure' (50) to be seasoned with 'Grateful digressions' (55) and 'conjugal caresses' (56) from her husband, since 'from his lip/Not words alone pleased her' (56–7). Milton gives Eve a positive role in this relationship by stressing that it is her choice, 'of him to ask/Chose rather' (53–4), but it is a choice apparently predicated on sex. The caesura in line 57 gives Milton the opportunity to re-enter the poem as its narrator and indulge in a little golden age nostalgia. He turns his exclamation into a rhetorical question, suggesting their relationship was in every way a model future generations of lovers have failed to live up to, unable to find couples today 'in love and mutual honour joined?' (58). The 'mutual honour' is the most interesting detail here, since it directly counters the inferiority charge.

The comparison with classical goddesses is made overtly in describing her 'demeanour' (59) and in the retinue that accompanies her, but this retinue, 'a pomp of winning graces' (61), is not without its problems. First of all Milton insists she is 'Not unattended' (60), where the verb's primary meaning refers to those who accompany her, but it has a secondary meaning which is hard, given the circumstances, to avoid – which is 'not unattended to'. However we respond to the 'winning graces' and their regal associations, 'pomp' (61) and 'queen' (60), we are clearly meant to admire them so much that we, presumably like Adam and Raphael, 'wish her still in sight' (63). (Although as we noted earlier, neither Raphael nor Adam say anything or show any sign of even noticing her leave.) Milton doesn't hedge but says, unequivocally, 'all eyes' (63). That is awkward enough if we were dealing with 'winning graces' alone but we are not because 'from about her shot darts of desire' (62) which are the very reason that 'all eyes' feel her loss. Milton doesn't imply Eve is in any way culpable in this, that she behaves like some kind of divine flirt. The 'darts of desire' shoot from her 'winning graces', not from Eve herself. Yet it is difficult to extract 'desire' from its sexual context and see the innocent, ravishing vision Milton seems to want us to see. At its crudest we are left with this question. If Eve is so ravishing that anyone who sees her yearns for her to stay, what makes Adam and Raphael impervious?

Teaching Adam

The next section selected for detailed analysis (179–223) throws a strong and clear light on Milton's theology and his interpretation of Christian obedience and trust. Adam and Raphael exchange words and ideas in a manner that is as close as the reader will find in the entire poem to ordinary human conversation. Their thoughts and conclusions are also central to the concept of original sin and to the Fall. The first thing to note is the untrammelled way Milton has Adam respond to Raphael's advice to restrain his thoughts. Adam is 'cleared of doubt' (179) and makes it clear himself that he values what Raphael has told him, 'How fully hast thou satisfied me' (180). The second is the hyperbole he uses in addressing Raphael as 'pure/Intelligence of heaven, angel serene' (180–1). You might well react negatively to language that sounds a little obsequious but 'Intelligence' is the important word and Adam uses it because it frames their intellectual relationship, affording Raphael the respect due to him as an angel whose mental faculties far exceed Adam's own. Given the context, a philosophical discussion about knowledge and understanding, this shouldn't be surprising and counters any charge of flattery against Adam.

The syntax here isn't easy but if you regard 'thou' (180) as the subject of both 'satisfied' (180) *and* 'taught' (183) then the otherwise awkwardly intervening phrase 'And freed from intricacies' (183) sounds less intrusive. Prosaically the meaning then becomes, 'You have both fully satisfied me *and* taught me to live the easiest way, free from intricacies…', by which Milton appears to mean a kind of nice philosophical speculation which has no religious faith underpinning it. From Raphael's advice, Adam extracts some precepts by which to live that will prevent 'perplexing thoughts' (183) from spoiling 'the sweet of life' (184). It's clear that Adam knows his life is pleasant and delightful, which 'sweet' implies, but to jump to the conclusion that he advocates a passive, intellectually arid life is wrong because Milton then takes pains to detail what Adam has learned from Raphael. Adam now knows God keeps their 'sweet life' unmolested, free from 'anxious cares' (185) and any disturbance is only the result of their own 'wandering thoughts, and notions vain' (187), but he also knows that man has a natural curiosity which needs divine guidance if it is not to perturb the state of happiness God has provided for them.

Adam's 'But apt' (188) acknowledges this natural tendency for the imagination 'or fancy' (188) to 'rove/Unchecked' (188–9). However, he also acknowledges the warning Raphael has issued on behalf of God to resist this natural tendency for the mind to overreach itself and seek knowledge and understanding beyond its proper bounds. His 'Till warned' shows he has understood Raphael well, but the qualifying clause 'or by experience taught, she learn' (190) is supremely equivocal. Milton seems intent on having it both ways. Adam is warned and so acts feely when he disobeys God's sole command, yet at the same time he must also be free to take advantage of the opportunities for learning created out of experience. Milton furnishes Adam with an antithesis to set the boundaries of his intellectual life. Things which are 'remote/From use, obscure and subtle' (191–2) are off limits, while those things that permeate their 'daily life' (193) merit contemplation and repay the effort invested in understanding them. That 'Is the prime wisdom' (194) and all else wasted speculation, 'fume,/Or emptiness' (195) or what is more even spiritually damaging, 'fond impertinence' (195), an insult to their creator. The concept of repayment is clear in the use of the term 'renders' (196), where Adam affirms that seeking things off limits only leads to incompletion and frustration. The return on such effort is only things 'Unpractised, unprepared, and still to seek' (197).

Having acknowledged Raphael's warning, Adam brings them both back to earth through an image that connotes both Icarus[1] and Satan in terms of ambition, 'from this high pitch let us descend/A lower flight' (198–9) and suggests they 'speak of things at hand' (199). But he isn't quite able to smother his natural curiosity completely and adds his hope that questions 'may arise' (200) in conversation which Raphael will feel both able and willing to answer. Adam's polite subservience is conveyed strongly in both 'sufferance' and the conclusive 'deigned' (202) and his subsequent suggestion that he relate Raphael his own story is equally deferential. At first he offers his account as a balance to Raphael's own, the caesura in line 204 operating as the fulcrum between the two accounts, 'Thee I have heard relating what was done' (203) therefore 'hear me relate/My story' (204–5). But Adam offers the traditional storyteller's excuse that they have ample time, 'day is yet not spent' (206), plus an extended metaphor that echoes earlier comparisons between food and knowledge (211–16).

One of the most intriguing features of life before the Fall in Milton's Eden is the quality of the friendship between men and angels. Adam openly admits his intention is to detain Raphael in language that would not be out of place in love poetry, 'till then thou seest/How subtly to detain thee I devise' (206–7), the heavy alliteration and tight connection between 'detain' and 'devise', both in terms of sound and seduction, combine to create a tone not unlike that of an ardent suitor. Similarly, Adam's choice of 'Fond' (209) is reminiscent of love poetry where 'fondness' is frequently the term used to describe the foolish acceptance of lovers. Adam appears to imagine himself sitting in the same enthralled way as a lover, were it not for the fact that he knows Raphael will speak to him. The sensation that we are listening to love poetry is even stronger in the next line which could easily come straight from the pen of any number of sonneteers, 'For while I sit with thee, I seem in heaven' (210), were it not for the literal possibility that, sitting with this particular individual, one has every right to think one could be in heaven. It's at this point that the extended metaphor continuing the theme of food as knowledge first appears, and Adam compares Raphael's 'discourse' (211) to the most delicious 'fruits of palm-tree' (212) which assuage both hunger and thirst after hard work, with the exception that, whereas the palm tree's dates 'satiate, and soon fill' (214), Raphael's voice 'with grace divine/Imbued' (215–16) is equally sweet but never satisfies. The lines again are redolent of intimacy, even passion. Compare, for example, the words of Shakespeare's Enobarbus describing Cleopatra:

> ... other women cloy
> The appetites they feed, but she makes hungry
> Where most she satisfies.[2]

When Raphael replies, his opening compliment may provide a clue as to Milton's own view of this relationship. Like Adam, Raphael is gentle and considerate, 'heavenly meek' (217), and he implies that Adam's voice is no less appealing, 'Nor are thy lips ungraceful...Nor tongue ineloquent' (217–18), but there is some danger in simply treating 'graceful' as a human quality. The word's connection with divine generosity and love can't be avoided and this shifts the tone away from love poetry to something more ethereal. Raphael stresses that Adam has been made in God's image, and that he is the recipient of many gifts, 'Inward and outward both' (221), on the one hand pointing to Adam's intellect and on the other to his physical beauty, the relatively innocuous image, 'his image fair' (221), hiding a witty ambiguity where 'fair' implies not just beauty but accurate reproduction. Whether 'Speaking or mute' (222) Adam is undoubtedly an impressive creature to Raphael who reproduces that significant noun 'grace' (222) once again to describe Adam's demeanour. It is far from an idle speculation, or even *waggish*, to compare Raphael's words with contemporary ideals of manners or indeed beauty. In Adam, 'each word, each motion' (223) is formed by the 'comeliness and grace' (222) which comes directly from his being made in God's image.

God Demands Adam's Obedience

Brought out of his first slumber by God to Eden, Adam instantly falls to his knees before his creator and Milton delivers us their first conversation (316–37). Adam's sense of wonder and delight at discovering himself alive and in this astounding place, this earth, is now brought up against God's own purpose. God's words and advice here are absolutely central to the poem's grand project and so it is very important to study them closely enough to gain a strong and clear understanding of what Milton's God intends.

Adam instinctively recognises God's divinity but it is perhaps a mark of the challenge Milton has created for himself that Adam falls to his knees in a turmoil of mixed emotions: joy, awe and submission. The syntax here mimics the abrupt action, the opening word 'Rejoicing' (314) balanced by the antithetical 'Submiss' (316), while the intervening phrase, 'but with awe/In adoration at his feet I fell' (314–15), signals the dramatic nature of the impact of God's presence on Adam through alliteration. The strong stress on 'Submiss' adds to this effect, punctuating the action and delaying the moment before God raises Adam to his feet. Echoing biblical syntax, God's first words are inverted, 'Whom thou soughtst I am' (316), emphasising the existential impact, and showing how coherent a dramatic poet Milton is because they directly answer the question Adam asked all creatures on his awakening (275–79). The assonance in 'Whom thou soughtst' is pronounced while the unity of the clause is carefully controlled by the 'm' sound, 'Whom...I am' that frames it. It is also worth noting that Milton uses the adverb 'mildly' (317) to describe their delivery. This is clearly not the Old Testament tyrant so often observed in the poem. And the mild, soft sounds carry over into the rest of God's opening sentence where he tells Adam that he is not only his creator, but the creator of 'all this thou seest' (317), where the equal stress on these four words resounds with divine force.

Milton keeps closely to the account in the book of Genesis here in making Eden God's gift to man, and from the very start Adam is given a duty to care for the garden, 'To till and keep' (320). God's generosity continues as he urges Adam to 'Eat freely with glad heart'; but perhaps the most overt statement of his love for man is embedded in the phrase that follows the caesura here, 'fear here no dearth' (322). It is another of those simple phrases easily overlooked, which on closer examination seems to be far more artful in its construction and intent. The distinct diphthong rhyme between 'fear' and 'here' is modified in 'dearth', but the slightest nuance in reading would make the latter closer to 'death'. And of course that is exactly what is at issue here. God's subsequent warning about the Tree of Knowledge relates specifically to death, the dire consequence of disobedience. There is heavy irony in the notion that, in granting Adam ample sustenance, no 'dearth', he is also guaranteeing him immortality.

A new sentence (323–33) separates the single condition God places on Adam from all else in his gift, and such is its significance for the poem as a whole that rereading it a number of times as a single unit is recommended. It is full of important detail that refers to events later in the poem. The first thing to note is the nature of the Tree itself. Eating the fruit of this specific Tree 'brings/Knowledge of good and ill' (323–4), and evidence of this knowledge in Adam and Eve after the Fall is therefore something we are entitled to expect. The second key idea is the symbolic power God has invested in the Tree. It is the single test he sets Adam and Eve, 'The pledge of thy obedience and thy faith' (325). That these two concepts are inextricably linked in God's mind cannot be ignored. In a secular age many students may genuinely struggle with the whole concept of faith, and time spent researching some of the great Christian theologians and thinkers on the topic, such as St Augustine,[3] would be well spent. The Tree of Knowledge is also located close to the Tree of Life because, as God now tells Adam, 'the bitter consequence' (328) of disobedience is simply death. God leaves no room for doubt, debate or questioning in issuing this warning to Adam, using the terse imperative 'for know' (328) to introduce the warning and signal its import. It is not that Adam eats the fruit which leads to his death, but that in doing so he disobeys and breaks faith with his creator. Milton spells this out as God interrupts the consequence with the key idea, 'my sole command/Transgressed' (329–30). He also avoids any quibbling about the timing of Adam's death with the qualifying word 'inevitably' (330) and by adding 'From that day mortal' (331). Having brought Adam into Eden and granted it to him with all the rich pleasure and joy it evokes, God now brings his warning back to the same point by reminding Adam that disobedience means the loss of Eden, all the joy and happiness it contains and a future full 'Of woe and sorrow' (333). Milton's choice of the verb 'loose' (332), where the more obvious 'lose' might well do, ought to grab any alert student's attention. The former is a far more powerful choice, connoting dissolution and decay rather than removal or absence. When Adam and Eve disobey God, they condemn an entire race to the woe, sorrow and ultimately death which God tells Adam will be his punishment – and in so doing undo the perfection of Eden forever.

God's warning over, Adam now recalls for Raphael how it was delivered 'Sternly' (333) and Milton stresses Adam's clear understanding of the warning through the way he describes it and responds to it. For Adam it was a 'rigid interdiction' (334), in effect a divine ultimatum which held such force it remains with him, 'which resounds/Yet dreadful in mine ear' (334–5). Milton emphasises that Adam understood the warning but perhaps, more significantly, he also emphasises that Adam grasped the concept of free will completely when he has him add, 'though in my choice/Not to incur' (335–6) before hastily returning us to a more benign atmosphere. God's sternness is quickly replaced by 'his clear aspéct' (336) and a renewed 'gracious purpose' (337): the naming and granting of authority to Adam over all the earth.

There is of course one key absentee from all of this: Eve. And the consequences of that absence form a large part of the narrative in the subsequent books.

Adam's Account of Eve's Creation

Adam's conversation with God then develops into a dispute about solitude and companionship, in which Adam's intelligent questioning and assertiveness seem calculated to demonstrate his possession of free will. The mild dispute over, and God having promised Adam the companion he seeks, Eve is created and brought to Adam for his approval. In this section (452–90) Milton imagines their first moments together. The simple deep sleep, which falls upon Adam in Genesis, is beefed up by Milton into quite a sophisticated state of mind more akin to a trance than unconscious slumber. He does this via a simile which is far from easy to grasp at first, partly because of the typically complex syntax, but also because it is not the most familiar of comparisons to draw. An ellipsis in line 453 may also cause some confusion, so it is worth starting this analysis by providing the missing word, which is something like 'nature' or 'will', and which should be inserted after 'earthly' and 'heavenly' (453). Adam's sense is of having been stretched to the limit of his understanding and capacity in his dispute with God, a dialogue he tellingly calls 'that celestial colloquy sublime' (456). The end result is exhaustion and sleep, 'called/By nature as in aid' (458–9). The difficult simile occurs in line 456, 'As with an object that excels the sense', where Adam compares his sense of depletion, of being 'Dazzled and spent, sunk down' (457), with the sensation of trying to sustain one's attention on an object which is beyond his sensual range. In need of 'repair' (457) Adam succumbs to sleep 'which instantly fell on me' (458) and then closes his eyes. It may also help if you back track here and note that the subject of the main verb in this sentence, 'strained' (454), is in fact the elliptical 'nature' or 'will', which is in turn replaced by the pronoun 'it' (454), also the subject of 'sought repair' (457). If you extract from the sentence the structure 'My earthly *nature* ... strained to the height ... and sought repair' you may find the whole construction more accessible. This may seem a stale and pedestrian approach, but in this particular case, where an ellipsis is followed by a pronoun, it may well prove helpful.

The repetition that begins line 460 is there to distinguish between Adam's visual sense and his internal, dream-like *vision*, a manifestation of his 'fancy' (461) afforded to him by God, who 'open left the cell' (460) so that Adam could witness the creation of Eve. Milton himself uses the word 'trance' as a simile, 'Abstract as in a trance' (462), to describe how Adam is able to see himself asleep, 'methought I saw,/Though sleeping, where I lay' (462–3). He is simultaneously awake and standing before God, since he saw too 'the shape/Still glorious before whom awake I stood' (463–4), but it is from the sleeping form of Adam that God removes the rib from which he then fashions Eve. Milton's dramatic sense is clear in the gory detail he supplies around the removal of Adam's rib, and the 'life-blood streaming fresh' (467) would have stirred contemporary readers to contemplate Christ's own sacrifice and death on the cross. The adoption by Christ of man's vulnerable, mortal form is of course a vital aspect of Milton's theodicy (468). In this way Milton also emphasises the severity of the invasion into Adam's own body, making his relationship with Eve much more powerful and intimate. The final half of line 467, 'wide was the wound', uses alliteration and a slower rhythm to draw out the image fully before a more urgent rhythm heightens the drama as the wound quickly heals, 'But suddenly with flesh filled up and healed' (468). This distinctive use of sound in the latter half or section of a poetic line is something we noted earlier in lines 316 and 322 and appears to be something of a favourite technique of Milton. Even a cursory scan of Book 8 reveals the following list: 'bud and bloom' (45); 'her spots thou seest' (145); 'be lowly wise' (173); 'Fast we found, fast shut' (240); 'Whom thou soughtst I am' (316); 'fear here no dearth' (322); 'No need that thou' (419); 'creator bounteous and benign' (492); 'here passion first I felt' (530).

Adam then watches as God literally moulds and shapes Eve with his own hands, 'Under his forming hands a creature grew' (470), until she resembles Adam, 'Manlike' (471). However, Milton distinguishes Eve by giving her the key attribute, 'but different sex' (471), which positions her as the representative of her sex and not simply another creature. More powerful by far is the manner in which Adam instantly responds to her appearance. In a Paradise full of beauty, Eve is 'so lovely fair' (471) that all other beauty now seems 'Mean' or is embodied by her, 'in her contained' (473). Eve does not speak, but she does seem to communicate with Adam 'in her looks' (474) which, like her form, seem to sum up all that is beautiful in Paradise since they immediately fill Adam's heart with 'Sweetness...unfelt before' (475). Milton concludes this revelatory moment for Adam with the highly provocative claim that by her essential nature, 'her air' (476), Eve is able to inspire 'The spirit of love and amorous delight' (477) 'into all things' (476). Put more bluntly, Eve is made for sex. If we step back a little in the poem, we will find God made a promise to Adam which here is merely being fulfilled:

> What next I bring shall please thee, be assured,
> They likeness, thy fit help, thy other self,
> Thy wish, exactly to thy heart's desire. (450–2)

The emphasis on Adam's desire is striking and is created through the repetition of the second person and a final statement which unambiguously equates Eve's being with Adam's *heart's desire*. Milton escapes the risk of cliché here because it comes at the end of the 'colloquy sublime' (455), between Adam and God, in which Adam has pleaded his case for companionship, and so Eve literally is made in accordance with Adam's wish. When she appears she is, unsurprisingly, as God foretold.

This is of course red meat for feminist critical practice. That Adam is besotted is clear when he vows 'To find her, or for ever to deplore/Her loss' (479–80) and abstain from all the other joys that Paradise provides. We can again see how skilfully Milton exploits moments in his narrative for dramatic effect as he then delays Eve's return momentarily through the rhythmically broken line, 'When out of hope, behold her, not far off' (481). But Eve's reappearance is perhaps a little more difficult to respond to poetically than her creation. She is 'as I saw her in my dream' (482), but the use of 'adorned' implies she is in some way clothed or something has been added to her until you perceive that Milton is really repeating his earlier idea that Eve is in some way naturally able not just to radiate all that is beautiful in heaven and earth, but to outdo it, and in so doing command Adam's attention and thus love. The crucial term 'amiable' (484) means literally 'lovable' and it is not being used in the more gentle way it might be today in an age more free with sexual language than Milton's.

As Eve approaches, Adam discerns God's presence accompanying her, although he remains tactfully invisible and guides Eve 'by his voice' (486). Aware of the sensual risks of this meeting, Milton takes care to frame it clearly within the bounds of his religious faith as a sanctified marriage, so Eve is not 'uninformed/Of nuptial sanctity and marriage rites' (486–7) and once more the potent noun 'grace' is played to undermine the libidinous tone, 'Grace was in all her steps, heaven in her eye' (488). However sensual or seductive we may have found earlier descriptions of Eve, at this moment Milton gently stifles any such tendency by allowing her 'In every gesture dignity and love' (489).

Sex in Paradise 490–559

Adam is so overjoyed at the sight of Eve being brought to him by God as his bride, he cannot remain silent even though God remains invisible, 'I overjoyed could not forbear aloud' (490), the infinitive 'to speak' or 'to cry' being elliptically absent after 'forbear'. Milton manages to weave Adam's exuberant gratitude together with the biblical authority necessary to situate Adam and Eve as the model for all future marriages and parents. So Adam calls God 'bounteous and benign' (492) and lauds him as the 'Giver of all things fair' (493) and celebrates Eve as 'fairest this/Of all thy gifts' (493–4) before echoing Genesis in 'Bone of my bone, flesh of my flesh' (495). The broken rhythm of Adam's statements in lines 495–9 creates an effect like a proclamation rather than the spontaneous outburst of joy the opening suggested, but perhaps the most interesting element here is the placing of the final two nouns, 'heart' and 'soul' (499). The Bible's narrow focus on 'one flesh'[4] is broadened to embrace the more lyrically acceptable 'heart and soul', countering any critical charge of misogyny and implying Milton was, as his essay *The Doctrine and Discipline of Divorce* suggests, a keen advocate of intellectual parity within marriage.

Eve hears Adam's eulogy and responds by turning her back on him. That might sound glib but it is literally true and has the advantage of focussing attention on the difficult aspects of this appropriately famous section of *Paradise Lost*. The first indication that this is an issue is 'and though divinely brought' (500), because the conjunctive sense initiated by 'and though' is not completed until much later at 'she turned' (507). In plainer terms, Milton openly acknowledges that *even though* she has been brought to him by God as his bride, she turns away. That response is Milton's answer to the challenge he inevitably faces when trying to describe sex before the Fall. He is writing within a centuries-long tradition of poetry, epic and otherwise, which has explored and detailed the passionate nature of sexual relationships, *ad nauseam* some might say. Sin and guilt are inextricably bound up in this tradition for Christian poets, as well as ecstasy and delight, and Milton has already carefully postponed the onset of the former pairing in Book 2. His challenge is how to convey the ecstasy and delight without resorting to unguarded passion or unbridled sensuality which would trigger anachronous charges of sin and guilt.

He does this by making Adam interpret Eve's actions for Raphael. If you now look at the intervening lines before we learn that 'she turned' (507) you will find that Adam stresses Eve's purity throughout, but he also gives her a noticeable degree of conscious power. She knows, for example, the 'conscience of her worth' (502) and 'would be wooed, and not unsought be won' (503). Milton appears comfortable with the idea that Eve's libido is entirely natural but for the avoidance of doubt adds that 'Nature' is 'pure of sinful thought' (506). Though in using 'sinful' Milton appears to make the error of giving Adam knowledge of sin *before* he has eaten the fruit of the Tree of 'Knowledge of good and ill' (324). Adam also gives Eve the universal female ability to judge the strength of male desire and time or measure her response to maximise her reward. This seems to underpin both the notion of her being unobtrusive and retiring, yet 'more desirable' (505), while simultaneously approving Adam's 'pleaded reason' (510). It may also account for the intensely awkward oxymoron, 'obsequious majesty' (509), which, given Milton's history as a regicide, is otherwise fraught with difficulty.

As Adam leads Eve 'blushing like the morn' (511) to their 'nuptial bower' (510) all nature joins in the celebration, the nightingale even urging the onset of night to speed them to their pleasure. But with appropriate tact, Milton leaves the couple to their carnal pleasures, safe in the belief that he has done all he can to sanctify their union. He returns instead to the present, and Adam distances himself a little from his recollections to dwell for a few moments on the change love has wrought in him. His post-coital musings occupy some forty lines before Raphael speaks again and admonishes him 'with contracted brow' (560) and they both further the narrative and the drama.

Adam tells Raphael that this account has brought him up to date, to the 'sum of earthly bliss/Which I enjoy' (522–3), but more ominously that his love for Eve has rendered his response to all else that is beautiful in nature as neutral in comparison. The list of sensual 'delicacies' (526) he produces – 'taste, sight, smell, herbs, fruits, and flowers,/Walks, and the melody of birds' (527–8) – revealingly lacks the sense of touch, and none of these things, Adam asserts, 'works in the mind no change' (525). But the phrase which exposes his vulnerability most fully is 'Nor vehement desire' (526) because it is unequivocally tied to Eve. His feelings for Eve seem now to overwhelm him. The repeated 'here' (528) is tantalisingly unclear and may indicate his head or heart, but what he is referring to is certainly his sense of himself. The sight of Eve, the touch of Eve, transports him beyond those pleasurable feelings previously stimulated by the rich nature of Paradise. He admits himself subject to 'passion' (530) and 'Commotion strange' (531), complaining to Raphael that he feels weak 'Against the charm of beauty's powerful glance' (533). Then in stark contrast with the praise he has only recently heaped on her in describing their nuptials, Adam criticises Eve as his inferior, although outwardly, physically, she far exceeds him. He speculates on whether nature is to blame for his lack or for Eve's excess, settling on the idea that

> Eve possesses, Too much of ornament, in outward show
> Elaborate, of inward less exact. (538–9)

If that were not enough to send feminist critics reaching for the sal volatile, he appears to seek agreement from Raphael for his speculation, 'For well I understand ... her the inferior' (540–1) 'in the mind/And inward faculties, which most excel' (541–2). To this explosive cocktail of failings Adam then adds the fact that Eve looks less like God than he does, and so must be inferior.

However blissful and harmonious their union was, by this stage in their relationship Adam is aware of an acute sense of weakness or indecision in Eve's presence. In the final outburst of his feelings which he shares with Raphael, it is as though Milton is setting him up to fail when Satan chooses Eve as the perfect means to tempt him. Adam cites Eve's 'loveliness' (547) as the source of his deference, the reason why, when she speaks or acts, what she says or does 'Seems wisest, virtuousest, discreetest, best' (550), surely one of the most unwieldy lines in the entire poem. Yet there may be hope for Adam in the forum of a modern classroom where gender politics are highly likely to fuel the flames. When he makes the claims that 'All higher knowledge in her presence falls/Degraded' (551–2) or that 'wisdom in discourse with her ... like folly shows' (552–3) is he necessarily accusing her of inferiority? And what of the notion that 'Authority and reason' (554) wait on her? Adam's final image is equally ambiguous. Such, he claims, is her 'Greatness of mind' (557) and nobility that they 'create an awe/About her' (558–9) like a guardian angel. Considering his interlocutor, this is a particularly poignant image.

What we can safely assume is that Milton's sense of the dramatic invests both Adam, and later Eve, with nuances of character that humanise them quite brilliantly, helping his reader take the huge imaginative stride necessary to enter Eden and face the arch tempter *with* them.

Exercises

Lines 64–178. This section contains some of the most complicated astronomical and metaphysical detail in the entire poem, but beneath Raphael's reply to Adam's question about earth's place in the universe lies a single, forceful message. Read through the section and try to isolate all the various questions Raphael poses before deciding what that single clear message is.

Lines 224–315. In this section Adam attempts to describe for Raphael how he came into being and first met his creator, God. Milton concentrates on Adam's viewpoint in this account and, although there are references to the beauty and plenitude of nature, everything is delivered through Adam's consciousness. What strike you as the dominant emotions that Adam experiences in this account?

Lines 338–451. God and Adam continue their dialogue after the naming of beasts in the same intimate and almost convivial fashion they began, but the subject of their discussion is problematic and Adam is shown by Milton to be quite capable of dispute. Read through this section and examine the way Adam disputes his case for companionship with God. How is this dispute resolved and what does it lead us to expect of Eve?

Lines 560–653. In the last part of Book 8, Raphael admonishes Adam for his apparent lack of spiritual perspective and, as he sees it, his vulnerability to the carnal aspect of his relationship with Eve at the expense of their higher love and mutual respect. He reminds Adam of the life led by the beasts in Eden and connects the higher emotions Adam feels for Eve with his love of God. Read through this section and decide for yourself how open to Raphael's advice Adam is. By the end of this book, how has Milton prepared Adam for the test he is to face from Satan?

9
Wiles and Wilfulness

Summary

Milton opens Book 9 in his own voice, again invoking aid from his muse, and asserts that the tragedy he has to recount in this book far outweighs those told in earlier, classical epics. Eight days after being driven from Paradise, Satan returns and, disguised in the form of a mist, finds a secret way into Eden through a fountain close by the Tree of Life. In the interim, he has pondered which of the beasts would most suit his plan and settles on the serpent as the most apposite for his deceit but, before he sets out to find Adam and Eve, he reflects on his dismal situation, provoked by the beauty of Paradise. Although he acknowledges the beauty of this new world, he cannot find any joy in it, only greater misery and a greater spur to seek revenge by corrupting man. He expands on his envy of man, who he sees as a replacement for the fallen, a favourite and a product of God's spite. He compares the furtive manner in which he has to move with the discourse and freedom man has with the angels. At last he finds the serpent sleeping and, without waking it, he enters into it and waits for the dawn.

At dawn, Adam and Eve begin the day, like all others, praising their maker before they discuss the day's labours. Eve begins by suggesting that there is so much work to be done just to keep the fertile garden in order that it would be best if they divide their labour. She argues that when they are close to each other, such is their love, they naturally seek each other's company and conversation and therefore don't accomplish as much as if they were physically apart. Adam responds lovingly, praising her for her practicality and her concern to help him, but he adds that God has not commanded them to restrict the pleasures of the day, whether eating, talking or loving, because all are part of their joyful life together – and he has made them in order that they will delight in life. Anticipating the birth of children, he adds that it won't be long before they have other hands to help them tend the garden anyway, but he agrees to separate if the absence is brief, turning it to a compliment since it will only make their reunion more pleasurable. Adam concludes his speech in doubt, reminding Eve of the warning Raphael has issued, that Satan is somewhere by, seeking their harm, and it is therefore much wiser for Eve to stay close by his side where he can protect her should Satan threaten them.

Eve exhibits slight offence when she responds, arguing further that she knows they are in danger, having been told by Adam and overhearing what Raphael said, but that, since they are immortal and the danger cannot be physical, it must be her susceptibility that Adam fears and this, she feels, demeans her. Adam reassures her that, far from doubting her, he merely wants to avoid creating a situation where any kind of attempt to harm her can take place without his being there to protect her. Even an attempt on her would, in Adam's mind, taint and offend her, and Satan is far more likely to attempt to harm Adam alone were he given the choice. He reminds her not to underestimate Satan, since he must indeed be powerful and subtle to have got this far, and adds that in her company he finds greater strength and courage and asks why she too shouldn't feel this way and so stay close to him.

Eve responds even more determinedly, stating that if they have to pursue their lives within boundaries created by Satan, how can they be happy? For her an attempt on her honour or virtue does not equal sin, and in fact such an attempt only harms the attacker and not the victim, who remains unsullied and even wins greater favour from God who, witnessing the event, can only approve their fidelity and firmness. Finally, she asserts that faith, love and virtue are valueless if not tested alone, and that the Paradise they inhabit would itself be a fraud.

Adam too is moved, and urges Eve to understand the nature of reason and free will, and that their existence means they are both vulnerable to deceit. It is not because he doubts her that he wants them to stay together, but because he fears Satan's unknown powers and thinks it unwise to do anything that might make his task easier. He urges her to demonstrate her obedience before her willingness to undergo any threat but finally relents, saying that were she to stay with him under duress, she is neither free nor present. Reminding her that she is God's creation he advises her to summon up all the gifts God has given her for her to remain obedient and true.

Eve then departs, but not before making it clear that she is going with Adam's permission and having heard his warnings. But she is full of confidence, saying she leaves more eagerly because she cannot imagine their enemy would attempt her alone, the weaker of the two, since to do so would only subject him to greater shame. They exchange loving looks and words as she departs before Milton intervenes to stress this moment is their last happy moment together, since Satan is already seeking Eve.

Satan hopes to find her alone, and is delighted when he does so. He moves towards her cautiously and is so deeply struck by her beauty, he is almost turned from his evil intent. However, his inherent corruption finally oversways him and, taking conscious advantage of Adam's absence, he approaches her. Speaking with a human voice, he flatters her and Eve responds not without some pleasure at his words, but also with surprise to hear an animal speak. She asks him how he came to possess both reason and speech. He narrates how he discovered a tree laden with richly appealing fruit which other animals too were attracted by, but could not reach. Winding himself around the trunk he ate his fill of the delicious fruit and immediately found himself able to reason and to speak and quickly deduced that the most beautiful object in the universe was Eve, and so hurried to find her so that he could admire and worship her.

Modestly suggesting the fruit has misled him, she nonetheless asks him where the tree is so that she can go and see for herself. Satan leads Eve to the Tree of Knowledge which she immediately recognises, telling the serpent he has had a wasted journey since this is the one fruit forbidden them to eat. The serpent then marshalls all his rhetorical skill to convince Eve that she will not come to any harm if she tastes the fruit, and indeed he is living proof of its power. He argues that man should not be denied anything free to beasts and tells her that God is more likely to praise her courage in tasting the fruit without fear of death, than in meekly obeying. He insists that knowledge of good and evil is in itself a benefit since it empowers man to be as gods and suggests that God's sole command was designed to keep Adam and Eve in subjection, as less than gods. He questions the very power of God to create anything, seeing evidence of creation all around him in nature, finally intimating that God's motive may be envy.

Eve is convinced by his rhetorical skill, not appreciating his entire narrative is not an exercise in reason but a lie. She rehearses all of the serpent's arguments, believing all he has said and concluding knowledge is something worth seeking and, because the serpent lives, that death cannot be the consequence. She then plucks the fruit and tastes it, greedily eating her fill and wondering at the new found knowledge she feels filling her. The serpent slinks silently away, unnoticed, having accomplished his task. For a moment she asks herself if she should keep her new found knowledge secret from Adam, but concludes that, if God has seen her action and death should result, Adam will find a new partner, something she cannot contemplate, and so she determines to persuade him to eat too.

Adam has woven Eve a garland of flowers and meets her close by the Tree, Eve carrying a bough laden with fruit for him to taste. Eve tells him the Tree was not as they had been told and recounts how the serpent had eaten its fruit and, not dying, had convinced her of its great powers which, tasting, she found to be true. She urges Adam to eat too so that they can be equal once again. Adam is instantly horrified and appalled. The garland withers in his hand and he pronounces her lost to death, and he with her because he cannot envisage life without her. He tells her that even if God were to create another Eve from his rib, she could never replace her. Acknowledging that what she has done cannot be undone, he convinces himself that since the serpent did not die and neither has Eve – then perhaps the serpent's tasting first has somehow lessened the danger and the offence. He tells himself that surely God wouldn't destroy that which he has just created and his favourite, and that to do so would allow his enemy to triumph.

Eve praises Adam's loyalty, superiority and good sense, tells him again that the fruit has opened her eyes and that he should not fear death but raise himself to the godlike heights she has reached by tasting the fruit. She then weeps on his shoulder at his demonstration of love and gives him the fruit to eat. Adam then eats and both soon become intoxicated not with love, but with lust and Adam tells her she has never appeared so beautiful as she does now, the fruit having opened his eyes too. They retire to a shady place and make love until sleep overcomes them.

When they wake, it is to be racked with shame and guilt. Adam immediately turns to blaming Eve, asking her how he can possibly now face either angels or God himself, tormented as they are with shame and true knowledge of evil. They then seek some leaves to hide their nakedness. Sitting down together they weep and rail against each other, bitterly feeling a host of negative emotions previously unknown in Paradise. Eve tries to defend herself, suggesting the same outcome might have occurred whether or not she had left him alone, finally asking him why he hadn't commanded her to stay, blaming him for being too weak. Adam is then angry and questions her love for him, reminding her of how hard he tried to dissuade her and finally declaring that from this time all men who let a woman's will rule them should expect evil to ensue, and their weakness to be cited as the cause. The book ends with the pair left wrangling painfully, each unable to accept their own part in the tragedy.

Satan's Inner Turmoil 99–178

Possibly the most popular book from *Paradise Lost* in terms of English Literature studies, either in schools or at undergraduate level, Book 9 contains the crucial tempting of Eve by Satan and the consequent Fall of both Adam and Eve. In the opening section (1–98) you will read how Milton consciously strives to shift the tone from one of innocent joy to impending tragedy, comparing his work as he does so with its literary models. A useful investigation is to look for other techniques he employs to achieve this change.

Once entered unseen onto earth, Satan's first reaction is not quite what we might have been expecting. His opening exclamation (99) shows that, though fallen himself, he is not at all immune to the beauty and variety of Paradise and, if anything, the sights around him whet his sense of loss. Satan is instantly reminded of heaven by what he sees and argues logically that earth, being created after heaven, must by definition be 'More justly' (102) 'preferred' (101) since 'what god after better worse would build?' (102). Logic is equally evident in the structure of the next lengthy sentence which culminates in the focus of Satan's parasitic envy, 'all summed up in man' (113). The subject of the sentence is the oxymoron 'Terrestrial heaven' (103), Satan's ironic recognition of earth's rich beauty and of its apparent centrality. He also uses the second person 'thou' (108) and later 'thee' (114) to address the earth – instead of the more neutral 'it' – which has the effect of personalising his sense of grievance further. From Satan's viewpoint, all the stars seem to shed 'their bright officious lamps' (104), and this for the benefit of the earth. He employs a faltering metaphor to convey his sense of awe. In the same way that God 'Is centre, yet extends to all' (108), Satan says, the earth too is the centre for all the stars and receives 'all their known virtue' (110) which is transformed into the chain of life, 'Productive in herb, plant, and nobler birth...all summed up in man' (111–13). The metaphor collapses when God is seen as extending, while the earth receives virtue from the heavens. By showing Satan preferring the logic of the chain of being which leads up to man, to the accuracy of his chosen metaphor, Milton may well be exposing Satan's hypocrisy.

There is certainly a rhythmical pattern to the list that also leads up to the emphatic final 'man' (113) as though Satan savours the drama of his own conclusion.

Even as Satan imagines himself enjoying the newly created earth, with all its rich landscape, he knows it is unavailable to him and that all joy is now beyond his reach, 'If I could joy in aught' (115). The impressive list he produces only magnifies his sense of torment at not being able to delight in them and he acknowledges the dreadful reality that, far from easing his pain, the sight of earth's magnificent landscape only worsens his state. The repetitious rhythm of 'the more I... so much more I...' and the subtle rhyming of 'see' and 'feel' in subsequent lines helps drive home his anguish, as though he is attempting to convince an imaginary listener to empathise with him:

> ... and the more I see
> Pleasure about me, so much more I feel
> Torment within me, (119–21)

The very essence of what it is to be Satan, to be the archetypal traitor that he is, is captured in his realisation that 'all good to me becomes/Bane' (122–3). He is eternally trapped in a paradox where, though still able to recognise and admire all that is good, good itself quickly mutates into an agony for him to contemplate.

But having indulged himself in his plight, Satan turns quickly to the attack once more and launches into an immensely lengthy sentence (124–62) which begins with his reminding us that neither heaven nor earth are worthy goals, 'unless by mastering heaven's supreme' (125), that is by destroying God. He is even honest enough to admit that he does not wish nor expect to lessen his torment, 'Nor hope to be myself less miserable/By what I seek' (126–7), but is rather intent on making others suffer too, because only in such wilful destruction can he 'find ease/To my relentless thoughts' (129–30). He next invites us to appreciate the scale of his design, and it is every bit as ambitious as his immense pride would lead us to expect. Although uncertain of the nature of his success, 'and him destroyed/Or won to what may work his utter loss' (130–1), Satan hopes that it will lead not just to the destruction of man but to the destruction of the earth which God has made for man too, 'all this will soon/Follow, as to him linked in weal or woe', where 'weal' is antithetical to 'woe' and infers prosperity or wealth (132–3). Here too is the same use of alliteration to create a clear emphasis at the end of a line which we noted in Chapter 8 (p. 165).

The pause here really is marked, and not just an effect of the alliterative ending but of the repeated phrase that follows, 'In woe then' (134),
which simply demands the reader takes stock and moves on to new
material.

That new material is Satan's imaginary best outcome, his ideal version of the future and, although 'destruction wide' (134) may be its
key manifestation, vanity is its real motivation. 'To me shall be the
glory sole among/The infernal powers' (135–6) is what Satan perceives
as reward. A 'glory' emanating from his being able to destroy 'in one
day' (136) what God has taken at least 'six nights and days' (137) to create. Throughout this prolonged diatribe, Satan again and again reveals
his intense enmity for his creator, choosing any name for him but God,
and frequently comparing himself with him in stature or achievement.
Here he sneers at the idea that it took God so long to create the earth
when he himself took merely 'one night' (140) to, in his terms, liberate
'From servitude inglorious wellnigh half/The angelic name' (140–1). The
irony is so obvious it risks missing its target, so it is worthwhile reminding yourself just what kind of freedom his followers now enjoy, as well as
noting the exaggeration, since we know from a number of places (most
notably VI, 156) that only one-third of heaven rebelled. Milton's fondness for the alliterative half-line appears again in 'and thinner left the
throng' (142), while 'adorers' (143) vibrates with petty jealousy.

A caesura at 'he to be avenged' (143) marks a change of direction
and a shocking interpolation by Satan which links the creation of man
and earth to God's desire to avenge Satan's rebellion. Satan can only
see the act of creation in crudely militaristic terms, 'to repair his numbers thus impaired' (144) and 'With heavenly spoils, our spoils' (151).
Or else utterly selfish terms, 'or to spite us more' (147) and 'Determined
to advance into our room' (148). He lacks the trust and faith which God
requires of Adam and of man to see his grand plan worked out to the
ultimate glory and salvation of mankind as a whole. He even casts doubt
on his own and the other angels' origins, 'if they at least/Are his creation' (146–7). But perhaps his greatest sense of grievance stems from,
unsurprisingly, his own vanity, because it is man's baseness, 'A creature formed of earth ... Exalted from so base original' (149–50), that
really exercises him. He reserves his exclamatory disdain, 'oh indig-
nity!' (154), for the idea that angels have been 'Subjected to his service'
(155), as though somehow he has been personally insulted by this new
arrangement. It is also intriguing to note the shift in the way Satan has
employed the word 'earth' in this diatribe. What began as a rich and
beautiful individual, to be admired and addressed intimately as 'thee'

(105) and 'thou' (108), has now become a term of abuse, 'their earthy charge' (157).

But the mention of the angels guarding Adam has a narrative function too, as it enables Satan to describe the means by which he enters Eden 'wrapped in mist/Of midnight vapour' (158–9) in order to avoid detection by them. This shift to his metamorphosis and his quest to find the serpent, re-establishes a sense of drama and immediacy, and we're invited to picture Satan transformed into a mist prying into 'every bush and brake' (160). The image of the serpent's 'mazy folds' (161) is wittily appropriate, since it not only describes the visual puzzle of a snake's coils, but the hidden nature of Satan's 'dark intent' (162). Satan himself is more concerned with the inappropriateness of the metamorphosis, exclaiming 'Oh foul descent!' (163) at the idea 'That I who erst contended/With gods to sit the highest' (163–4), and who is now reduced to the proportions and habits of a snake, 'and mixed with bestial slime' (165). But this transformation also provides Milton with an opportunity to contrast Satan with Christ, since the latter selflessly embraces his reduction through incarnation as man, while Satan whines and complains, 'This essence to incarnate and imbrute' (166).

The final section of Satan's speech is difficult, not so much through complex syntax or vocabulary, as through the perverseness of Satan's ideology. He starts with a rhetorical question few listeners would respond to as quickly and readily as he imagines they might, 'But what will not ambition and revenge/Descend to?' (168–9). He produces what sounds like a sententious observation, 'Who aspires must down as low/As high he soared' (169–70), but which simply doesn't ring true. Satan appears to be trying to convince himself that there is a direct proportion to be embraced and that the higher one's ambitions, the lower one's starting point. Yet immediately afterwards he also recognises the much more acceptable belief that revenge is only a temporary pleasure which soon turns sour. 'Revenge, at first though sweet,/Bitter ere long back on itself recoils' (171–2), the final word ironically connecting him to the serpent. It is quite possible that Milton is perfectly comfortable with Satan's inconsistency here, preferring to stress his recklessness when he decides to dismiss any bitter consequences, 'Let it; I reck not, so it light well aimed' (173). He is determined to concentrate his aim on God, even though he knows the missile might 'fall short' (174) and hit man, 'on him who next/Provokes my envy' (174–5). The brief list he then produces articulates that envy perfectly, 'this new favourite/Of heaven, this man of clay, son of despite' (175–6).

In any discussion about Satan it is important to acknowledge the precise nature of his failings and here Milton is completely unequivocal about them. The first is envy: he names it and Satan exemplifies it for us immediately. Contemporary students would benefit from researching and understanding exactly what envy is and why for Milton's readers, as for Dante, it was unshakably one of the seven deadly sins (see p. 60).

Satan's second great weakness is pride and Milton returns finally to his sense of insulted pride to close this speech, 'Whom us the more to spite his maker raised/From dust' (177–8), as though man's base origin represented a direct, personal insult that God aimed at him. In the end, it seems Satan's logic is merely that of the playground, 'spite then with spite is best repaid' (178).

Eve Persuades Adam to Allow Her to Work in the Garden Alone

One of the most infamous sections of *Paradise Lost* is the section of Book 9 that contains the conversation between Adam and Eve which ends with Eve seen skipping blithely off into the trees alone, her husband looking longingly after her (205–384). In any critical discussion about blame or fault, it inevitably figures highly, and the analysis here will focus on the line of argument each pursues.

Eve opens this conversation with a clear request. Instead of their working together to 'tend plant, herb and flower' (206) she wants them to split up so that they work more effectively and stop their garden 'Tending to wild' (212). She asks for Adam's advice, 'Thou therefore now advise' (212), but immediately offers her own suggestion, which may remind you of what Adam told Raphael about how he responded to her thoughts and words (VIII, 546–59):

> All higher knowledge in her presence falls
> Degraded, wisdom in discourse with her
> Looses discount'nanced, and like folly shows; (VIII, 551–3)

and of course how Raphael subsequently warned Adam to temper his desire for Eve with reason. Eve's suggestion points them towards differing plants which have emblematic connotations any decent edition of the poem will detail, but what is unavoidable and more challenging than these emblems is the basis Eve uses for her suggestion. Her view is that, being so close, they are inevitably drawn to look at each other and then converse, so that the day ends not just with little work accomplished, but crucially 'the hour of supper comes unearned' (225).

Adam responds initially with loving compliments, playing with the word 'sole' (227) to stress their union and assuming from her request that her motive was all to do with good husbandry, 'to study household good/And good works in her husband to promote' (233–4). His rejection of her request is based on his belief that God has not forbidden any of the loving communication, the shared thoughts and food – what he sums up as 'this sweet intercourse/Of looks and smiles' (238–9) which Eve viewed as time wasted – and he points out that 'smiles from reason flow' (240) which distinguishes them from the animals 'and are of love the food' (240). Adam turns Eve's suggestion about work efficiency into a love test, reminding her that love is 'not the lowest end of human life' (241). He does return to her point, by reminding her that God has created them not for 'irksome toil, but to delight' (242).

There is something euphemistic about this whole conversation and, although Eve never mentions sex, Adam appears to understand that is what she is really talking about, and if that is the case, then what Milton is describing is a demonstration of the tension between carnality and rationality that Adam told Raphael he felt in Eve's presence ever since their nuptial union (VIII, 530–53). Adam makes one more attempt to dissuade Eve when he suggests that her anxiety about the garden's grow-ing wildness is unfounded, 'These paths and bowers doubt not... Will keep from wilderness with ease' (244–5), but then he suddenly acqui-esces. This abrupt leaning Eve's way could be seen as reinforcing the argument that this entire conversation is euphemistic. Is too much con-versation really a credible reason to agree to Eve's request? That is what Adam implies when he says 'but if much convérse perhaps/Thee satiate' (247–8). 'Satiate', with its implication of excess, seems infinitely more suited to a discussion about sex than gossip and one doesn't have to be a schoolboy to take the step from convérse to intercourse. The paired lines which Adam next uses to justify a brief sojourn from each other's company are also quite noticeably lyrical:

> For solitude sometimes is best society
> And short retirement urges sweet return. (249–50)

There is a quite clearly lyrical balance created between 'solitude' and 'society' which is then paralleled by 'retirement' and 'return' and if you examine these two lines more closely, you will see a permeating use of assonance gives them a memorable, sententious feel.

The next stage in their argument is clearly signalled by the phrase 'But other doubt possesses me' (251), and Adam now openly refers to the danger they both *know* they face from Satan, 'for thou knowst/What hath been warned us' (252–3). Even Adam understands that envy is motivating Satan, 'Envying our happiness' (254), and, so acute is his sense of danger, that he predicts accurately the idea of Satan watching them to find an occasion to make his attempt on Eve alone. His essential point is that together they are safer, and he appears to use their mutual happiness as a rhetorical device to win Eve over to his view. Adam doesn't know whether Satan's aim is to break their faith with God, destroy their shared joy 'or worse' (265), but whichever it might be his argument melts into something more akin to pleading when he says 'leave not the faithful side/That gave thee being, still shades thee and protects' (265–6). Again there is a note of sententiousness in the way Milton constructs his final three lines (267–9), as though Adam were Eve's teacher, and draws from their particular dilemma a truth about wives in general: a bizarrely anachronistic tactic for the only husband on earth to employ and one which reveals how tightly bound by seventeenth-century social mores and his own Puritan faith Milton was. In his acceptance that his role is to guard her, or 'with her the worst' (269) endure, you might see prolepsis, heavy irony or even a hint of courage.

The simile Milton employs to describe the way Eve now replies, 'As one who loves, and some unkindness meets' (271), is both subtle and provocative. It certainly implies that, however we as readers respond to Adam's argument, Eve is hurt. The question most readers now face becomes: is Eve right to leave her husband's side? However, the simile isn't unsupported and if you also take into account the frame Milton places around it, 'the virgin majesty of Eve' (270) that speaks 'with sweet austere composure' (272), the answer to the key question is far from clear cut. Does Eve compose herself because she feels she has to? And what, in Eve, does Milton point us to by using the oxymoron 'sweet austere'? How on earth does she suddenly become a virgin and what does Milton want us to understand from his use of this apparently inappropriate adjective? Is chastity an attitude of mind or a sexual *fait accompli*? Possible answers to these questions start to form themselves once we look at Eve's words and the line of argument she now pursues with Adam.

In a series of noticeably terse sentences that seem designed to match her 'sweet' austerity, she starts by praising Adam in a way which emphasises his superiority, calling him 'all earth's lord' (273), then agrees that they are in danger, but how she knows this is in itself intriguing. She says she learned this not just from what Adam has told her, 'by thee informed' (275), but also by overhearing Raphael, 'As in a shady nook I stood behind' (277). Eve then expresses clear disappointment in Adam by telling him that just because 'an enemy we have, who seeks/Our ruin' (274–5) does not mean that he should 'doubt' her 'firmness' (279). She even spells out for Adam why she is disappointed, explaining that since they are immortal, 'not capable of death or pain' (283), he has no reason to fear Satan's 'violence' (282) and therefore he can only be afraid of Satan's 'fraud' (285) and consequently of her inability to resist it. The lines are so vital they merit reproducing here:

> His fraud then is thy fear, which plain infers
> Thy equal fear that my firm faith and love
> Can by his fraud be shaken or seduced; (285–7)

This idea is what she finds so objectionable. But the way she sums up her feeling abandons the syllogistic logic she has so far pursued. She says she simply cannot understand how Adam entertained such thoughts, 'how found they harbour in thy breast' (288), since they were 'misthought of her to thee so dear?' (289). Put in a colloquial fashion that makes the point about her abandonment of logic very succinctly, she argues that he thought... wrong.

It's clear that Adam sees she is hurt since when he next responds it is with 'healing words' (290), and, just as Eve addressed him, he addresses her in placatory terms, adding very markedly his belief that she is 'from sin and blame entire' (292), where 'entire' carries the meaning, unmarked or untouched. He refutes directly her charge that he doubts her, instead stating that his wish is 'to avoid/The attempt itself, intended by our foe' (294–5). To Adam, then, there seems no reason to put themselves in danger or to invite 'dishonour foul' (297) which would be the result of even allowing Satan an opportunity to tempt Eve. Appealing then to Eve's own potential feelings, he tells her that 'thou thyself with scorn/And anger wouldst resent the offered wrong' (299–300), even were it to be futile, 'Though ineffectual found' (301). This gives him the opportunity to respond directly to her charge of *misthinking* as he asks Eve not to 'misdeem' (301) his desire to protect her from 'such affront' (302) when he is prepared to suffer any assault himself. Adam believes, rightly as it turns out, that Satan will not attempt anything while they are together and that, even if he did, it would give Adam the chance to defend Eve by taking the brunt of any such attack himself. He adds a new warning; not to underestimate Satan's 'malice' or 'false guile' (306), since anyone who could 'seduce/Angels' (307–8) is to be feared, and he pleads with Eve not to undervalue the help he offers, 'nor think superfluous others' aid' (308).

At this point the dialogue takes yet another direction and, having in his mind clearly refuted all her charges, he turns to flattery and shared love to try and persuade her to stay. In her presence, 'in thy sight' (310), Adam tells her he becomes 'More wise, more watchful, stronger' (311) and the fear of shame, were he to fail any test in her presence, would spur him on, 'would utmost vigour raise' (314) and, through being shared, would unite them. Adam ends this speech with what he hopes is a rhetorical question, asking Eve why she does not feel exactly the same and choose to face any trial with Adam beside her, since he is 'best witness of thy virtue tried' (317). You need only reflect on the ambiguity in 'virtue' to appreciate why Eve may not respond as he hopes. So far this dialogue has proceeded largely unnarrated, but at this moment Milton's narrator steps in, and does so with both feet. The narrator supplies two strong leads as to how he wishes us to react to Adam's argument, 'domestic' (318) and 'matrimonial love' (319), both hinting at Adam's selflessness and familial care, before fielding a powerful 'but' (319) that instantly undermines Eve by implying she has neither understood nor valued these qualities in Adam. When the narrator states 'but Eve, who thought/Less attribúted to her faith sincere' (319–20), he is intervening directly on Adam's behalf by depicting Eve as failing to listen. Prosaically, the effect is like saying: in spite of all Adam has said, yet Eve still felt he didn't trust her. This apparent subjectivity also appears in the 'accent sweet' (321) with which she takes up the argument.

Yet the series of three questions she now asks are so intelligently worded and incisive that the narrator's interpolation itself sounds ill thought out and unhearing. The first (322–6) challenges the foundation of all Adam's objections, that they are happy. How can they be happy, Eve asks, if their life is lived in fear, under the constraints imposed by their enemy, however violent or cunning he may be, and if they are not equally able to defend themselves? Her second question (327–32) asks why they should fear or avoid their enemy when any assault on them he might attempt is merely an affront on their integrity and can neither dishonour them nor lead directly to sin. In effect (she adds to this question) by repelling their enemy they 'double honour gain' (332) by proving him false, find peace for themselves and earn God's favour as he is their ultimate witness. The third and final question is the most challenging of all, since it is God's own (III, 103–11). What value or use are 'faith, love, virtue' (335) if never tested by external forces? In attempting to draw a conclusion from these three questions, Eve now makes a huge and dangerous assumption. She asks Adam to assume, as she does, that God has not made their world so 'imperfect' (338) that they need to act jointly to secure it. If that were the case, she states, their happiness would indeed be 'Frail' (340) and, in a final rhetorical flourish, 'Eden were no Eden thus exposed' (341).

One of Milton's great achievements in *Paradise Lost* is the rich characterisation he achieves from such intransigent raw materials and in this lengthy dialogue we can see how he does it. They may be the first man and woman on earth and be immortal, but, as they exchange views here, we see them behaving in ways any married couple would recognise, or even wryly acknowledge as representative of the condition. When Adam replies 'fervently' (342) his anxiety is growing, a condition captured in his addressing Eve now simply as 'O woman', as he firmly rejects her assumption by reminding her that nothing God makes is imperfect, 'much less man' (346). The nature and subtlety of free will has occupied us elsewhere in this book and it now receives one of the most valuable treatments in the entire poem. Rejecting danger from 'outward force' (348), Adam spells out for Eve exactly where the danger for her is, 'within himself/The danger lies, yet lies within his power' (348–9). If there was a single line from the poem which every student should memorise and be prepared to exploit, in either written or verbal debate, it is Adam's assertion that 'Against his will he can receive no harm' (350). He now returns to logic as a tool, connecting free will to the faculty of reason since 'what obeys/Reason, is free' (351–2) and explaining to Eve that this relationship necessitates the possibility that reason may be fooled 'by some fair appearing good surprised' (354). Which in turn means there is always a risk that reason may 'dictate false, and misinform the will' (355) such that man disobeys God. Adam then breaks off from his 'fervent' words and adopts a more intimate, loving tone, assuring Eve that he is not mistrustful of her at all and that it is out of 'tender love' (357) that he desires to protect her, and that he expects the same from her. The paired lines (357–8) form a single sentence where the opening terse phrase, 'Not then mistrust', is sharply contrasted with the gentle fluency of 'tender love enjoins' (357) and the harmonious balancing of minds in 'That I should mind thee oft, and mind thou me' (358).

After this brief, lyrical appeal, Adam picks up the thread of his argument to restate that they risk falling 'into deception unaware' (362) if they do not, as they were warned, keep 'strictest watch' (363). Given that is the case, it is better that Eve should not 'seek temptation' (364) which will be more likely if they separate, and, in a clearly ominous note, Adam assures her that temptation will inevitably come, 'trial will come unsought' (366). Ironically, it is enormously tempting to wish that Adam had left off there, since what he now says is guaranteed to fuel Eve's intent but it also reinforces the critical view that admires Milton's ability to humanise his key characters. If you wish to prove your 'constancy' (367), the very thing Eve took deepest exception to his having impugned, he says, prove you are obedient first. Which leaves the reader with the thorniest of questions: does he mean obedience to him or to God? It is easy to prove obedience, he concludes, but constancy has to be tested; and he has not witnessed Eve being tested: 'who can know' (368) whether or not she is able to resist?

The final exchanges between the couple (370–84) are some of the most fiercely disputed lines in *Paradise Lost*, partly because the language is so richly ambiguous, and partly because they seem to have abandoned listening to each other. Syntax, as so often, is also an issue but if you connect 'If thou think...us both securer' (370–1) with 'seemst' (371), Adam appears to be acquiescing and saying something along these reductively prosaic lines: 'If you think that the coming and unsought for trial will find us both more secure than you *seem* to think, given the warning I have given you, then go'. But he adds a confusing reason, 'for thy stay, not free, absents thee more' (372). If we lose the latter phrase then it does seem entirely consistent with everything Adam has said about free will. Were she to stay it would be under duress and without the free will so crucial to their happiness and relationship with God. But 'absents thee more' sounds almost petulant and risks making Adam's tone weakly reluctant. He also repeats the imperative 'Go' on subsequent lines, in a manner which invites critics to see him ultimately as the positive agent, a view reinforced by his final words, which are equally imperative, 'do thine' (375). Yet simultaneously Adam seems willing to accept that God has made Eve sufficient for whatever trial awaits her, 'For God towards thee hath done his part' (375).

If all that were not enough to exercise the reader, the narrator steps in once more with two lines that seem precision engineered to criticise Eve. 'So spake the patriarch of mankind' (376) invests Adam with near biblical authority, but that authority is instantly undermined by the challenging 'but Eve/Persisted' (376–7) and the paradoxical 'yet submiss, though last', as though Eve is determined to have the final word, whatever Adam's advice or commands. And when Eve utters those last words, they are no less puzzling and provocative than Adam's. She assumes, first of all, that Adam has granted her permission, 'With thy permission then' (378), an assumption inviting challenge. She adds that she has understood his warning, 'and thus forewarned/Chiefly' (378), but her understanding goes only so far as 'Chiefly' takes her, and that is to an agreement that they are both likely to be most vulnerable when least seeking temptation. A key question is: does Eve believe that she is leaving at this point expecting a trial and is therefore more secure? But perhaps the most challenging idea here is her confident assertion 'The willinger I go' (382), which implies that, after hearing everything Adam has had to say, she is even more certain that her decision to work apart is right. 'Go in thy native innocence' (373) was the valedictory injunction Adam used, and something of that innocence may be what we hear in her confident, final belief that their enemy is far less likely to seek the weaker out, since his shame in being defeated would be so much greater. Eve may be confident that she is capable of resisting but her notions about Satan are strikingly, and of course tragically, ill judged.

The Serpent Converses with Eve

Satan first gains Eve's attention through his lavishly sensual physical appearance and then through extreme flattery, 'A goddess among gods' (547), before his gift of speech engages her in conversation. When she asks him how he came to be able to speak when all other animals are mute, he constructs a skilfully baroque deceit (567–612).

The flattery in Satan's opening 'Empress' is clear, but he is also eloquent, as the rhythm invites a heavy stress on the 'splendidness' of 'resplendent' and on the final 'Eve' (368). Satan is also tactically subservient, acknowledging her command and ironically professing obedience. Milton reminds us that Satan is the 'guileful tempter' (567) and that guile is put to work immediately as he takes the first opportunity available to shift their conversation towards his ultimate object, the fruit of the Tree of Knowledge. But before analysing the various steps in his temptation of Eve, we shouldn't overlook the most obvious but least frequently commented on strategy that Satan uses: deceit. Lies trip off the serpent's forked tongue at a bewildering pace, and with not the least sign of self-consciousness.

The serpent tells Eve that he was like all other grazing animals, 'of abject thoughts and low' (572), a life he reinterprets for her as one driven essentially by food and sex, 'nor aught but food discerned/Or sex' (573–4), and then pursues his tale in an almost jovial manner:

> Till on a day roving the field, I chanced
> A goodly tree far distant to behold (575–6)

choosing images and words drawn from a distinctly pastoral palette. Besides the richness, colour and odour of the fruit, he refers with equal savour to the milking of sheep and goats. He relates how powerfully the fruit played on his appetite, describing the sensation as a 'sharp desire' (584) he is unable to resist as 'hunger and thirst at once' (586) urge him on. The now familiar use of alliteration in the latter half of a line is reversed to produce 'Powerful persuaders' (587) and his lurid account is designed to stimulate a similar response in Eve. So persuasive is he, it is easy to forget that God has not invested the fruit of the Tree with any such qualities at all. His words are all lies. In an image that echoes the way he weaves language around Eve, he describes how he then wound himself around the Tree in order to reach the fruit, 'About the mossy trunk I wound me soon' (589). There is a touch of Satan's overweening arrogance in his depicting the scene as witnessed by 'All other beasts' (592) and of his own trademark weakness in imagining them 'Longing and envying' (593). A wittier Eve might have responded by asking where the giraffe was.

Rhyming 'got' (594) with 'not' (596) punctuates the action dramatically and allows a moment's pause before he can wax even more lyrical about how delicious the fruit was, 'for such pleasure till that hour/At feed or fountain never had I found' (596–7). Intriguingly the alliteration 'feed or fountain' occurs again in the first half of the line, as though Milton were singling out the serpent's speech. Undoubtedly, in comparison with the earlier sophisticated exchanges between Adam and Eve, his conversation is mundane, even crude, but nonetheless serves its purpose superbly. So seductive is his account, Eve even fails to notice the obvious use of 'Tempting' (595) which less well hidden should have rung deafening alarm bells given the dream she related to Adam (V, 28–93).

Maintaining the parallel between food and sex which underpins his story, Satan enjoys a moment of post-coital satisfaction, 'Sated at length' (598), before he relates how he then felt the growth 'Of reason in my inward powers' and realised he had the power of speech, though still a serpent, 'though to this shape retained' (600). When the serpent turns his new found intellect to 'speculations high or deep' (602) we ought to recall the advice Raphael gave Adam (VIII, 172–8) which included the apposite phrase 'Think only what concerns thee and thy being' (VIII, 174). The serpent's idle speculation is of course neither speculation nor idle, since it never took place and is merely a ploy to flatter Eve further. The hyperbole is obvious, as his 'capacious mind/Considered all things visible' (603–4) not just in heaven but on earth and 'middle' (604) by which we must assume he means everything between them. In contemplating all creation, 'all things fair and good' (605), he concludes with the blasphemy that Eve is the epitome of everything beautiful and good, 'no fair to thine/Equivalent or second' (608–9). This allows him to account for his presence and their conversation, while flattering her even further. Knowing what he now knows, he was 'compelled' (609) to seek Eve out to 'worship thee' (611), 'Sovereign of creatures, universal dame' (612), which is of course more blasphemy. So outrageous is his hyperbole, that Eve herself reacts to it as soon as he ends his speech, although not with the condemnation Raphael's warning (had it been heeded) would have rendered. Instead Eve jokes with him in a way that signals how successful his flattery has been. 'Serpent, thy overpraising leaves in doubt/The virtue of that fruit, in thee first proved' (615–16).

The Temptation of Eve

Perhaps the first thing to remind ourselves when looking closely at the way Satan persuades Eve to follow his example and eat the fruit (679–732) is that everything he says is predicated on a fundamental deceit. Eve is not conversing with a serpent and neither has that serpent eaten the fruit. Given the almost tortuous lengths Milton's God has gone to in order to warn them and pave the way for the temptation of Adam and Eve to take place on a free will footing, it is mildly surprising that Eve doesn't seem to even entertain the possibility that a talking snake is a tad suspicious. However, Milton has to work with his chosen material, at least to some extent, and it is precisely where he chooses to elaborate on his source that a lot of the critical interest lies.

In the preamble to Satan's carefully structured argument, Milton uses an elaborate simile to describe the way the serpent prepares himself to speak:

> As when of old some orator renowned
> In Athens or free Rome, where eloquence
> Flourished, since mute, to some great cause addressed, (670–2)

He pursues the simile in some detail, describing the serpent summoning all his oratorical skill and indignation in a zealous determination to pursue truth. It is full of irony which works on a number of levels and tells us a lot about the kind of education Milton had received,[1] but the main point to make is that, in acting in this way, Satan cleverly disarms Eve because he treats her as an intellectual equal. He opens his assault on her by pretending that the power of the fruit, which he apostrophises as 'O sacred, wise, and wisdom-giving plant,/Mother of science' (679–80), is operating there and then, in front of Eve. He is also far from reserved in estimating the power it gives him, telling Eve it affords him the godlike power to 'discern/Things in their causes' (681–2), but, more cunningly, that it has given him the ability not just to understand God, but actually to question his omnipotence, 'to trace the ways/Of highest agents, deemed however wise' (682–3). Flattering her further, 'Queen of this universe' (684), he tackles God's word head on by asserting that the threat of death he made is a lie and that if Eve eats the fruit as he has done, she will not only live but gain the immense knowledge he has done.

He does this in a series of briefly phrased questions that are designed to convince as much by their simplicity as their appeal to the evidence of Eve's senses, 'ye shall not die:/How should ye? By the fruit?' (685–6), 'By the threatener?' (687). Between these comes the potentially diffi-cult sentence, 'It gives you life/To knowledge' (686–7), where 'to' simply means 'in addition to'. The way he chooses to diminish God as 'the threatener' after reinterpreting his 'sole command,/Sole pledge of his obedience' (III, 94–5) as 'rigid threats' (685) is equally a clever, yet bold strategy, especially when followed up by his appeal to Eve to see for her-self. 'Look on me' (687), he advises, and the mere fact that he is still very much alive and apparently able to converse with her on such a demand-ing level is proof that God is, indeed, merely a *threatener*. The serpent doesn't let the momentum lapse, embellishing his argument with a wonderfully well targeted enticement to Eve: that by eating he has ven-tured 'higher than my lot' (690). Another example of Satan using alliter-ation in the first half of a line, 'Shall that be shut to man, which to the beast/Is open?' (691–2), invites Eve to feel not just neglected, but duped. The heavy irony connected to Satan's use of 'beast' is possibly more modern than historical, but nonetheless present for today's readers.

Having built up a head of rhetorical steam, the serpent speeds on, firing more questions at Eve (there are no fewer than twelve in this speech) designed progressively to undermine her belief in God's power over her. We can chart this movement very easily. The serpent suggests that far from displaying anger, 'For such a petty trespass' (693), God will 'praise/Rather your dauntless virtue' (693–4), which is as fine an exam-ple of bathos as one will find in the entire canon of English poetry, original sin being reduced to a 'petty trespass'. The parenthetic 'what-ever thing death might be' (695) interrupts his flow for a moment but is equally bathetic, trivialising the hugely significant as unknown (he has after all met Death) in comparison with the known benefit of the 'knowledge of good and evil' (697) to be gained from eating the fruit.

Knowledge of good, he argues, has to be 'just?' (698) while knowledge of evil he discounts as fictitious, 'if what is evil/Be real' (698–9), and surely something more easily avoided if known, 'why not known, since easier shunned?' (699). This barrage of seemingly self-evident logic now brings him to the climax of his assault, 'God therefore cannot hurt ye, and be just' (700).

It is here now that Satan finally names 'God' (700) but only to negate his authority and power 'Not just, not God' (701). If God is *not*, then Eve has no reason to either fear or obey him and, with something of the Greek about him, perfectly matching the simile Milton used to introduce this speech, Satan produces the quite brilliantly rhetorical conclusion, 'Your fear itself of death removes the fear' (703). It is a simple step from there to surmise as to why God issued Adam and Eve with this single command, 'why then was this forbid?' (703). The serpent's deduction is pure Satan. Unable to see beyond selfish gain and vanity it has to be because God wished to keep them 'low and ignorant' (704) in order that they may worship him. If they eat the fruit, they will gain the knowledge of good and evil that distinguish the 'gods' (note the plural) from man, 'and ye shall be as gods' (708). In order to reinforce this, the serpent returns to himself as the example, suggesting it is only right and proper, 'but proportion meet' (711), since through eating the fruit, a serpent has become man: that men, through eating the fruit, should become gods, 'I of brute human, ye of human gods' (712). That might be interesting, had the serpent ever eaten the fruit, but as we stressed earlier Satan's entire assault on Eve is predicated on this one, potent lie.

The rhetorical fireworks continue as he then tells Eve that this may indeed be death, 'So ye shall die perhaps' (713), but it is a 'death to be wished' (714) if it renders them gods. The questions now come thick and fast. Apart from the profound reductionism in referring only to 'gods' in the plural, he challenges the very concept of their pre-eminence, denying that they are creators when it is evident that the earth itself, 'Warmed by the sun' (721), is the more fertile. And if they were the creators of everything, who 'enclosed/Knowledge of good and evil in this tree' (722–3), making it possible for anyone who eats the fruit to gain the wisdom he has gained, 'without their leave?' (725). Satan makes the error of assuming that the fruit has the power he imagines when God has never said so. God only ever requests Adam and Eve's obedience. Why would eating the fruit cause offence? How can the tree give out its power 'against his will if all be his?' (728). The lapse back into the singular possessive pronoun may be a deliberate choice by Milton to expose

Satan's deceit, before he transfers to God his own, self-destructive flaw, envy, 'Or is it envy, and can envy dwell/In heavenly breasts?' (729–30). As Milton explained before the serpent gathered himself for this rhetorical tour de force, he would exploit every trick and strategy employed by classical orators, and the repetition, 'These, these' (730), with its lengthy stresses, combined with the alliterative sentence ending, give greater force to his suggestion that Eve actually *needs* 'this fair fruit' (731). So confident is he, that in his final sentence Satan even risks a joke and uses the dangerously witty oxymoron, 'Goddess humane', as he exhorts her to 'reach then, and freely taste' (732). The oxymoron flatters in two directions by raising Eve's status and acknowledging her compassion, but the heaviest irony by far falls on his encouragement to taste 'freely'. Having worked so hard to persuade her and remove all doubt, fear or caution from Eve's mind, in the end Eve is as God intended, free to choose.

Eve Succumbs

The serpent ends his assault on Eve here and Milton then allows us access to her immediate thoughts and the reasoning that brings her to the point where she chooses to eat. Eve is left with the serpent's words ringing in her ears, 'With reason, to her seeming, and with truth' (738), while the sensory appeal of the fruit is heightened by her noontide hunger. Yet she does not immediately eat, instead she reflects on what she has heard, 'Pausing awhile, thus to herself she mused' (744). The efficacy of Satan's chief lie is clear as Eve doesn't question the idea that the fruit is responsible for the serpent's gift of speech but sees it as evidence of the fruit's power. God's naming and 'forbidding' (753) is equally proof to her that the fruit has the power the serpent says it has, but what *is* new is Eve's then reasoning that God's forbidding them to eat is in itself an enticement, 'his forbidding/Commends thee more' (753–4), because it confirms the fruit's virtue. In addition, she asks herself what good there is in knowing the virtue of the fruit without enjoying or benefiting from it. That is tantamount to not knowing it exists at all. You may already have noticed Eve makes no mention now of evil but acts as though the Tree were named the Tree of Knowledge of Good. She deduces, unaided by the serpent, that in essence then God has simply forbidden them to know what is good, and therefore it follows that he also 'forbids us to be wise?' (759). Eve appears to have picked up the serpent's trait of avoiding God's name too and consequently is less afraid of concluding that 'Such prohibitions bind not' (760).

For a moment she rediscovers her fear of death (760–2) but immediately relinquishes it because the serpent is alive and he has eaten, proof perfect it appears. Throughout this interior monologue, Eve uses quite short, simple sentences clearly connected to the preceding ideas, but the list she produces, held together by *ands*, 'He hath eaten and lives,/And knows, and speaks, and reasons, and discerns' (764–5), undermines the quality of her reasoning because it sounds very much as though she is trying to convince herself. She also asks herself a number of rhetorical questions, the most poignant of all being her next one, 'For us alone/Was death invented?' (766–7), because while assuming the rhetorical answer to be 'Of course not' she has unknowingly, amidst a welter of deceit, uttered an absolute truth. God did create death for man (III, 208–16). We can see too that the serpent's words have struck home when Eve voices frustration at being 'denied/This intellectual food' (768). There is more heavy irony on show as she assumes from the serpent's eagerness to share his good fortune that he is not envious but joyful, and is in fact 'Friendly to man, far from deceit or guile' (772).

With some speed, Eve's reasoning has brought her to the point where she is genuinely unafraid, 'What fear I then' (773), because knowing nothing of good and evil she paradoxically has nothing to fear. Again a list exposes the shallowness of her reasoning and the influence of the serpent, since she rejects not just fear of God, but of 'death, of law or penalty?' (775). In Eve's mind, God has become merely one of a number of potential influences on her. Having reasoned thus, nothing remains to hinder Eve from feeding 'at once both body and mind?' (779) and 'in evil hour' (780) she reaches for the fruit and eats it.

You will be able to find ample evidence of Milton's desire to signal the scale of this disastrous act in the reaction of nature:

> Earth felt the wound, and nature from her seat
> Sighing through all her works gave signs of woe,
> That all was lost. (782–4)

But how explicit the criticism is, in his description of 'her rash hand' (780), may be less straightforward. The caesura (784) puts an abrupt end to the dramatic tension that has been building since Eve left Adam's side; and Satan exits unceremoniously, 'Back to the thicket slunk/The guilty serpent' (784–5). Eve is left to relish the fruit and Milton allows her ample space to indulge herself while emphasising her self-deception, before we are once more party to her thoughts. You should be able to locate plenty of words in this short section (785–94) which stress her greed and pleasure, and Milton's puritanical taste settles on drunkenness as the dominant image. But the most damning indication that Eve has indeed been seduced by the serpent's skilful words is the idea that 'nor was godhead from her thought' (790) as 'Greedily she engorged without restraint' (791). One question ought to surface above many potential ones, and that is: why does Eve not experience utter disappointment, since the fruit does not have the power the serpent claimed?

Such is her conviction in its virtues that she praises it in hymn-like terms, promising to tend and care for it 'Not without song, each morning' (800), an action which is near blasphemous since it supplants their worship of God that begins each day. Eve anticipates being very liberal with the Tree's fruit, intending to offer it 'free to all' (802), and imagines that the more she eats, the more she will achieve divine status:

> Till dieted by thee I grow mature
> In knowledge, as the gods who all things know; (803–4)

She curiously praises 'Experience' (807), personified as though a mentor or guide who has led her out of 'ignorance' (809) to wisdom, yet that wisdom does not preclude her using 'perhaps' twice in the space of three lines (811–13) as she wonders whether or not 'Our great forbidder' (815) has seen her disobedience. Her adoption of the serpent's reductive vocabulary is taken further in the use of 'spies' (815) for angels, but Eve betrays the real effect of eating the fruit most shockingly in her questioning what she is to tell Adam. Instantly she perceives a dilemma which before eating would not have occurred to her. On the one hand she could tell Adam in order that he can share 'Full happiness with me' (819); on the other hand she could withhold the truth and 'keep the odds of knowledge in my power/Without copartner?' (820–1). Eve considers, in effect, exchanging love for superior knowledge, and the speed with which she adds a reason, 'the more to draw his love' (822), only serves to expose it as an afterthought.

For the first time she expresses a sense of inferiority, 'And render me more equal' (823), and ambition, 'sometime, Superior' (824–5), but her deduction that a hierarchy by definition negates freedom, 'for inferior who is free?' (825), is entirely fallacious. The questions reveal a growing uncertainty as well as the onset of an impulsive jealousy:

> Then I shall be no more
> And Adam wedded to another Eve,
> Shall live with her enjoying, I extinct;
> A death to think. (827–30)

The caesura marks the moment of her appallingly selfish decision to ensure Adam shares her fate, whatever it may be, 'Adam shall share with me in bliss or woe' (831), all signs of the wisdom only moments before she was so proudly exhibiting, gone. It is worth noting as well the final two lines of this section since they will be so poignantly echoed by her husband:

> So dear I love him, that with him all deaths
> I could endure, without him live no life. (832–3)

Adam's Free Will

As in the moments after Eve has tasted the fruit, Milton opts for an interior monologue to detail Adam's first thoughts on learning that Eve has disobeyed God. The reversal in their joint fate is captured in the build-up to this monologue by his symbolic dropping of the garland of flowers he had made to crown her with and its instant withering, 'and all the faded roses shed' (893). That motif is picked up by Adam in his first thoughts where Eve becomes a perfect creature 'on a sudden lost' (900). Adam apostrophises Eve as 'the last and best/Of all God's works' (896–7) and lists her good qualities before asking himself what looks like the most pertinent question:

> How art thou lost, how on a sudden lost,
> Defaced, deflowered, and now to death devote! (900–1)

but which is in effect a statement of incontrovertible fact. The harshly alliterative line sounds almost as though Milton designed it to be quoted. His language contrasts starkly with that used by the serpent and Eve, 'transgress' (902) and 'violate' (903) evoking the gravity of her fault while the fruit itself is 'sacred' (904). Adam then makes the most revealing of deductions, 'Some cursèd fraud/Of enemy hath beguiled thee, yet unknown' (904–5), not just because it is correct, but because it exposes the depth of his love for Eve. Given the accuracy and subtlety of their marital conversations this far, you could be forgiven for expecting Adam to launch into either anger, blame or both, but Milton invests his first man with immense generosity and civility. His assumption is that Eve has been tricked. His second assumption appears equally generous:

> And me with thee hath ruined, for with thee
> Certain my resolution is to die; (906–7)

The highly organised use of sound and rhythm of these two lines provides a strong example of Milton's poetic skill at work. The rhyme between 'me and 'thee', and that between the stressed syllable of 'ruined' and resolution' (picked out here in bold), glue the two lines tightly together, while the tight enjambment from 'thee' to 'Certain' forces the reader to pause before 'my' and puts all the stress on the dire consequences and immutability of Adam's decision.

It is clearly Adam's love for Eve that drives this decision and he cannot imagine replacing her even 'Should God create another Eve' (911). Yet what seems initially noble and generous, even touching, is fraught with difficulty. He calls Eve 'flesh of my flesh,/Bone of my bone' (914–15), but this is an overt anachronism and Eve is a separate being with a free will, and Adam's will is every bit as free as hers. A valuable topic for discussion is to consider all the options open to Adam at this point, particularly given the easily overlooked fact that he has not fallen and remains completely free to obey or disobey God. But as he reaches the end of this interior monologue, it is clear Adam has gone beyond the point where he understands this himself, 'from thy state/Mine never shall be parted, bliss or woe' (915–16). The narrator steps in for a moment with another helpful simile that conveys simultaneously Adam's demeanour and the reality of his state:

> So having said, as one from sad dismay
> Recomforted, and after thoughts disturbed
> Submitting to what seemed remediless,
> Thus in calm mood his words to Eve he turned. (917–20)

Obvious though it may seem, Adam's mind is made up before he ever speaks to Eve, removing her from any further accusations of influence and therefore blame.

Considering the words he chose to praise Eve with in his opening apostrophe (896–9), Adam is more objective now, calling her 'adventurous Eve' (921) and addressing her in terms more appropriate for a heroic figure returning from a quest. It is in this speech to Eve that Adam is faced with, and fails, his own test. Like Eve he runs through a list of rationalisations which we can extract here, although each will reward closer study. For example, at first he tells Eve what she has done cannot be changed either by God or fate. Is this in fact true? And if not, what does it imply about Adam's faith? He grasps at the hope that maybe Eve will not die because the serpent tasted the fruit first and may have lessened the crime, using the same conditional adverb Eve employed to bolster her desire, 'perhaps the fact/Is not so heinous now' (928–9). With no evidence beyond Eve's words, like her he views the serpent's survival as evidence that Eve too might live and follows the same ambitious route she took. If the serpent has gained a 'Higher degree of life' (934) then it follows that they too will win a 'Proportional ascent' (936), making them 'gods, or angels demigods' (937). Adam's choice of the phrase 'inducement strong' (934) is especially culpable since it is so radical a travesty of what he is really proposing: disobeying God.

Adam's determination to justify what he has already made up his mind to do, now extends to anticipating God, who he decides will not destroy them because to do so would destroy the natural world too, since it was 'For us created' (942). This would be 'Not well conceived of God' (945) since, although he could recreate everything, he would also be allowing Satan an opportunity to challenge his authority:

> lest the adversary
> Triúmph and say; Fickle their state whom God
> Most favours, who can please him long? Me first
> He ruined, now mankind; whom will he next? (947–50)

One has to admire Milton for the rational contortions Adam performs to reach the point where he is able to justify disobedience on the grounds that he is protecting God from Satan! When he finally ceases listing the various reasons why eating the fruit would be a good thing, or in other words justifying his disobedience, his use of the simple conjunction, 'However' (952), seems to dismiss it all as so much froth. At the heart of it all is his love for Eve. He adopts a heroic tone himself, 'if death/Consort with thee, death is to me as life' (553–4). We know from Book 2 (790–95) that Sin is Death's consort and so by wedding himself to Eve in this way Adam is embracing sin. In the end he makes the same crucial error he made earlier (914–15) in failing to perceive Eve as a separate being and maintaining himself as a free individual:

> Our state cannot be severed, we are one,
> One flesh; to lose thee were to lose myself. (958–9)

Before we leave this key moment in the poem, there is another aspect of Adam's thinking well worth your further thought. Is it love he is describing when he says the following?

> So forcible within my heart I feel
> The bond of nature draw me to my own,
> My own in thee, for what thou art is mine; (955–7)

The Immediate Aftermath of Sin

As on other occasions, Milton precedes a passage of speech (1134–89) with a comparison designed to set the atmosphere or tone, in this case it is a storm metaphor that dictates the way both Adam and Eve speak, conveyed in phrases like 'high winds' (1122) and 'tossed and turbulent' (1126), culminating in Adam's 'distempered breast' (1131). Adam's opening accusation takes them both back to the pivotal moment of their separation, now replete with irony since Adam's decision to eat the fruit was based on his belief that 'Our state cannot be severed, we are one' (958). The first thing that might strike you is how mundane and human Adam's complaint is. Gone is the intense thinking, the logical connection of ideas to form a single argument that both Adam and Eve employed in the build up to her departure. In its place is the simplest of complaints: I wish you had listened to me. Yet however mundane, Adam chooses some unpredictable words, describing Eve's departure as 'that strange/Desire of wandering' (1136), a word she challenges in her response, 'or will/Of wandering, as thou callst it' (1145–6). There is a hint of jealousy in the term and of weakness in his futile reminder, 'as I besought thee' (1135), and even comedy, 'I know not whence possessed thee' (1137), which is uncomfortably like 'I don't know what came over you', in our modern, colloquial equivalent. Resignation and bitterness permeate his whole speech as he seeks to draw a sententious conclusion from Eve's behaviour that sounds pitifully inadequate:

> Let none henceforth seek needless cause to approve
> The faith they owe; when earnestly they seek
> Such proof, conclude, they then begin to fail. (1140–2)

The last word, 'fail' (1142), like 'wandering', barely masks a barbed, personal criticism. Eve is quick to respond to the charge, dismissing it on the grounds that her separation was not the cause and that the same, miserable outcome might have taken place had she stayed. In the true spirit of marital conflict everywhere, she not only refutes the charge but issues one of her own, 'thou couldst not have discerned/Fraud in the serpent, speaking as he spake' (1149–50), adding that she had no reason to imagine his evil intent, 'No ground of enmity between us known' (1151). Eve's next, pragmatic question exemplifies how mundane this squabble is, 'Was I to have never parted from thy side?' (1153).

The charge Eve makes which is most likely to stimulate excitable debate is her accusation of weakness in Adam, 'Being as I am, why didst not thou the head/Command me absolutely not to go' (1155–6). One response might be to ask Eve what chance was there of her heeding

Adam when she failed so spectacularly to follow God's sole command. But building on her accusation, she insists not only did Adam fail to prevent her, but in fact he 'didst permit, approve, and fair dismiss' (1159), which is an interesting interpretation of the words they exchanged earlier (364–84). Eve closes the first round of this bruising encounter by hurling the blame fully back in Adam's face, telling him that had he 'been firm and fixed in his dissent' (1160) neither of them would have 'transgressed' (1161), a word noticeably absent from her interior monologue but precisely the one Adam chose in his, on learning she had eaten the fruit (902).

Milton tells us that this quarrel has intensified, 'To whom then first incensed Adam replied' (1162), and Adam's anger is evident both in his repetition, 'Is this the love, is this the recompense' (1163), and in the epithet he chooses, 'ingrateful Eve' (1164). Such is Adam's frustration, he is moved to remind Eve that, unlike her, he 'willingly chose rather death with thee' (1167), when he might have 'lived and joyed immortal bliss' (1166). The rhythm places considerable emphasis on the key fact coming at the end of the line, 'when thou wert lost, not I' (1165). For Adam it now seems infuriatingly unjust to have Eve accuse him of being 'the cause/Of thy transgressing?' (1168–9). In his 'Not enough severe,/It seems, in thy restraint' (1169–70) one can almost hear the mockery underneath the 'seems'. A caesura in subsequent lines (1169–70) breaks up any rhythm and fluency, rendering this part of Adam's speech, however poetic, startlingly close to credibly angry speech. 'What could I more?' (1170) he asks, almost in desperation before accurately listing the steps he took to try and persuade Eve to stay, using repetition as a vocal weapon:

> I warned thee, I admonished thee, foretold
> The danger, and the lurking enemy
> That lay in wait; (1171–3)

One charge Eve never refutes is Adam's claim that he passed on to her Raphael's warning about their enemy having entered Eden, and indeed if there is any scope for criticising the dramatic credibility of Milton's narrative, it may be that moment when Eve acts in ignorance of any such discussion or conversation and chats to a passing snake.

Yet Adam's most powerful rebuttal is his reminder to Eve that had he restrained her further 'this would have been by force,/And force upon free will hath here no place' (1173–4). It is central to Milton's entire theodicy that both Adam and Eve act freely and this study has identified numerous examples of where Milton exerts himself to weave this concept throughout the entire epic. Recalling their exchange in more detail, Adam reminds Eve that in the end she was supremely confident, and left his side expecting either not to encounter danger or, in the event, 'to find/Matter of glorious trial' (1176–7). This may be a particularly bitter pill for Eve to swallow, but it is a fair account of how she finally resolved their difference (330–6). Adam's fondness for Eve (synonymous with foolishness) is evident on a number of occasions, most significantly when the narrator, in the briefest of digressions, tells us:

> he scrupled not to eat
> Against his better knowledge, not deceived,
> But fondly overcome with female charm. (997–9)

That fondness Adam now regards as a culpable fault because it led to his

> overmuch admiring
> What seemed in thee so perfect, that I thought
> No evil durst attempt thee, (1178–80)

which in a moment of confession he calls 'my crime' (1181). It is clear from this that Adam has more to learn before he can begin the long journey back to redemption for himself and all mankind. Following a pattern set earlier (1140–2), from the specific case he tries to draw a sententious conclusion but only succeeds in making himself seem weaker and grudging. His 'Thus it shall befall' (1182) sounds weakly hollow and motivated more by shame than wisdom. Book 9 ends with the unedifying spectacle of the couple continuing their 'mutual accusation' (1187) endlessly, neither prepared to admit their essential guilt. And with somewhat surprising wit, Milton renders the scene even more pitiful with a pun on 'fruitless hours' (1188) that reaches right back to the book's opening lines and Eve's ardent interest in efficient gardening.

Exercises

Lines 179–204. In this brief interval before Adam and Eve are shown discussing how best to divide their labour, Satan finds and enters the serpent. How does Milton depict the serpent before and after its invasion by Satan?

Lines 385–566. One of the richest sections of the poem in terms of sensual description combined with classical allegory, Satan, disguised as a serpent, searches for Adam and Eve and is delighted when he discovers Eve alone. There is nothing rushed or cheaply dramatic about the way Milton handles the narrative here, and a lot of poetic effort goes into preparing Eve for the trial she and Adam agreed was inevitable. Read the section as a whole and consider how Milton couches Satan and Eve's entire encounter as a seduction. Look carefully at how Satan reacts to Eve and the various stages he moves through before she starts to speak to him.

Lines 613–78. The success of Satan's deceit is immediately evident as Eve asks the serpent to show her the tree which has had such a miraculous effect on him. Milton concentrates on the serpent's actions and behaviour in this short interlude before recommencing his temptation. How does this focus on Satan and impact on the dramatic tension?

Lines 834–95. In this relatively short episode, Adam encounters Eve on his way to find her, returning from the Tree with a branch laden with the fruit for him to eat. She explains that she has eaten the fruit and suggests Adam now does the same. That is a deliberately neutral precis of a moment in the epic which is loaded with dramatic significance and power. Read through it and consider carefully both the way Eve delivers her difficult message and the way Adam responds to it.

Lines 960–1133. Once Adam has vowed to endure the same fate as Eve, she expresses her delight in a way that shows she has herself taken all of Adam's reasoning as proof of his love. Man's love for God, his creator, has been noticeably absent throughout the temptation of Eve and beyond, so it should not surprise us that, once Adam too has eaten the fruit, Milton uses sex to seal their compact. There are two tasks which you can complete that will further your understanding of the poem considerably in this section. The first is to focus wholly on the narrator's voice and from it adduce the judgements the reader is encouraged to make about Adam and Eve's relative culpability. The second is to contrast the period immediately following Adam's eating of the fruit with the post-coital dawn when they both awake to face the real consequences of having disobeyed God.

10
Crime and Punishment

Summary

The angels protecting Adam and Eve return to heaven where God absolves them of any fault since he had foreseen man's fall and Satan's success. Addressing all the inhabitants of heaven he tells them not to despair and all that remains is for the judgement on Adam and Eve to be pronounced. He summons the Son to carry out the judgement for him and to act as man's mediator as well as their judge, since it is the Son who will save mankind by becoming man himself and dying on the cross. The Son accepts the task and his future role as saviour, saying he needs no one to accompany him, since the only two to be judged are Adam and Eve, Satan having escaped and the serpent being guiltless of any crime.

Adam and Eve hear the Son's voice in the garden but hide from him in shame until he calls to Adam and asks him what has changed that they do not greet him joyfully as before. Adam and Eve come from their hiding place, their appearances betraying their guilty, fallen state and their unresolved bitterness. Adam tells the Son he was ashamed to come out since he was naked and the Son asks him who told him this, and if he has eaten from the forbidden tree. Adam is torn between confession and blame, and in his defence says that, since God created Eve, he could not think anything she did could result in evil and so accepted the fruit from her hand. The Son asks him if Eve was his God that he felt he must obey her, and reminds him that Eve was made for love, not subjection, and that he was made her superior and it was his responsibility to act as her guide and protector. He next asks Eve what she has done and Eve replies simply and with none of the confident, determined loquaciousness she displayed with Adam, that she was deceived by the serpent and ate the fruit.

The Son then pronounces his judgement on the serpent and then on Eve, condemning her to pain in childbirth and subjugation to her husband. Adam is judged next, and the Son condemns him to a life of labour in the fields in order to feed himself and his children, telling them that death, though due, is merely postponed. Taking pity on them, he then clothes them in skins and with his grace, before he returns to heaven.

Meanwhile Sin and Death had observed earth from their place at hell's now wide open gate, and Sin thinks that Satan must have succeeded since he has not been returned to hell by God. She expresses her sense of growing power and attraction towards earth and suggests they now build a bridge together between earth and hell, across chaos. Death scents the vast numbers of prey now waiting for him on earth and urges her on, readily agreeing to help her in her task. Strengthened by the power given them through man's fall, they construct a broad and solid bridge between hell and earth, making it fast at each end with indestructible pins and chains. On the edge of chaos they encounter and recognise Satan, returning to hell after his success, and he rejoices at the sight of their new construction. Sin breaks the silence and tells him how she sensed his success and embarked on the creation of the bridge, stressing the inseparable bonds that unite him with her and their child, Death. She praises him as the new monarch of this new world, flattering him as the victor over God. Satan is triumphant and encourages Sin and Death to haste to Paradise and possess the earth, enthralling and ultimately killing man, while he hastes to celebrate his success with his companions in hell.

Satan finds hell near deserted, the sentinels vanished, and reaches the very throne of Pandaemonium without being noticed. At last his presence is felt and his counsel clamour to hear him speak. Satan, at his most boastful and triumphant, tells them he has succeeded beyond his dreams and is ready to lead them out of hell over the causeway made by Sin and Death, to possess their new realm. He describes earth and its rich beauty, whetting their appetite and mocking both man and God, the former for being tricked by an apple, the latter for punishing the guiltless serpent. As he awaits the expected uproar from his counsel, he is met by the disparaging sound of hissing from all sides and finds himself and all his companions transformed into serpents. They writhe out of the palace behind Satan who has been transformed into the largest serpent of all, where the remaining fallen angels witness the sight with horror and fear, even as they are themselves similarly transformed. Burning with thirst, they are lured to a grove of trees laden with delicious fruit, close by which they greedily eat, only to find themselves chewing on ashes.

Meanwhile Sin and Death reach earth and Sin asks Death what he thinks of their new realm. Death remarks that such is the vastness of his hunger, all places are alike to him, and, although earth seems rich with prey, it still seems too little. They then separate, Sin to corrupt mankind and Death to feed on all living things. Witnessing this, God explains how mistaken Satan, Sin and Death are in thinking themselves victorious because they are only parts of his plan to save mankind, renew the earth and close up hell forever on the last day. The angels sing his praises and then carry out tasks he sets them to change the physical conditions of the universe, such that it accords with the world we know. The natural world turns against itself and, through Sin's influence, the prelapsarian harmony Adam and Eve had enjoyed with nature is replaced by a world of predators and prey.

Adam's new found conscience leads him to voice misery and despair at the sight of all the ruin and misery he has caused and he struggles to find the justice in what has happened, seeing only a future full of pain and suffering, not just for him but for all his descendants. He finds himself unable to understand the nature of death and wonders whether this misery is now eternal, concluding eventually that on him and him alone rests all the blame. Finding him lying on the cold ground, wishing for death, Eve attempts to comfort him but he rejects her angrily, calling her a serpent and predicting all kinds of pain and suffering that man will suffer in future at the hands of woman. Eve falls to his feet and begs him not to forsake her, pleading for his forgiveness, accepting that though he may have offended God, she has offended him and God. At the sight of her distress Adam relents and his anger wanes.

Adam advises patience and hopes that, perhaps through the remnants of their love, they can at least share in each other's misery and lighten each other's suffering. Eve then raises the possibility of their preventing the suffering of their descendants by the taking of their own lives. Adam reminds her that it is impossible to escape God's justice and such actions would not only be futile but demonstrate pride and continued disobedience. Seizing on the Son's kindly judgement and his words pertaining to the serpent, he suggests that they should now seek God's help through prayer and penitence. Adam and Eve then return to the place of judgement and, falling on their knees, beg God's forgiveness, confessing all their faults humbly and contritely.

Adam and Eve Face God

One potential confusion to remove before we undertake an analysis of the highly significant meeting between God, and Adam and Eve (103–62) is precisely who it is Adam and Eve are talking to. During the heavenly council which opens the book, all three persons of the holy trinity are differentiated and God directly addresses his Son before sending him to Eden to pronounce judgement. 'Mercy colleágue with justice' (59) is how God describes it. From the point at which we pick up our analysis of the poem, when the Son arrives in the garden and seeks out Adam and Eve, God has reassumed a single, divine identity and speaks as one being, while Adam and Eve address him as such.

Milton builds on the bare, factual account to be found in Genesis (3:9), 'Then the LORD God called to Adam and said to him, "Where *are* you?"', so that from the outset the focus is on the relationship between man and God. Used to Adam's eager greeting, 'wont with joy to meet/My coming seen far off?' (103–4), God is not of course surprised, but the loss of love is observed and felt, 'I miss thee here,/Not pleased' (104–5). The chain that binds creator and created appears broken, so that 'where obvious duty erewhile appeared unsought' (106), God now has to search for Adam. Milton's choice of 'obvious' implies ingratitude and immediately reminds Adam and Eve of the duty they have so dramatically failed to meet. God's first question, 'Where are you?', is entirely reasonable because practical, but his next two questions, 'What change has taken place?' and 'What event has detained you?', seem close to taunts because he links them directly to an implied third question, 'Am I any different?', 'Or come I less conspicuous' (107). The very idea that God could be 'less conspicuous' sounds like irony which makes this whole dialogue a challenge for critics keen to attack Milton's God as an Old Testament tyrant.

When Adam and Eve do appear, Eve is the more reluctant, 'more loath' (109), but Milton quickly places them on an equal footing in terms of guilt by adding 'though first/To offend' (109–10). Adam was merely second to offend. There is no suggestion that he is in any way less culpable here. Guilt undermines their looks and demeanour, 'discount'nanced both, and discomposed' (110), the repetition of the harsh prefix, as well as the contrasting stress patterns in the verbs, combine to create a strikingly inharmonious line that suits the discomfort of their situation. The absence of love already noted is now spelled out, 'Love was not in their looks, either to God/Or to each other' (111–12), before Milton looses a battery of devastating nouns against them, linked by a repeated 'and' to reinforce our sense of their shame and loss. Each of those nouns will repay your consideration, but in the interests of brevity I have chosen only the last, 'guile' (114). Apart from its clever aural proximity to 'guilt', ending line 112, it is last because it is the chief characteristic Adam will display when he finally speaks to God.

Milton's fine sense of poetic antithesis and balance is clear in the single sentence that introduces Adam's speech, 'Whence Adam faltering long, thus answered brief' (115). Adam's first words lack guile and are poignantly simple and pathetic, contrasting dramatically with the eloquence he displayed before the Fall, 'I heard thee in the garden, and of thy voice/Afraid, being naked, hid myself' (116–17). This is a pitiful change from the divine ambition he displayed with Eve in their discussion before eating the fruit. The mercy God has preordained from his Son is there in 'The gracious judge, without revile' (118) and in the pure logic of his three questions which seek first for an explanation of Adam's newly discovered fear, next for his shame, before finally and directly asking Adam if he has disobeyed God's sole command. It is here that Adam's new found guile exhibits itself. The first sentence of Adam's answer is typically Miltonic, lengthy and complex (125–36). The second is much shorter and simpler (137–43), but both display the effects of the Fall dramatically.

He begins with an exclamation, 'O heaven!' (125), that seems to appeal to the only figures who might sympathise or intercede on his behalf: the angels themselves. Even before admitting to the crime, Adam recognises his status as a criminal before God, in acknowledging he is standing 'Before my judge' (126). But he then presents himself as facing an agonising dilemma. He can either 'undergo/Myself the total crime' (126–7) or 'accuse/My other self, the partner of my life' (127–8). Does he describe Eve as 'My other self' in an attempt to make his imminent accusation against her less deplorable? The choice he speculates on that he faces portrays him as generous or selfless in taking on himself all the guilt instead of accusing Eve. Equally curious is his belief that it is morally correct to protect Eve:

> Whose failing, while her faith to me remains,
> I should conceal, and not expose to blame
> By my complaint; (129–31)

This fallacious choice he finally abandons under 'strict necessity' (131) 'and calamitous constraint' (132) because he does not wish to endure all the blame and all the punishment. His only admirable moment in this speech is his accepting all such speculation is futile since, whatever he might attempt to conceal, God 'Wouldst easily detect' (136). But then we come to the second, briefer sentence in which Adam finally confesses. Understanding the structure of the sentence helps appreciate its shocking effect, and it is one of those sentences where there is considerable space between the subject and its operative verb. This looks like 'This **woman**... **gave** me of the tree, and I did eat' (137–43). Eve has become the derogatory 'This woman', and between subject and verb Adam interjects a stream of excuses. He even comes close to blaming God, since it was God who created Eve 'to be my help' (137) and made her 'so good,/So fit, so acceptable, so divine' (138–9) that he was unable to imagine anything she did could lead to evil, 'That from her hand I could suspect no ill' (140). This last claim is especially ignominious since it is untrue. Milton went to some trouble to convey the instantaneous dismay and despair that incapacitated Adam when he realized Eve had disobeyed God (IX, 888–95).

God's measured and detailed response (145–56) retains his merciful tone but also exposes starkly the precise nature of Adam's sin, disobedience: 'Was she thy God, that her thou didst obey/before his voice' (145–6). But God exposes Adam's sin further, explaining very clearly that whatever Eve may have done, Adam was her 'Superior' (147) and that his 'perfection far excelled/Hers in all real dignity' (150–1). The diction and tone throughout this speech, though gravely judgemental, is never harsh and there is nothing the least rhetorical in what God says about Adam's failure to govern Eve:

> Adorned
> She was indeed, and lovely to attract
> Thy love, not thy subjection, (151–3)

At the close, God reiterates for Adam the precise nature of his error. It is as Raphael had cautioned him: a failure to discern between emotion and reason in his response to Eve, 'hadst thou known thyself aright' (156). God turns to Eve and asks simply, 'Say woman, what is this which thou hast done?' (158).

The contrast between Adam and Eve's confessions is one of the most dramatic shocks in the poem. The narrator intervenes for a moment to describe Eve's pitiful state, 'sad Eve, with shame nigh overwhelmed' (159), and to stress she is neither 'Bold or loquacious' (161). Then Eve, whose loquaciousness and grace entranced Adam before the Fall, utters the few, but admirably truthful, words, 'The serpent me beguiled, and I did eat' (162).

Sin and Death Forge a Bridge to Earth

After God's brief and clinical sentencing of Adam and Eve, the story-teller's age old 'Meanwhile' (229) reintroduces the key characters from Book 2, where Satan had left Sin and Death sitting hungrily by the wide open gates of hell. Sin is first to speak and she questions their still waiting for Satan's return while he 'thrives/In other worlds' (236–7). It's difficult to resist at least noting the irony of Sin calling Satan 'our great author' (236), but more plangent is her describing them both as 'his off-spring dear?' (238), which situates Satan as their provider and earth their prey. Sin is sure Satan has succeeded because, had he failed, by this time God and the angels would have driven him back to hell, 'since no place like this/Can fit his punishment, or their revenge' (241–2). Suffused with a sense of burgeoning power, Sin feels her 'Wings growing' (244) and anticipates a 'dominion given me large/Beyond this deep' (244–5). Her sense of being drawn by 'sympathy, or some connatural force' (246) is ironically a command from God, not Satan, since she and Death now figure centrally in the fate of all mankind. Sin produces a memorable epithet for Death, calling him 'Thou my shade/Inseparable' (249–50), before she suggests they both begin the work of building a bridge across chaos to earth, 'a path/Over this main from hell to that new world' (256–7). Her entirely pragmatic reason is that Satan may not be able to find his way back 'over this gulf/Impassable, impervious' (253–4) and she uses the same alliterative pattern at the start of a line, which we have noted before is a feature of Satan's own language. This path or bridge she regards not just as a practical means by which she, Death and indeed 'all the infernal host' (259) will be able to reach earth 'as their lot shall lead' (261), but (dutiful daughter that she is) as 'a monument/Of merit high' (258–9) to her victorious father. Again Milton exploits the irony of Sin's misplaced sense of her growing power coming from Satan, 'this new-felt attraction and instinct' (263), when it is God's will that is drawing her earthwards 'so strongly' (262).

Allegory, which is in essence a metaphor so extended, now becomes a story in itself, though it has conventionally been regarded as a lesser form than the epic. Some readers see the personification of Sin and Death as detracting from the epic tone of the whole poem but, in passages like this, it is difficult to sustain that criticism. Milton exerts himself to humanise Adam and Eve, and his personification of Sin and Death as incestuous monsters, born out of Satan's rebellion, is a power-ful counterpoint to that. It's wonderfully evident in the way Death, 'the meagre shadow' (264), now responds to his mother. He exudes a terri-ble confidence, 'I shall not lag behind, nor err/The way, thou leading'

(266–7). There is an audible savouring in the sound of his chosen words, 'such a scent I draw/Of carnage, prey innumerable' (267–8). When he ends with a promise to 'afford thee equal aid' (271) in constructing the path, we feel his cooperation with Sin will hardly end there.

Like the dreadful predator he is, he then sniffs the air, 'with delight he snuffed the smell/Of mortal change on earth' (272–3), the less common verb 'snuff' cleverly emphasizing his deadly function through its link to the candle light ubiquitous in Milton's world. The extended simile which follows, of scavenging birds scenting the thousands of corpses on the eve of a battle, is not original but in Milton's hands becomes terrifying. The birds become 'ravenous fowl' (274), the pun matching Death's careful characterization. He uses rhythm to create a generous pause before the most potent verb 'lured' (276), giving it even greater emphasis than it already has by merit of its long vowel sound. There is a subtle interplay of sound in the 'scent of living carcasses designed/For death' (277) and a harsh finality to the placing and short stress that ends the simile, 'in bloody fight' (278). One has the sense that Milton relished his subject matter. Captivated by the image he has created of Death scenting death, he repeats it in a highly visual, baroque way, 'So scented the grim feature, and upturned/His nostril wide into the murky air' (279–80), picturing Death in an ecstasy of anticipation, 'Sagacious of his quarry from so far' (281).

Sin and Death Reap the Rewards of Satan's Success 585–615

After the dramatic bathos of Satan's triumphant return to hell, Milton turns to the pathos of earth's despoliation by Sin and Death (585–615). This is comparatively quite a short passage but its significance is considerable. The tragedy of Sin and Death's arrival on earth is conveyed by the understated phrase, 'Too soon arrived' (586). A good example of ellipsis occurs here and one which helps to explain why poets use it. 'Sin there in power before,/Once actual, now in body' (586–7) is terse to the point of incomprehension, but with a little thought it yields its fairly obvious meaning. Before Adam and Eve ate the fruit, Sin was only a potential presence but, now that they have acted, actually eaten the fruit, sin is a reality and, in keeping with Milton's allegorical strategy, a body present here on earth. You can see how much more elegant is Milton's expression of the idea. Similarly, consider the richness of meaning compressed within the alliterative and witty line opening, 'Habitual habitant' (588).

When Sin addresses Death, who is as ever 'Close following pace for pace' (589), she relishes the prospect before them, and again begins a line with an alliterative phrase, 'Second of Satan sprung' (591). When you study Milton in depth, a poet whose early education was entirely dominated by classical Greek and Latin, you should be able to observe and comment on the often astonishing skill he displays in terms of verse construction. Sin's little speech here is a perfect example. If you read it aloud with the aim of articulating its meaning clearly and fully to the listener, connections and patterns you may not have seen when reading silently should emerge. Look, for example, at the internal rhyme, 'thou' and 'now' (592), and the way that the rhythm of her speech and sound binds 'all-conquering Death' (591) to 'travail difficult' (593). It is impossible to read her speech effectively without a generous pause after 'difficult' which, combined with Milton's favourite use of the negative prefix 'Unnamed, undreaded' (595), invites the reader to wallow in the latter half of the speech. No part of this speech lacks interest as verse, so when you look at the superficially simple 'and thyself half starved?' (595) you should hear the subtle shift between 'self' and 'half' and the alliterative 's' effect in 'self' and 'starved'.

Death's response is every bit as chilling and tragic as his mother's speech when read as part of the lengthy, complex narrative of *Paradise Lost*, and not in isolation. The dreadful paradox that confronts Death is the realisation that not 'hell, or Paradise, or heaven' (598) can ever satisfy his infinite hunger. 'There best, where most with ravin I may meet' (599) is another fine example of Milton's prosodic skill at work. The unusual word 'ravin' (599) might cause you some hesitation and it implies a violent robbery, or seizure of goods or prey, but note how subtly the first half of the line rhymes, 'There best, where most', and how the 'm' sound is carried through to the line's end at 'may meet', pulling the whole line tightly together as a single unit. Although Death sees plenty to prey upon, 'all too little seems/To stuff this maw, this vast unhidebound corpse' (600–1). The hyperbole is highly effective and the coined word 'unhidebound' adds to the horror by making Death's conventionally emaciated skin grotesquely loose and detached through the addition of Milton's favourite negative prefix.

The consequences for all life and for mankind are spelled out finally by Sin as she invites her son to 'Feed' (604) on all livings things in a rising scale starting with 'herbs' (602) and ending with 'man' (607). And although we may find the image of all flora and fauna being mown down by 'The scythe of time' (606) distressing, how much more so is the notion of Sin 'residing through the race' (607) so insidiously that she will 'His thoughts, his looks, words, actions all infect' (608). All this for love of her monstrous son, 'And season him thy last and sweetest prey' (609).

Inseparable till this moment of triumph, Sin and Death now separate to wreak the havoc Satan promised them and Milton stresses once more the immense loss the Fall has brought about for mankind through adding 'unimmortal' to 'destroy' (611), spelling out that, though all things now die, 'for destruction to mature/Sooner or later' (612–13), mankind has lost immortality too. There is a sense in which *Paradise Lost* is a poem that fluctuates between extremes: Satan's discovery on the floor of hell is followed by his epic journey to Paradise; Adam and Eve's blissful love is exchanged for cruelty and bitter loneliness; and now, after the tragic sight of Sin and Death's despoliation of the earth, what is arguably the poem's nadir, we are treated to God's omnipotent reassurance.

God's Promise of Salvation 616–40

Witnessing Sin and Death's dispersal on earth, God addresses the entire host of heaven and makes sense of this apparently wilful act of devastation by foretelling Man's ultimate triumph over evil through Christ's Incarnation and Death on the cross. God's pronouncement (616–40) consists of one challengingly Miltonic sentence of twenty-one lines and an unusually brief sentence of three lines. God invites his listeners, the reader among them, to witness the destruction, 'See with what heat these dogs of hell advance/To waste and havoc yonder world' (616–17). Ellipsis helps make the most of the alliteration so that the conventional 'lay waste' or 'make havoc' are abandoned. Milton leaves no room for ambiguity as God asserts that the world would have remained 'fair and good' (618) were it not for 'the folly of man' (619). No distinction is implied here between Adam and Eve, 'man' standing for the race and not the individual. More significantly God refutes absolutely the claim made by 'these wasteful furies' (620) and Satan that this disaster is the result of his folly. The 'furies' (620) or Eumenides (which ironically translates as 'the kindly ones') were the ancient Greek goddesses of vengeance, portrayed as grotesque and frightening female figures intent on punishing the guilty.[1] The key to unpicking the structure of this lengthy sentence is to recognise that God is the main subject and the chief object is 'the prince of hell/And his adherents' (621–2), specifically Sin and Death. God contrasts those actions which are consciously his with the false interpretations put on them by Satan, Sin and Death. Each of the three separate uses of the personal pronoun 'them' that occurs is a reference to Sin and Death directly, but Satan is implied too, and in the second part of the sentence it is Sin and Death who 'know not that I called and drew them hither' (629).

Sin and Death are mistaken in imagining that God connived, 'quitted' (627) or 'yielded' (628) anything to them, and there is even an element of God mocking them for their mocking him in the simile he employs to describe their laughter, 'That laugh, as if transported with some fit/Of passion' (626–7). In a dramatic reversal of the Satanic narrative, God claims Sin and Death as his own, 'My hell-hounds' (630), assigning to them the duty of cleaning up the mess Adam and Eve have bequeathed mankind through their sinful disobedience. In an image that is redolent of Greek tragic drama, and which sustains the imagery of hunger and greed that surrounds Sin and Death, God invites us to picture them as they 'lick up the draff and filth/Which man's polluting sin with taint hath shed' (630–1). The relatively neutral phrase, 'On what was pure' (632), ends with a distinct caesura followed by a sequence of long vowel sounds which force the reader to dwell on the horrors they convey, accentuating the greed and grossness proper to Sin and Death, 'till crammed and gorged, nigh burst/With sucked and glutted offal' (632–3).

The sentence comes to a close with an even more baroque picture of the Son stopping up 'the mouth of hell' (636) forever with the corpses of Sin and Death: 'and yawning grave' (635) as with one gesture, 'at one sling/Of thy victorious arm' (633–4), he hurls them 'Through chaos' (636) at the end of time.

The second sentence takes us beyond that final, immense act of revelation and, in calmer tones, God promises that 'heaven and earth renewed shall be made pure' (638) indefinitely and immutably 'To sanctity that shall receive no stain' (639); but this vision, he reminds us, is some way off, and 'Till then the curse pronounced on both precedes' (640). The slight word 'both' embraces the vastness of heaven and earth as well as the individual tragedies of Adam and Eve, and it is given divine force through the connected sound of 'pronounced' and 'precedes'.

God's grand design revealed, in one of the most astrologically dense passages of the poem, Milton next describes how the stars, seasons and motion of the earth relate to one another, before turning to the changed relationship between other living creatures. For the first time we hear of prey and predator, and of the terror man's presence creates in what was formerly a landscape imbued with harmony and joy. Nothing living escapes the consequences of Adam and Eve's original sin.

Adams Grieves Alone

Alone and intensely troubled with shame and guilt, Adam voices his feelings in another interior monologue of some length and complexity (719–844). His opening complaint is riddled with paradox, 'miserable of happy!' (720), 'Accursed of blessed' (723), but he also links his personal tragedy to that of the world around him, 'Is this the end/Of this new glorious world' (720–1). In an echo of his last encounter with God, he exhibits the same intense shame which drives him to hide his face. What previously was his greatest happiness, his relationship with his creator, is now his greatest misery. It is important to appreciate that Adam's misery extends far beyond self-pity or personal guilt. He knows that by his action he has brought death and ruin to all things in Paradise and to all the generations that will follow him. That is a truly appalling prospect and one Milton exerts himself to convey. When the thought of suicide or at least death as some kind of release strikes Adam, 'yet well, if here would end/The misery' (725–6), he is immediately stung by the knowledge that even that won't serve to undo the curse he is doomed to pass on:

> ...but this will not serve;
> All that I eat or drink, or shall beget,
> Is propagated curse. (727–9)

A caesura emphasises the terribly irony, 'Oh voice once heard/ Delightfully, *Increase and multiply*' (729–30). On one level Milton is dramatising Adam's tale for us in an intensely human, sympathetic fashion, but on another level he is rattling the chain that binds us, the reader, to Adam and his sin, 'For what can I increase/Or multiply, but curses on my head?' (731–2). Adam imagines what future generations will say of his eating the fruit, 'Ill fare our ancestor impure' (735). A phrase which is truly elegant in its use of subtle, internal rhyme.

In an image that plays almost too cleverly with ideas of rejection and backward flow, 'all from me/Shall with a fierce reflux on me redound' (738–9), Adam tries to articulate the extremity of his despair whilst simultaneously acknowledging his guilt through another extreme paradox, the oxymoronic 'light/Heavy' (740–1). Heavy though the generations' curses might be, they alight 'on their natural centre' (740), Adam. Milton continues to put Adam through a series of inner torments, making him turn for a moment on God and complain that he never asked to be created or to be given Paradise, 'this delicious garden?' (746). Using his gift for logic, he decides that since he had no say in his making, 'As my will/Concurred not to my being' (746–7), it is only right that God 'reduce me to my dust' (748) and lets him repay willingly all he gained because he has found the deal too dear by far:

> ... unable to perform
> Thy terms too hard, by which I was to hold
> The good I sought not. (750–2)

The imagery Adam draws on here, from commerce and the law, pulls us into the dilemma with him, perhaps because Milton wished to pull us up as shortly as he does Adam when he admits, 'yet to say truth, too late,/I thus contest' (755–6). If we recall the deal God made with Adam, his request that the fruit of one tree, in the whole vastness of Paradise, remain inviolate, untouched, because to disobey would bring ruin, Adam's 'terms too hard' take on a very different perspective.

Adam's tormented diatribe against his creator steps up a pace when he asks 'why hast thou added/The sense of endless woes?' (753–4) to what seemed the 'Sufficient penalty' (753) of his death, and it reaches its climax with the hastily withdrawn statement, 'Inexplicable/Thy justice seems' (754–5). Adam's sudden use of 'Thou' (757) for himself might cause some confusion, but he is still caught up in his own logic, trying to work his way through the despair with what reason he can still summon, and so he takes on the role of an imaginary second party, challenging his own views. He knows that he accepted God's gifts readily and joyfully and retains the legal imagery in the rhetorical question, 'wilt thou enjoy the good,/Then cavil the conditions?' (758–9). His slow progress on the arduous path to redemption begins when he shows signs of being able to empathise with his creator by asking a second rhetorical question which places him in the same position:

> ... And though God
> Made thee without thy leave, what if thy son
> Prove disobedient, and reproved, retort,
> Wherefore didst thou beget me? I sought it not: (759–62)

Not only does Adam name his own sin, disobedience, he rejects the theoretical objection as a 'proud excuse?' (764) using the most Satanic adjective of all.

Another caesura marks a dramatic change in Adam's thinking and two brief sentences underline the decisiveness which begins to characterise his shift in thinking and behaviour. The crucial difference Adam now recognises between God and himself as father is that between choice and necessity. Any son of Adam is the result of the latter while the essence of God's relationship with Adam is choice, 'God made thee of choice his own' (766); though, even more significantly in terms of Milton's theodicy, 'thy reward was of his grace,/Thy punishment then justly is at his will' (767–8). In the scales of justice he has been struggling to balance, Adam has finally placed the most essential condition of happiness, God's grace, and in so doing he has instantaneously grasped the essential justice of God's punishment. A series of unusually short phrases, punctuated by lengthy pauses, make Adam's acceptance clear: 'Be it so, for I submit, his doom is fair' (769), before he reproduces the curse from Genesis, 'That dust I am, and shall to dust return' (770).

However, his torment and despair still have some way to run and so he immediately asks himself why God has delayed the punishment. In other words, having accepted the justice of the punishment, why is he still alive? Why does God seem to prolong his suffering? In harmony with suicidal figures throughout literature,[2] Adam imagines death as a blessed release, 'How gladly would I meet/Mortality my sentence' (775–6), and the earth becomes an image of his missing parent, his mother, 'how glad would lay me down/As in my mother's lap!' (777–8). That release would remove forever not just the fear of an unknown future for him and his children, but, more poignantly, 'his dreadful voice no more/Would thunder in my ears' (770–80). God's voice and presence had formerly been Adam's greatest joy but in the depths of his shame and guilt it is turned into something to be shunned and terrified by.

Adam's continuing logic takes him now into pure metaphysical speculation. Unlike Hamlet, whose infamous 'To be or not be' fear of suicide stems from the pure unknown,[3] Adam's stems from a fear that the 'pure breath of life' (784) that God literally breathed into him, 'Which God inspired' (785), may not die with his physical body and that he might suffer 'a living death?' (788) trapped in 'the grave,/Or in some other dismal place' (786–7). In this way Milton manages to shift the ground from Adam's personal dilemma to mankind's and hence the Christian readers' spiritual health. What Adam is struggling to understand here is something Milton's readers would take for granted, that he has an immortal soul. Adam himself falls back on Raphael's lesson that there are some things simply beyond human comprehension, 'let this appease/The doubt, since human reach no farther knows' (792–3).

Milton exploits the irony he has created very skilfully in the next stage of Adam's interior monologue. While Adam ponders whether or not God's anger will last for all eternity, 'For though the Lord of all be infinite,/Is his wrath also?' (794–5), and struggles to equate that with his own mortality, the reader of course perceives the difference between Adam and hence mankind – and between Satan and his fallen associates. In this way Milton dramatises Adam's dilemma effectively, depicting him struggling to acknowledge his guilt and accept God's justice, while simultaneously lifting the reader above him in spiritual awareness and hence health. Adam's paradoxical question, 'How can he exercise/Wrath without end on man whom death must end?' (796–7), is an invitation to the reader to recall the sacrificial role of the Messiah and ultimately the possibility of redemption. While we can see Adam's weakness and failing, we are ourselves still free to choose the immortal life as yet denied him.

Finding a brief respite in the notion that God cannot undo his own natural laws, 'That were to extend/His sentence beyond dust and nature's law' (804–5), Adam suffers a new wave of despair when it occurs to him that what lies beyond the moment of death is still unknown:

> ... But say
> That death be not one stroke, as I supposed,
> Bereaving sense, but endless misery
> From this day onward, (808–11)

His emotional state is conveyed in the exclamatory 'Ay me' (813) and in the elegantly concise fear that 'both death and I/Am found eternal, and incorporate both' (815–16). It is there again where he shows the first glimmers of his own redemption in immediately thinking not of himself, but of the as yet unborn generations he is to father because

> ... in me all
> Posterity stands cursed: fair patrimony
> That I must leave ye, sons: Oh were I able
> To waste it all myself, and leave ye none! (817–20)

Gone are the lengthy, complex, rational sentences he exchanged with Raphael in Books 6 and 7, now replaced with terse outbursts of high emotion. Milton has also managed to maintain the legalistic imagery and tone through the idea of inheritance as well as the repeated use of paradox, 'So disinherited how would ye bless/Me now your curse!' (821–2).

Adam's persistent self-interrogation leads him to a number of significant conclusions which only serve to deepen his despair. All men, he believes, will inevitably inherit his fallen nature, 'both mind and will depraved' (825), and, if that is the case, how can they ever find justice, 'How can they then acquitted stand/In sight of God?' (827–8). He admits the fallacies of his own internal debate and makes the simple but powerful statement of guilt that he must do in order to fulfil God's will, 'Him after all disputes/Forced I absolve' (828–9). He dismisses his earlier thinking as 'evasions vain' (829) and 'mazes' (830) and affirms, not least through repetition, but also through the antithetical imagery he uses, that he and he alone is to blame, 'first and last' (831) he is 'the source and spring/Of all corruption' (832–3). The familiar alliterative line ending (832) adds weight to his conclusion and his selfless wish to endure all the punishment, 'all the blame lights due/So might the wrath' (833–4). A caesura gives Adam ample time to pause at this thought before rejecting it outright with another terse exclamation, 'Fond wish!' (834).

The reason why Adam rejects the idea of his bearing all God's wrath contains the only mention of Eve in this monologue and it is hardly a flattering one, to either party. Thinking of the vast scale of destruction their sin has brought into the world, 'That burden heavier than the earth to bear' (835), he finds it unimaginable that he could carry such a burden, even were he to share it with 'that bad woman?' (837). There is some way to go yet in the poem before Adam and Eve achieve the reconciliation that enables them to leave the garden hand in hand. Milton once more uses paradox to expose Adam's emotional state:

> ... Thus what thou desir'st
> And what thou fearst, alike destroys all hope
> Of refuge, and concludes thee miserable
> Beyond all past example and futúre, (837–40)

The only model Adam has to compare himself with is Satan, and so he decides, wrongly, that he is 'To Satan only like both crime and doom' (841). In both cases he is wrong. Whereas Satan chose rebellion, Adam was, in the crucial words God uses in Book 3, 'deceived':

> The first sort by their own suggestion fell,
> Self-tempted, self-depraved: man falls deceived
> By the other first: man therefore shall find grace,
> The other none: in mercy and justice both, (III, 129–32)

God's gift of grace to man places Adam and mankind on an entirely different footing to the eternal damnation reserved for Satan and his followers. The 'abyss of fears/And horrors' (842–3) into which Adam finds himself 'plunged!' (844), however dismal, is hardly to be compared with where we discovered Satan at the poem's opening. The monologue closes with the same exclamatory emotion that has permeated it throughout, coming to a dramatic end with another of Milton's artfully constructed clauses, 'from deep to deeper plunged!' (844).

Finding Adam in the state we have just left him, despairing and alone, Eve is at first bitterly rejected by him. The overt misogyny Adam exhibits will exercise many students educated under post-feminist legislation, but it really is important to understand Adam's predications about the future roles of husbands and wives in the light of Milton's era (888–908). Perhaps even in the light of his own complicated experience of marriage. When Eve tries a second time, falling in tears at his feet, claiming sole guilt and suggesting she will return to their place of judgement and plead with God to punish only her, Adam relents.

Eve Attempts to Frustrate Death

Adam's anger is finally neutralised by the suppliant figure of Eve, and when he next speaks it is 'with peaceful words' (946) that he admonishes her. Adam quietly gives Eve's wish to accept punishment its proper perspective. As formerly, she is both 'Unwary, and too desirous' (947) of things she does not understand. Her self-evident inability to cope with her own suffering and Adam's 'displeasure' (952) implies she is hardly likely to bear God's ire, 'His full wrath whose thou feelst as yet least part' (951). But though he makes her limitations clear, Adam does not mock Eve, instead moving closer to her ground by telling her that if prayer could have moved God, as she suggested (931–7), 'I to that place/Would speed before thee, and be louder heard' (953–4). In telling her this, he also reveals how much further than Eve he has travelled in understanding and acknowledging guilt:

> That on my head all might be visited,
> Thy frailty and infirmer sex forgiven,
> To me committed and by me exposed. (955–7)

At this moment Adam takes a major step in achieving reconciliation and bids Eve 'rise, let us no more contend, nor blame/Each other, blamed enough elsewhere' (958–9). Just as Christ will raise Mary Magdalene from his feet to hers, so Adam's action is equally symbolic of forgiveness. It is a moment that many readers find something of a relief after witnessing the emotional savaging Adam and Eve loose on each other.

Adam generously reminds Eve that, through their love, they may be able to lessen their suffering:

> ... but strive
> In offices of love, how we may light'n
> Each other's burden in our share of woe; (959–61)

He ends his speech with a flurry of alliteration which serves a joint purpose, giving his words greater force and closing down debate, as well as adding a lamentable tone that matches the fate they are consigning their children to, 'this day's death denounced' (962) and 'A long day's dying' (964) are the most noticeable examples; but Milton also produces the intensely compact 'And to our seed (oh hapless seed!) derived' (965), while using 'sudden' (963) to weld the dominant alliterative sounds together.

Adam's gentler words lift Eve's spirits sufficiently for her to now speak with greater calm, eloquence and palpable sincerity. Her first sentence is moderately lengthy by Milton's standards, but is nonetheless extremely complex and is well worth rereading in its entirety in order to master the structure. The fulcrum around which the sentence balances is 'nevertheless' (970). In its first half Eve acknowledges the weakness of her position in attempting to persuade Adam to any course of action and, in the second, she asserts her determination not to hide her thoughts. In recognising that her words are unlikely to impress Adam, since her earlier, successful attempt at persuasion led to such disaster, Eve also accepts the justice of God's punishment, 'by just event/Found so unfortunate' (969–70). The repetition of the phrase 'Found so' (969–70) connects her former eloquence directly with their downfall and begins Eve's own journey to a better life. She also acknowledges Adam's generosity when she contrasts his restoration of her immediately with her own opinion of herself, 'vile as I am' (971). There are also the faintest glimmers of a rekindled love when she adds to her 'place/Of new acceptance' (971–2) the idea that it is incumbent on her to earn Adam's love, 'hopeful to regain/Thy love, the sole contentment of my heart' (972–3).

Having prepared the way, Eve continues tentatively. Whether she lives or dies, with or away from Adam, she is determined to share the thoughts that trouble her 'unquiet breast' (975). Those thoughts, she believes, may offer them some escape or relief from the misery they currently endure, 'Tending to some relief of our extremes' (976). It may be that Milton deliberately constructed Eve's words here in an opaque way because what she is ultimately suggesting is shocking and indeed wicked to the Christian sensibility of the period. For Milton's readers all children were a blessing and suicide is simply a sin. Some of that opacity might be relieved if you connect the phrase 'Or end' (977) with the earlier 'I will not hide' (974) so that Eve is saying she isn't going to hide either her thoughts or the end that might result from those thoughts. That 'end' may be 'sharp and sad' but it may also be 'tolerable' (976), given the miserable situation they face, 'As in our evils' (978), and, ultimately, an 'easier choice' (978).

Eve's next sentence (979–88) is also quite opaque but its structure is less complex, being chiefly a simple proposition broken by a lengthy parenthesis. Eve asks Adam if his feelings concur with hers, 'If care of our descent perplex us most' (979), and if, being the cause of so much misery to their descendants, then he should consider that

> ... in thy power
> It lies, yet ere conception to prevent
> The race unblest, to being yet unbegot. (986–8)

Typically Milton opts for the negative prefix to maximise impact and the alliterative play is obvious. The parenthesis is also richly alliterative: 'devoured/By death' (980–1), 'miserable ... misery' (981–2), 'begotten ... bring' (983), 'world a woeful' (984) and 'food for so foul' (986). Eve expresses her dismay at the thought that they must bring into the world a race of beings destined for death, sententiously noting that 'miserable it is/To be to others the cause of misery' (981–2) and exploiting the image he has carefully built up of Death as a 'monster' (986).

If up to this point she has been circumspect, then here Eve makes it very clear what she is proposing, 'Childless thou art, childless remain' (989), and there may even be a hint of them beginning to fight back in her image of Death: 'deceived his glut, and with us two/be forced to satisfy his rav'nous maw' (990–1). It's rarely possible, or indeed valuable, to speculate realistically about a poet's choice of specific words, but in this case we are almost invited to ask the question why Milton didn't choose the more obvious verb 'denied'? One possible answer may lie in the underlying idea of 'conception', which would make 'deceived' the natural or more appropriate choice.

As Eve shares more of her own mind with Adam, Milton uses rhythm quite brilliantly to underscore her words and reinforce her argument. What happens here is qualitatively different from the rhetoric and oratory we have heard elsewhere in the poem, making Eve seem intensely human and sympathetic. If you read the next sentence she speaks

(992–1006) as a single unit, focusing on the rhythm, you will find it impossible not to be led by the strong shifts and changes. The long stress on 'hard' and its marked contrast with the staccato 'difficult' (992) force the reader to dwell on the idea of arduousness itself before Eve's rhythm changes into a more languid list, 'Conversing, looking, loving' (993), that invites us to reflect on what is to follow. The perfectly equitable stress on each element of 'love's due rites' is set against the more fluent 'nuptial embraces sweet' (994), where the elision between the last two words entices the reader even as it does Adam. The sense of listless, timeless frustration Eve anticipates in an imaginary, sexless marriage is conveyed in the continued use of the sibilant sounds and longer stresses, 'And with desire to languish without hope' (995). And she is noticeably self-deprecating in her choice of the coldly practical image, 'the present object' (996), to describe herself, though Adam seems implied too. Milton rarely misses the opportunity to exploit a powerful word once he has found it and it isn't surprising therefore to see 'languishing' (996) immediately cropping up again, with almost onomatopoeic impact.

Rhythm isn't the only powerful feature of Eve's appeal. Knowing she is still far from reconciled in love with Adam, she manages gently to convey her own desire by assuming the frustration she anticipates in a sexless future is mutual, 'Before the present object languishing/With like desire' (996–7). Although she has reduced herself to a mere thing, the neutral term implies Adam, as well as signifying herself. Having created this image of a cold and loveless future for them both, she recapitulates it hyperbolically as 'misery/And torment less than none of what we dread' (997–8), before launching back into the thrust of her argument with renewed vigour, underscored by the sustained regular rhythm of 'Then both ourselves and seed at once to free/From what we fear for both' (999–1000). That regularity is broken by the more abrupt and shocking climax of the sentence, 'let us make short' (1000), with its two, final, long stresses and the repeated pattern in the next line, 'Let us seek death' (1001). Her most 'unquiet' (975) thought now laid bare, Eve ventures further and suggests that if they cannot find death then they should kill themselves, 'supply/With our own hands his office on ourselves' (1001–2).

In a final, passionate flurry, 'Why stand we longer shivering under fears' (1003), Eve poses the concomitant question. Why should they continue to suffer, knowing death is their ultimate end, when they can foreshorten their suffering through suicide? Her closing paradox may be a poetic gem, but it is also an audacious attempt at justifying the unjustifiable, 'Destruction with destruction to destroy' (1006).

Adam Advises Reconciliation with God

It would be a mistake to see anything manipulative or especially rhetor-ical in Eve's call for a suicide pact. Milton leaves it open as to whether or not she consciously completes her speech, or if 'vehement despair' (1007) terminates it for her, and depicts her turning pale from too much contemplation of death, 'so much of death/Her thoughts had enter-tained, as dyed her cheeks with pale' (1008–9). But when Adam responds it is without fear or passion and his calm decisiveness closes the book. Adam speaks in a measured way, without any of the rhythmical variety and force given to Eve.

His initial challenge to Eve is immediately turned into a compliment. Adam tells her that her 'contempt of life and pleasure' (1113) indicates she is really 'more sublime/And excellent' (1014–15) because it masks her true feeling, her 'anguish and regret/For loss of life and pleasure overloved' (1118–19). This is a long way from his earlier rejection of her as 'this fair defect/Of nature' (891–2) and is indicative of the 'better hopes his more attentive mind/Labouring had raised' (1011–12). Adam has begun to see a possible life for them rooted in the conditions of God's punishment. He gently rebukes Eve for thinking that death could be a way to avoid their punishment, telling her that

> ... doubt not but God
> Hath wiselier armed his vengeful ire than so
> To be forestalled; (1022–4)

It is a timely and rational reminder of their fundamental relationship with their maker. Not only does Adam understand the infinite range of God's omniscience, he fears that, were they to do as Eve suggests, in effect rebel against their just punishment, their act

> Of contumacy will provoke the highest
> To make death in us live: (1027–9)

His advice is to 'seek/Some safer resolution' (1029–30), which he then describes for Eve in detail. It is in this resolution that Adam displays the depth of his learning and the signs of sincere penitence that will lead to a tolerable future for them both on earth, and a restored relationship with God.

Adam has understood that God's reference to the serpent, and to Eve's children bruising the serpent's head, is metaphorical, and he sur-mises correctly that Satan, 'our grand foe' (1033), is the serpent. If it were meant literally, then in Adam's mind treading on a snake's head would be 'piteous amends' (1032). This leads him to sense the possibility of vengeance, 'to crush his head/Would be revenge indeed' (1035–6): a revenge they can never accomplish through suicide or childlessness. The critical element in Adam's understanding then follows because he reasons that if it were not as he surmises, then Satan would go unpunished, 'so our foe/Shall scape his punishment ordained' (1038–9), and he and Eve would suffer a double punishment.

Having reasoned this far, Adam closes down any further discussion with Eve, showing also that he has learned a bitter lesson from his earlier tolerance:

> No more be mentioned then of violence
> Against ourselves, and wilful barrenness,
> That cuts us off from hope, and savours only
> Rancour and pride, impatience and despite,
> Reluctance against God and his just yoke
> Laid on our necks. (1041–6)

In these few lines Milton has embedded perhaps the single most significant realisation in the entire poem. Adam's former disobedience is replaced by a humility and wisdom that can ironically now discern the truth. Adam understands Eve's suggestions as the weak and fearful choices that they are, and it is surely no accident that he cites Satan's identifying weakness, 'pride' (1044), among the sins such a course of action would involve. From this point it is possible for Adam to begin to paint some kind of future for Eve which is rooted completely in God's word. He reminds her how gently

> God delivered his judgement,
> Remember with what mild
> And gracious temper he both heard and judged
> Without wrath or reviling; (1046–8)

and then seeks out the good in what his faith and obedience tells him was God's wholly just pronouncement. Instead of 'Immediate dissolution' (1049) God foretold pain in childbirth to Eve but pain immediately 'recompensed with joy' (1052). To Adam he foretold 'with labour I must earn/My bread' (1054–5), but Adam reasons quite elegantly, 'what harm? Idleness had been worse' (1055).

Adam's course of action is now determined and continuing his education of Eve he points out that God has already begun generously to provide for this existence:

> ... his timely care
> Hath unbesought provided, and his hands
> Clothed us unworthy, pitying while he judged; (1057–9)

and then introduces the idea that, through prayer, they may gain even more:

> How much more, if we pray him, will his ear
> Be open, and his heart to pity incline, (1060–1)

This consideration of the conditions under which post-lapsarian life can be made tolerable are at the forefront of Adam's thinking and Milton dramatises this by having him observe the changing weather around them and note the onset of a more wintry climate. The natural world is made to suffer in harmony with them:

> ... while the winds
> Blow moist and keen, shattering the graceful locks
> Of these fair spreading trees; (1065–7)

while Adam speculates on how God might teach them to keep warm through the use of fire. He imagines himself using lenses or flint to kindle a fire and makes the connection himself between that and the natural fire caused by a lightning strike which 'Kindles the gummy bark of fir or pine' (1076). You might be puzzled by the unusual term 'Tine' (1075) to describe the lightning, but a 'tine' is the prong of a fork or antler and Milton has turned it into a verb to create the visual effect he wants.

Confident now in God's mercy, Adam envisages a liveable life forti-fied by prayer and crucially God's grace, 'sustained/By him with many comforts' (1084), ending at some distant time in their death, 'till we end/In dust, our final rest and native home' (1084–5). He has reached the final stage of his journey to penitence, full contrition, and urges Eve to join him as he seeks God's forgiveness at the very place where their judgement was made:

> What better can we do, than to the place
> Repairing where he judged us, prostrate fall
> Before him reverent, and there confess
> Humbly our faults, and pardon beg, (1086–9)

Gone is any vestige of pride or truculence. Adam sees them watering the ground with their tears and filling the air with their sighs, 'sent from hearts contrite' (1091), signifying the sincerity of their 'sorrow unfeigned, and humiliation meek' (1092). Sure of God's mercy, Adam tells Eve that God 'will relent and turn/From his displeasure' (1093-4), reminding her of their former, joyful relationship with God:

> When angry most he seemed and most severe,
> What else but favour, grace, and mercy shone? (1095-6)

In the last few lines of the book, Milton's narrator steps in to link us with Adam directly, 'our father penitent' (1097), and replays word for word the instructions Adam has just given Eve (1099-1104), reaffirming their contrition and leading the way ultimately to the possibility of redemption.

Exercises

Lines 1-102. Book 10 opens with a clearly worded summary of events and the divine design of which they form a part. The narrative picks up again with the angels returning to heaven where the news of the Fall is greeted with sadness and sympathy, before God sends his Son to Eden to pronounce judgement on Adam and Eve. When you read through this section, ensure you have a clear understanding of the relationship that God outlines between the Fall, Christ's sacrifice and man's ultimate redemption.

Lines 163-228. As soon as Eve confesses, God proceeds to judgement, since her honesty requires nothing to match the correction he gave Adam. The judgement itself occupies little space in the poem and is closely linked to the account in Genesis. Read this section and make sure you understand the different ways in which the serpent, Eve and Adam are punished.

Lines 282-584. This is a lengthy and in many ways exciting section of the poem, and one well worth close inspection and analysis. Satan meets his grotesque children on his flight back to hell and, somewhat prematurely, bequeaths to them his newly conquered territory. But before dealing in any detail with the despoliation of the earth, Milton takes us back to hell with the triumphant Satan, parodying classical literary models of returning conquerors and dealing out to Satan and his followers the punishment decreed by God. Read through the section and ask yourself what effect the description of Satan's punishment, the hollowness of his triumph and subsequent torment all his followers endure has on you.

11
Loss of Paradise

ᢙ

Summary

Through the power of God's grace, Adam and Eve are able to feel penitent and pray for forgiveness. The Son intercedes for them, asking the Father to accept their prayers and to mitigate their punishment, letting him sacrifice himself for them and ultimately redeem those worthy of redemption. God immediately grants him this wish, reminding us that it was his decree already, but then tells the Son that Adam and Eve can no longer live in Paradise. Sin has corrupted them to such an extent that the pure, natural world of Paradise cannot stomach their presence and they must be cast out of Eden. The Son then summons all heaven's inhabitants for them to hear God's judgement too. The Father repeats his judgement on Adam and Eve, expelling them from Paradise to till the earth and survive by their own means, in case, having sinned once, they sin again and taste the fruit of the Tree of Life.

The Father instructs Michael to carry out the sentence and to drive Adam and Eve from Paradise, but because he has heard their prayers and knows their penitence, to carry out the act without harshness or violence. He tells Michael he will let him know the future, so that Michael can allow Adam some sight of what is to come and the hope that comes with it. Having done that, Michael is then to set a guard over Eden to make sure the Tree of Life is never threatened in the same way by man or devil.

While Michael and four cherubim prepare to carry out God's will, Adam and Eve awake on earth. Adam explains to Eve that, since praying, he has felt the benefit of contrition and senses God's forgiveness, so much so that he believes their sentence of death has been commuted and he praises Eve as the mother of all mankind. Eve responds meekly and sadly, showing none of Adam's renewed sense of hope. She acknowledges her guilt and God's inestimable forgiveness, allying Adam to God in his forgiveness of her failing. She notes the irony of being made the mother of all life yet having brought death into the world, and then calls Adam's attention to the dawn and the day of labour that awaits them. She promises Adam she will never stray from his side again and ends her speech content to live as God commands.

As she ends her speech, they both witness ill omens: an eclipse of the sun, an eagle attacking other birds and a lion hunting deer, all things impossible before the Fall. Adam reads them as presaging some ill news for them and wonders at how much longer they might have to live before they must return to the dust from which they came. Michael and his companions reach the garden and Adam perceives Michael approaching, though with none of the delight and joy he previously felt, telling Eve to retire while he goes to meet the visitor and to expect more news and possibly new laws for them to obey, since Michael's aspect is solemn.

Michael appears as a man, dressed as an imperial figure, but armed with the same sword and spear with which he attacked Satan. Michael launches straight into his business, telling Adam that God has heard their prayers and postponed their death so that, in the interim of life, they may compensate for their one bad act by many good ones. He tells Adam that God might ultimately redeem them, cheating Death of his prize, but that they cannot live in Paradise any longer, and that his purpose is to send them from the garden to begin a life of toil. Adam is struck senseless by the news and, overhearing it, Eve too bewails their expulsion from Paradise.

Eve laments her departure as worse than death, and asks who will tend the flowers and maintain order in Eden. She asks how she can leave her nuptial bed and breathe the less pure air of a lesser world. Doing as God commanded, Michael gently reminds her of the justice of this judgement and advises her to seek solace in her husband, who will go with her. Adam recovers his sense and humbly acknowledges the rightness of Michael's words, accepting this new demand from God with patient obedience. He tells Michael the greatest loss will be the loss of God's company. Michael responds by reminding Adam that, since all heaven and earth are his, God is omnipresent and will not be absent in the lives that they are now to lead. To show him this, he tells Adam he has been instructed by God to foretell events in the future, so that Adam has some knowledge of the race he is to father with Eve. Michael induces sleep in Eve and invites Adam to ascend a hill close by where he will relate the future events in order to teach Adam how me may best endure the life which he must now lead outside Paradise.

Michael takes Adam to the summit of the highest hill in Eden and there applies herbal remedies to clear Adam's sight so that he can see clearly, untainted by the effects of the forbidden fruit. Induced into a trance by Michael, Adam is then gently woken and invited to see the effect of his original sin on his children. Adam views a pastoral scene and watches as a shepherd and a reaper both bring and prepare sacrifices to God, one which is well received and the other not, because the supplicant lacks sincerity. Moved to rage, the reaper strikes the shepherd with a rock and kills him, leaving Adam horrified at such violence. Not recognising death, he naively asks Michael to explain what has happened to the shepherd whose sacrifice was so proper and acceptable to God. Michael tells him the men are brothers and his sons, and that death is the answer to his question.

Adam is repelled and dismayed at the sight, thinking this must be the way he too will die, but Michael tells him death comes in many forms, though all are dismal. Michael tells of death by violence and disease, and prepares Adam to see the latter. Adam's vision changes into a place housing many people suffering every kind of disease and sickness, some so ill they cry for death to ease their pain. So great is their suffering Adam is moved to weep so much he cannot speak. When he recovers enough to speak, he wonders why life would be worth living if such suffering ends it, and why man should, being made in God's image, have to endure such disfiguration. Michael connects this loss of divine similitude for all men to the moment Eve abandoned her own likeness to God by allowing Satan to deceive her. Adam again accepts the justice of this but asks is there no other way to die except through illness and suffering.

Michael describes for Adam the alternative. After leading a life of temperance and moderation, he can expect a slow weakening into a melancholy old age, lacking the vigour and strength of youth, but at least having the compensation of a calm and easeful death. Adam says Michael's words have taken away his fear of death, however short a period it proves to be, and he can look forward now to living what life remains to him well and in God's good grace. Michael tells him not to love nor hate life, but to leave the timing to God. Instead he should do his best to live that time well. Michael then invites Adam to view another vision.

The third vision shows Adam a happier prospect, the fruitful, pleasant, Godly lives led by the descendants of Seth who he sees actively farming, making music and forging metal. Loving, marital sex is also a feature of this vision and Adam is moved to remark on the hope and peace he witnesses, seeing nature fulfilled in the lives of the figures in the vision. Michael warns him not to judge what he has seen by nature alone but to remember that man was made to praise and glorify God. He denounces the seductive female figures as decadent and lustful, lacking the domestic duties and qualities of a good wife, and predicts how the men become enslaved to them and neglect their duty to God. Adam acknowledges the pity and shame of such a weakness but cannot resist connecting this to his own disappointment in Eve. Michael corrects him, reminding him that it was his effeminate weakness that led to the Fall and not simply Eve's naivety, and that he should have shown more wisdom and firmness as her husband. He then introduces a fourth vision.

The fourth vision is of violence, war and civil strife with armies battling it out on the plains for ownership of livestock, leaving a field strewn with corpses. He sees a city besieged and then the intervention of the prophet Enoch, who strives to pull men back to peace and godliness only to be turned on by the mob before he is taken up to heaven by God. Adam is once again moved to tears, denying the manliness of those he sees as bringers of death. He asks Michael who the just man was who tried to reverse the decline. Michael tells Adam the warring men were sons of the immoral marriages seen in the third vision, men belonging to a time when war and strength of arms was the only virtue and what was truly virtuous remained hidden from most men's eyes. Only the seventh in line from Adam, Enoch, sought a better way and was therefore saved from death by God as a sign of what awaits the good, and evil, the subject of the fifth vision which Michael now reveals.

The war having ended, Adam is shown all manner of sinful behaviour, the emphasis on luxury and sexual immorality linking this vision strongly to the royal courts Milton despised. Amidst the scenes of excess, one man again stands out. This time it is Noah, who tries to challenge the ubiquitous wickedness, only to give up at last and begin building the Ark. Adam sees him fill the Ark with every animal, bird and insect and his own immediate family and their wives before God seals the Ark's door in advance of the Flood. Adam sees the world destroyed by the Flood, only the Ark containing a remnant of man and nature. So great is the loss, he is distraught and Michael has to raise him to his feet. Adam is scarcely able to speak such is his grief at seeing his descendants wiped out. He expresses his despair at ever having been shown the future, advising future men to avoid falling into a similar trap because it is far better to be ignorant of the suffering and misery of the future than to have to live knowing it will take place. He says he hoped the few survivors might have been saved but imagines they too succumbed to death and asks Michael to let him know their fate. Michael does not answer immediately, but retells the events of the fifth vision, stressing how both conqueror and conquered ultimately grow corrupt until Noah tries to save them. He tells Adam how God commands Noah to build the Ark and how he then destroys everything except the Ark and its inhabitants to teach man that nowhere is sacred unless man makes it so through his virtue and obedience. He invites Adam to look once more.

The sixth and final vision depicts the Ark's voyage and final resting place on dry land and Noah's joy at being saved by God, and the creation of the rainbow as a symbol of God's renewed covenant with man. Adam joyfully thanks Michael for showing him future things as though they were present and is glad to know that one man at least will merit God's grace and so preserve mankind and the rest of the creatures preserved in the Ark. He ends by asking Michael what the rainbow means and Michael ends the book by describing the terms of God's renewed covenant: that he will never again drown the world and that the rainbow will always be there at any season and hour of the day to remind man of that, until the world finally ends, which it will do in fire and not in flood.

Michael's Mission

One of the most frequently repeated criticisms you will read of *Paradise Lost* is that once Adam and Eve have been punished in Book 10, the narrative falters and Milton draws it out for two more books unnecessarily. A pertinent response is to point out that the poem ends with Adam and Eve's expulsion from Eden, and that *that* is the real climax of the story Milton tells. Book 11 returns us to heaven and a conversation between Christ and God in which Christ intercedes on Adam and Eve's behalf, embodying the route through which man can seek God and find grace. Prayer and grace play a key part in the Son's intercession but less obviously in God's words. It is important when you read this part of the poem (1–125) to make sure you understand what the Son offers to do and what God commands Michael to do. It is interesting to compare God's decrees and behaviour here with Adam's description of him towards the end of Book 10 (1046–8; 1093–6).

At God's command, Michael departs for earth with a 'cohort bright/Of watchful cherubim' (127–8) on a mission to expel Adam and

Eve from Eden. Likening them to the Roman god Janus, whose double face looked in different directions and gave him authority over gates and entrances, beginnings and endings, signifies ominously the end of one world and the start of another for Adam and Eve. As so often, Milton uses classical analogy, here that of Io, the watchful Argus and Mercury, to make his characters even more impressive. As dawn breaks, Adam and Eve wake with renewed courage and hope, although Leucothea, the Roman goddess of the dawn, does bring light, paradoxically she also 'with fresh dews embalmed/The earth' (135) and reminds us that Death now holds sway here. Eve is noticeably now a 'matron' (136) and Milton asserts the efficacy and power of prayer, 'their orisons' (137), by stating that it is 'Strength, added from above' (138) which brings them renewed 'hope' (138) and even 'joy, but with fear yet linked' (139). Adam's words to Eve then embellish this fundamental tenet of Christian faith further.

With a new humility born out of sin, he tells her it is easy for them to appreciate that 'all/The good which we enjoy' (141–2) comes from God, but that faith might be a two-way street is less obvious, 'Hard to belief may seem' (146). The syntax is quite difficult and rereading his first sentence (141–8) will undoubtedly help, especially if you can see that it is determined by the phrase, 'yet this will prayer' (146), which is a compact way of saying, more prosaically, 'yet prayer has the power to do this'. Adam's humility is evident in his doubting that they could express anything through prayer which could 'ascend to heaven' (143) and actually be of interest to God, 'So prevalent as to concern the mind/Of God high-blest' (144–5), let alone bring about a response, 'or to incline his will' (145). But he tells Eve that the experience of praying has confirmed his absolute faith in its power and in God's love. Even 'one short sigh of human breath' (147) sincerely expelled will be 'upborne/Even to the seat of God' (147–8). Faith now becomes a dramatically significant concept in Milton's theodicy. The nature of faith lies right at the heart of the religious controversy of Milton's age and Adam's words to Eve here are an object lesson in what Milton understands by it.

Adam binds his renewed hope to his act of contrition. It was when he 'sought/By prayer the offended Deity to appease' (148–9) and 'humbled' (150) himself that he saw God was indeed 'placable and mild' (151). Not only did this convince him that he 'was heard with favour' (153), but more ironically, considering Michael's current mission, 'peace returned/Home to my breast' (153–4). In addition, Adam then recalled God's promise 'that they seed shall bruise our foe' (155), which in his despair he had forgotten. But what Adam takes from this is an over-optimistic belief that they have somehow cheated death:

> ... yet now
> Assures me that the bitterness of death
> Is past, and we shall live. (156–8)

This burst of optimism leads to a shocking pronouncement, 'Whence hail to thee,/Eve rightly called, Mother of all Mankind' (158–9), because Milton's readers would have only ever heard the salutation 'hail' applied to the Virgin Mary, sometimes referred to as the second Eve. In an echo of God's promise to Adam that the world and all things in it have been created for him, he brushes aside the presence of death and eulogises Eve in religious and therefore ironically almost sacrilegious terms as 'Mother of all Mankind,/Mother of all things living' (159–60). His concluding words contradict the reality that Eve, by her sin, has brought about, 'since by thee/Man is to live, and all things live for man' (160–1).

If in the moment of a new dawn, burnished with renewed faith, Adam has forgotten what Eve did, she has not, and she shows no sign of matching Adam's vitality and hope. Instead when she speaks, it is with 'sad demeanour meek' (162), one of those short phrases Milton frequently produces at the end of a line which at first sight may not seem especially interesting, but on closer inspection display a quite brilliant interplay of assonance and alliteration. She gently rebuffs Adam's praise with the terse, 'Ill worthy I such title' (163), describing herself as both a 'transgressor' (164) and 'snare' (165) when she was 'for thee ordained/A help' (164–5). Showing by her words the sincerity of her own contrition, Eve says Adam should rather 'reproach' (165) her since all she has earned is 'distrust and all dispraise' (166), Milton once again deploying a negative prefix for emphasis. However, like Adam, Eve does acknowledge God's generosity and love, 'But infinite in pardon was my judge' (167), connecting this generosity with Adam's praise of her. The irony Adam missed is not wasted on Eve, 'That I who first brought death on all, am graced/The source of life' (168–9). The depth of Eve's contrition can be measured by what she then adds, because she likens Adam to God in his generosity:

> ... next favourable thou,
> Who highly thus to entitle me vouchsaf'st,
> Far other name deserving. (169–71)

This is a dramatically different Eve from the figure Adam wistfully watched walking away from him (IX, 385–403), like some ardent peasant in a social realist fantasy determined to divide their labours and be more productive.

Milton himself picks up the very same thread after the caesura when Eve reminds Adam that, under God's will, they now have hard work to complete, 'But the field/To labour calls us now with sweat imposed' (171–2). Although Eve is far from fully restored, 'Though after sleepless night' (173), she is resigned to her punishment, and Milton hints at this, not just in her instigating their joint labour, but in her poignant image of the sun continuing its progress irrespective of their condition:

> ... for see the morn,
> All unconcerned with our unrest, begins
> Her rosy progress smiling; (173–5)

The principal difference on this occasion is of course in Eve's promise, 'I never from thy side henceforth to stray' (176), even though their activity together is evidently 'Laborious' and unremitting, 'till day droop' (178). In Eve's ironic resignation, we are reminded of Michael's mission to expel them, 'while here we dwell,/What can be toilsome in these pleasant walks?' (179–80), and of their inability to appreciate the new world and existence they face outside of Paradise, 'Here let us live, though in fallen state, content' (180).

Adam and Eve Hear their Fate from Michael

When Michael explains the reason for his visit, that he has come to expel them from Eden (251–62), the effect on Adam is dramatic. He is stunned into a kind of paralysed silence and it is left to Eve, hidden from Michael's view, to voice their joint sorrow at such unexpected news. As Michael (who we should recall was Satan's principal adversary after Christ) begins to deliver his message, he is pragmatic and clinical, ignoring the pleasantries Raphael and Adam exchanged. Michael wastes no time on greeting, choosing instead simply to deny the appropriateness of such formality given the significance of his message, 'heaven's high behest no preface needs' (251). The one crumb of comfort he offers is the assurance that 'Sufficient that thy prayers are heard' (252), because this now means the death sentence Adam so feared has been subtly changed. Michael tells Adam Death has been 'Defeated of his seizure many days' (254), which clearly indicates a postponement, not a reversal. He also acknowledges that this addresses Adam's uncertainty when he states, 'Then due by sentence when thou didst transgress' (253). More significantly, he uses the concept of grace to lead into the slim possibility of a future reversal. It is through God's grace, Michael insists, that Adam has been granted the unspecified 'many days' in order for him to 'repent' (255) and through 'many deeds well done' undo the 'one bad act' (256). This done, he adds crucially, 'well may then thy Lord appeased/Redeem thee quite from Death's rapacious claim' (257–8). The words offer hope but not certainty, the quintessential condition of the Christian believer, whatever faith they profess.

Having qualified God's sentence in this way, Michael again loses no time on delivering the other half of his message in an equally unemotional way. He tells them not only that they can no longer live in Eden, but that it is his task to expel them, 'to remove thee I am come' (260), so that they can live the remainder of their days on 'fitter soil' (262). Besides the fulfilment of God's will that Adam should now labour and till the soil to provide the means for life, Michael's final image (261–2) reminds us, through contrast, of the perfection of Paradise and of the blissful life Adam and Eve shared within it. We have noted Milton's skilful grasp of sound repeatedly throughout this study, but this final couplet of Michael raises an intriguing possibility. If you listen closely you will hear the connections made between 'garden' (261) and 'ground' (262) and the alliterative use of 's', 't' and 'f' sounds which holds the two lines tightly together. So strong is this effect, that it is almost possible to hear the unvoiced word 'toil' overlaid onto the voiced word 'soil' because both meet the requirements not just of sound, but of sense.

Adam is physically paralysed by the mortifying news, 'Heart-strook with chilling gripe of sorrow stood/That all his senses bound' (264–5), and it is Eve who responds, spontaneously, bursting into an 'audible lament' (266) which betrays her whereabouts to Michael, 'Discovered soon the place of her retire' (267). Exclamation and exaggeration convey her shock, 'Oh unexpected stroke, worse than death!' (268), but the essence of her despairing question, 'Must I thus leave Paradise?' (269), pulls us right into the heart of the epic itself, *Paradise Lost*. Eve's lament takes the form of a series of four questions, which, though equally futile, highlight her acute sense of loss. The first points to two key characteristics of Eden that mankind loses by the Fall. The first is that Eden is man's 'native' (270) home and the second is that it is 'Fit haunt of gods?' (271). You might find yourself a little bemused or even amused by Eve's selection of strolling in the garden (of all the various paradisial joys available to her) as the one she first cites, but Milton lived in an age where the garden was a powerful symbol of civility and order, and only recently Voltaire had concluded that tending one's garden was the secret of a happy life.[1] Our age is possibly the most mercilessly urbanised in human history.

Eve then asks who will replace her in her office as head gardener in Eden, 'Who now shall rear ye to the sun, or rank/Your tribes, and water from the ambrosial fount?' (278–9). Her interest in flora is really far from trivial, since it stresses fertility and her maternal role, which is why Milton reminds us that the flowers have been Eve's 'early visitation, and my last/At ev'n' (275–6). In one sense her substitute children, Eve has reared these flowers, 'bred up with tender hand/From the first op'ning bud, and gave ye names' (276–7). What at first may have seemed a somewhat arbitrary choice of losses, now appears to betray a clear and significant pattern. From garden walks to flowers and to fertility, it is a short step to Eve's greatest loss, 'Thee lastly nuptial bower' (280). Whether this ranking of questions exhibits Milton's advanced feminism or quite the opposite, a conventionally masculine vanity, is unclear. What *is* clear is that Eve (unlike Shakespeare)[2] is deeply moved by the loss of her marriage bed, 'from thee/How shall I part' (281–2). The value she placed on it is conveyed lyrically, 'by me adorned/With what to sight or smell was sweet' (280–1), and through contrast with that 'lower world' (284) into which Michael has come to banish her. In her final few words Eve's fear of the unknown shows itself as she imagines outside Eden to be so 'obscure/And wild' (283–4) that she doubts their ability to survive there, 'how shall we breathe in other air/Less pure, accustomed to immortal fruits?' (284–5). Given the care with which Milton linked and ranked Eve's series of questions, it seems highly unlikely that her shift from 'air' (284) to 'fruits' (285) is accidental or unintentional, and Fowler's suggestion[3] that Michael's 'interruption mild' (286) is triggered by Eve's 'impudence' in mentioning 'fruit' is dramatically and entirely justifiable.

Michael's rebuke, though undoubtedly mild, does bring Eve back to reality and reminds her of the justice of her loss, 'Lament not Eve, but patiently resign/What justly thou hast lost' (287–8). He also accuses her of excess, 'nor set thy heart,/Thus overfond, on that which is not thine' (288–9), before offering her a comfort which she should, by rights, have discovered for herself, given the final question she asked: 'Thy going is not lonely, with thee goes/Thy husband' (290–1). Then in keeping with the underlying theme which has permeated this entire exchange – mankind's rightful home – Michael advises Eve to revise her entire concept of belonging, 'Where he abides, think there thy native soil' (292), which is possibly the starkest image of subservient femininity in the entire poem.

Adam Accepts their Punishment

Michael's advice to Eve appears to draw Adam out of the sudden, intense stupor, which gripped him at the news of their expulsion, and he speaks to Michael in 'humble words' (295). This new humility and Adam's post-lapsarian subservience are indicated by his addressing Michael as a high-ranking spirit, 'Prince above princes' (298), and by his thanking the visiting angel for delivering his harsh message, considerately, 'gently hast thou told/Thy message' (298–9). Adam continues for some time before reaching the definitive statement, 'to his great bidding I submit' (314), and repeating Eve's complaint that the loss of Eden is the loss of their home, 'all places else/Inhospitable appear and desolate' (305–6), adding the compact image, 'Nor knowing us nor known' (306). Although his presumption may be misplaced, it is chiefly humility and penitence that leads him then to assume that no amount of prayer, 'I would not cease/To weary him with my assiduous cries' (309–10), can undo God's 'absolute decree' (311) expelling them from Eden. There is certainly an impressive acknowledgement of God's power in his chosen image 'breath against the wind,/Blown stifling back on him that breathes it forth' (312–13).

However, loss of habitat is for Adam less deplorable than loss of God's company, and it is this then which he bemoans to Michael:

> This most afflicts me, that departing hence,
> As from his face I shall be hid, deprived
> His blessèd count'nance; (315–17)

Although Milton exploits Adam's somewhat Catholic tendency towards idolatry, 'So many grateful altars I would rear' (324), and has Michael remind him that God is ubiquitous, it is perhaps more significant that, in regretting the loss of companionship he formerly had with his creator, Adam is exhibiting a greater sense of self-knowledge. It was Adam's uncharacteristic shyness, after all, that God commented on when he first entered Eden after they had tasted the fruit (X, 103–8). In Adam's nostalgic list of mounts, trees and fountains (320–2) that he imagines one day recounting to his children, 'and to my sons relate' (319), we get the faintest reminder of the Paradise he and Eve enjoyed before the Fall, although the sacrificial 'sweet-smelling gums and fruits and flowers' (327) convey little of its former, sensuous richness. Adam belittles the external world as 'yonder nether world' (328), a place devoid of God, 'where shall I seek/His bright appearances, or footstep trace?' (328–9).

Improved self-knowledge is also very discernible in the way Adam describes his new relationship with God. He admits his earlier guilt and fear at the sight of God's ire, 'For though I fled him angry' (330), but now that he understands he has a life to live and a race to beget, 'yet recalled/To life prolonged and promised race' (330–1), he would be grateful for the briefest glimpse of God, however distant. It is a pitiful shift in perspective and one which Michael responds kindly to, 'with regard benign' (334). He reminds Adam that heaven and earth are God's creations and provides him with an instructional antithesis:

> Not this rock only; his omnipresence fills
> Land, sea, and air, and every kind that lives,
> Fomented by his virtual power and warmed: (336–8)

The adjective 'virtual' is simply derived from the noun 'virtue', and it is God's essential goodness and life giving capacities that Michael is interested in.

Michael is there to remove them from Paradise, but not before issuing them with further guidance from God and the first example of this is his reassurance that God is to be found in all created things. He reminds Adam of God's generosity, 'All the earth he gave thee to possess and rule' (339), and therefore of how inappropriate it is to attempt to limit him to Eden, 'surmise not then/His presence to these narrow bounds confined' (341–2). Though Adam has lost the 'pre-eminence' (347) granted to him via Eden, and must 'dwell on even ground now with thy sons' (348), Michael introduces the first hint of Christ's role as mankind's model when he tells Adam that the earth will nonetheless be full of signs of God's presence, 'Yet doubt not but in valley and in plain/God is as here' (349–50). The image of 'his face/Express' (353–4) clearly prefigures Christ, and 'of his steps the track divine' (354) not only reflects Adam's concern to follow in God's footsteps, but leads Milton's Christian readers to reflect on Christ as the model on which they are to build their own path to redemption.

Michael is then very precise about his purpose, outlining for us the material which is to occupy much of the remainder of the poem in a series of carefully balanced lines. He tells Adam that, before they leave Eden, he will show him the future, good and bad, and in so doing teach him how best to prepare for death when it finally comes. Michael will show Adam a world in a constant state of war, 'supernal grace contending/With sinfulness of men' (359–60), but out of that state man will be able to find for himself the means to seek redemption. The first of these is 'True patience' (361), a state of mind mankind must learn, just as he must learn to 'temper joy with fear/And pious sorrow' (361–2). However 'Prosperous or adverse' (364) the events of one's life, Michaels advises that through 'moderation' (363) mankind will learn to bear either state equally well and in so doing prepare himself for death. In summing up the rewards for living life as he advises, Michael isn't exactly what one would call cheerful or even optimistic, but it is the best a Christian of Milton's puritanical leaning is likely to get:

> ... so shalt thou lead
> Safest thy life, and best prepared endure
> Thy mortal passage when it comes. (364–6)

This said, he invites Adam to higher ground where this vision of the future will be presented to him while he leaves Eve in a sleep Michael has induced, '(for I have drenched her eyes)' (367) just as God once made Adam sleep when Eve was created from his side. If Eve's absence from the vision reads to you rather like a red rag to a feminist bull, be patient, because Eve will receive her instruction from Adam in the final book of the poem (XII, 595–605).

Adam Sees a Vision of Death

With restored sight, Adam is invited by Michael to view the first of a series of six historical events selected for a number of reasons but primarily because they all demonstrate, eloquently, the impact of original sin. Looked at from outside Christian literature or theology, original sin as a concept can seem unjust and even utterly bizarre, but in Milton's poetic hands it is almost a natural, even perfect explanation for the presence of evil in human affairs. The murder of Cain by Abel depicted in this brief dramatic account is neatly and obviously a continuation of the threads of pride and envy we have witnessed Satan plait together since he first appeared writhing on the burning lake in hell.

Michael's didactic strategy is to tell Adam the reason for the vision before he sees it, simultaneously aligning our vision with Adam's and telling us how original sin has impacted on our own world. Although Michael uses 'thy' (424) he is not singling Adam out and later is to tell him to impart all he has seen to Eve. It is their joint guilt which is punished by this tragic and painful sight. Milton stresses the tragedy by pointing out that the 'some' (425), those sinners whom Cain represents, have neither 'touched' (425) the tree nor 'conspired' (426) with Satan, 'Nor sinned thy sin' (427), yet nonetheless the evil behaviour they exhibit has its very source, 'spring' (425), in 'man's first disobedience'. The virulence and widespread nature of the effect are conveyed in the image of sin as 'Corruption' (428) and in its changing form, burgeoning from what might once have been euphemistically downplayed as scrumping, to murder and even 'more violent deeds' (428).

Like Adam, we open our eyes and witness the brief event with the same sense of drama at the shocking action. Milton sets his stage with easily recognisable pastoral props, a 'field/Part arable and tilth' (429–30), some 'sheaves' (430) and 'sheepwalks and folds' (431), even the altar is 'Rustic' (433). The broken rhythm allows us to digest the scene, 'Rustic, of grassy sward' (433), before the more fluid movement of the figure into the scene:

> ... thither anon
> A sweaty reaper from his tillage brought
> First fruits, (433–5)

It's not surprising to find Milton injecting colour into something so crucially visual, 'the green ear, and the yellow sheaf' (435), but more significantly these first offerings are 'Unculled, as came to hand' (436), which, as Milton's readers would instantly appreciate, signals insincerity. In contrast, the second shepherd, who is also 'More meek' (437), brings choice offerings, 'the firstlings of his flock/Choicest and best' (437–8), an image not without irony when applied to Adam and his two sons.

The sacrifice of the animals' innards and fat, 'with incense strewed' (339), is instantly consumed by lightning, 'propitious fire from heaven' (441), while the first offering remained cold, untouched, 'for his was not sincere' (443). All this, Adam can *see*, allowing him not only access to the physical action but to the characters' emotions, 'Whereat he inly raged' (444), an image which links Cain closely with Satan and his determining weakness, envy. Milton uses rhythm again to punctuate the action, the gently matter of fact 'and as they talked' (444), which is immediately usurped by the rush of 'Smote him into the midriff with a stone/That beat out life' (445–6). There is a subtle chime between 'Smote' and 'stone' and a similar connection between 'Smote' and 'beat'. The caesura is followed by the briefest of phrases, 'he fell' (446), accentuating the pause even further and contrasting with the renewed fluency of 'deadly pale/Groaned out his soul with gushing blood effused' (446–7), another line which, the more closely one examines it, the more one admires its subtle interplay of sound.

It is this shocking loss of life, not the first murder so much as the first death, which moves Adam to protest, although he is yet to learn the dreadful truth that these are his two sons or to understand fully the connection with his own sin. Acknowledging his ignorant status, he calls Michael 'O teacher' (450) and tries to understand exactly what he has just witnessed, 'some great mischief hath befall'n/To that meek man' (450–1), since to Adam's eyes it seems as though the violence was the reward for the sincere sacrifice, 'Is piety thus and pure devotion paid?' (452).

Michael, himself moved by what he has seen, calmly identifies the two as 'brethren, Adam, and to come out of thy loins' (454–5). Although he does not name them, he does teach Adam the tragic truth, 'the unjust the just hath slain' (455), motivated not by Adam's original sin, disobedience, but by Satan's original sin, envy, 'For envy that his brother's offering found/From heaven acceptance' (456–7). There remain two key ideas, which Michael has yet to teach from this first drama. The first is that faith does not go unrewarded, as Adam feared, 'and the others' faith approved/Lose no reward' (458–9). This implies the ultimate primacy of God's justice too since 'the bloody fact/Will be avenged' (457–8). The second leads onto the second vision, because Michael now names for Adam the 'great mischief' they have just witnessed as death itself, 'though here thou see him die/Rolling in dust and gore' (459–60).

The efficacy of Michael's teaching is clear in Adam's horrified response. Milton makes Adam ask desperately, 'But have I now seen death?' (462), but only after acknowledging his own part in the tragedy, 'Alas, both for the deed and for the cause!' (461). Since his death sentence was first pronounced, Adam has speculated unhappily about the nature of death and his fear here is that this bloody and brutal spectacle is the specific manner in which he will himself return to the soil, 'Is this the way/I must return to native dust?' (462–3). Responding now as he should to the vision, with fear and horror, he exclaims finally:

> … Oh sight
> Of terror, foul and ugly to behold,
> Horrid to think, how horrible to feel! (463–5)

his final word eloquently capturing his tragic change from immortal to mortal being.

Adam's second vision shows the many forms death takes through illness and intemperance, while the third describes the cultural practices of the irreligious descendants of Cain and Seth, while appearing to offer Adam some hope of a better future. The fourth deals with war and strife between nations and cities before the flood, introducing the biblical figures of both Enoch and Noah, who both seem to have had a strong, personal appeal to the politically active Milton. In each case it is Adam's reaction that gives Michael the opportunity to instruct him further, but it is the fifth vision which repays close analysis the most and as such is the one I've chosen to look most closely at.

Adam's Vision of Sensual Excess

The fifth vision dramatised for Adam by Michael (712–86) moves antediluvian mankind from the violence and savagery of war, to the wasteful excesses of purely sensual pleasures. Milton captures the change in a single line that is a fine illustration of his ability to balance sound and compress meaning into few words, 'The brazen throat of war had ceased to roar' (713). On one level the 'brazen throat' is literally a cannon but, metaphorically, 'brazen' equally conveys shameless impudence, exactly the kind of behaviour he is about to describe. The striking stress placed on the 'r' of 'brazen' gives the line its dominant sound, picked up in the internal rhyme between 'war' and 'roar' which is itself echoed in the assonance between 'throat' and 'roar'. Given that Milton's own political life had been almost entirely dictated by a similar antithesis in the life of his own small nation, it is difficult to avoid his puritanical assault on royalist mores and attitudes in this section of the poem. The hedonism that leads to the destruction by the Flood is given almost peremptory treatment in a single sentence made up of a series of paired behaviours, the first of which are anathema to the Puritan mind: 'jollity and game' (714), 'luxury and riot, feast and dance' (715). These are followed by pairs which imply a loss of moral perspective and come with qualifying phrases, 'Marrying or prostituting, as befell' (716) and 'Rape or adultery, where passing fair/Allured them' (717–18). The end of all this sensual excess is drunkenness and brawling, 'cups to civil broils' (718).

Into this scene steps Noah, 'a reverend sire' (719). One of the interesting aspects of these visions is how dramatic they are. The murder of Abel by Cain required little staging or background and what we saw, with Adam, was a series of very closely connected actions in a short space of time. The subsequent visions lacked that intense dramatic focus, although in parts Milton clearly strove to achieve it; and, when we reach the fifth, it is the building of the Ark, and the Flood, that Milton puts most effort into. Noah's attempts to persuade lack drama, not least because they are spread over an indeterminate length of

time: 'he oft/Frequented their assemblies' (721–2). When he realises he is
preaching to the unreachable, Noah 'ceased/Contending, and removed
his tents far off' (726–7), but in using anachronistic imagery to convey
this, 'as to souls/In prison under judgments imminent' (724–5), Milton
loses the intensity of Adam's point of view which had so strongly driven
our own in the first vision.

In describing the building of the Ark and its population, Milton
adopts more comfortable, dramatic ground. The Ark is built from 'tim-
ber tall' (728) and is of 'huge bulk' (729), the emphasis on the latter
adjective adding to our sense of the immense scale of Noah's project,
as does the repetition of the conjunction in 'Measured by cubit, length,
and breadth, and height' (730). The construction of the single door and
loading with provisions is followed by an exclamation which reminds
us that we are borrowing Adam's point of view, 'when lo a wonder
strange!' (733). The practical construction of the Ark is followed by an
orderly embarkation 'Of every beast, and bird, and insect small' (734)
and by Noah, 'last the sire' (736), with 'his three sons/With their four
wives' (736–7), before the curiously practical detail that 'God made fast
the door' (737), which is far less easy to envisage and undermines the
drama.

Milton's fondness for alliterative line endings has been noted repeatedly throughout this study but here we find the technique being
combined with enjambment, 'Meanwhile the south wind rose, and with
black wings/Wide hovering, all the clouds together drove' (738–9). The
effect is to mimic the build up of the storm clouds to which are added
the vast quantities of water necessary to flood the entire earth:

> ... the hills to their supply
> Vapour, and exhalation dusk and moist,
> Sent up amain; (740–2)

Matching the 'black' (738) clouds, the moisture itself is given the
unusual adjective 'dusk' (741) or shadowy, and this immense natural
accumulation of cloud and water culminates in the striking and unchar-
acteristically terse simile, 'the thickened sky/Like a dark ceiling stood'
(742–3). A caesura marks the moment before the deluge, 'down rushed
the rain/Impetuous' (743–4), but instead of attempting to depict the
effect on the race of men Adam has seen already, Milton sweeps the
entire world aside in one tremendously understated image, 'till the
earth/No more was seen' (744–5), to concentrate instead on the effect
on Adam.

But before we are treated to Adam's spectacular grief, Milton ensures the Ark and its strange crew are safe, imbuing it with almost anthropomorphic qualities:

> ... the floating vessel
> Swum uplifted; and secure with beakèd prow
> Rode tilting over the waves, (745–7)

Of the race of men we see nothing, instead Milton's puritanism leads him to dwell pensively on their vanity, their habitats and habits, 'all dwellings else/Flood overwhelmed' (747–8), while 'all their pomp/Deep under water rolled' (748–9). Their luxurious palaces are reduced to stables for 'sea-monsters' (751). Hyperbole combines with repetition to convey the universality of the disaster, 'sea covered sea,/Sea without shore' (749–50), the surviving handful of humanity held in 'one small bottom swum embarked' (753).

The shift in dramatic narrative from the Flood back to Adam is unannounced and may cause you some confusion because it is the poem's narrator, not Michael, who asks, 'How didst thou grieve then, Adam,/To behold the end of all thy offspring, end so sad' (754–5). Milton boldly deploys the kind of scientific word which rarely finds its way into poetry, 'Depopulation' (756), to demythologise the event and signal a moment for reflection before he fields hyperbole again to convey Adam's grief, having him drown in 'another flood/Of tears and sorrow' (756–7). Michael, ever the gentle teacher, lifts the distraught Adam to his feet again, 'till gently reared/By the angel' (758–9), but the most poignant image of all used to convey the terrible human cost of the Flood is left for last, 'as when a father mourns/His children, all in view destroyed at once' (760–1). Such is Adam's grief he is barely able to speak, 'scarce to the angel utterdst thus thy plaint' (762), but when he does, it is to loose a stinging assault on fate common to many Protestants of the age, driven to despair by Calvin's belief in predestination.[4]

First of all there is a rather black wit in his opening exclamation, 'O visions ill foreseen!' (763), before he expresses the wish that he had remained in ignorance and been able therefore to endure his own guilt and not now feel the terrible guilt of so much amassed sin and evil he and Eve have loosed into the world. Challengingly for feminist critics, his complaint is riddled through with images of birth, culminating in the shocking oxymoron, 'birth/Abortive' (768–9). The thought of having to endure knowing this future but being unable to prevent it leads him to voice his quintessentially Protestant complaint, perhaps the most significant Protestant issue Milton rejected:

> ... Let no man seek
> Henceforth to be foretold what shall befall
> Him or his children, evil he may be sure,
> Which neither his foreknowing may prevent,
> And he the future evil shall no less
> In apprehension than in substance feel
> Grievous to bear: (770–6)

If you were looking for a definition of Protestant despair, it would be difficult to find one more articulate than this pitiable desire of Adam. If you find the use of 'neither' (773) without a subsequent 'nor' to be confusing, this is because the 'And' (774) has exactly the same function as 'nor'.

In one respect this moment of the entire poem is Adam's nadir because he cannot see any future beyond the sin, evil, death and destruction of the Flood. He imagines no hope for the Ark's few souls:

> ... those few escaped
> famine and anguish will at last consume
> Wandering that watery desert: (777–9)

the oxymoron before the caesura so brilliantly apt as to be easily overlooked. However, Michael has responded to each of his reactions to the visions with consolation and Adam seeks that again. He tells Michael that, after the fourth vision, his hope had been that mankind could have found peace and happiness but that he believes what the vision taught him is that peace is just as destructive as war, 'for now I see/Peace to corrupt no less than war to waste' (783–4). The vision left the scraps of all the beauty and richness that had populated Eden, floating vulnerably in a crude wooden vessel, and recapturing a little of the drama, Adam asks, 'How comes it thus? Unfold, celestial guide/And whether here the race of man will end' (785–6).

Michael retells the fifth vision for Adam (787–869), spelling out for him the process that led to a degenerate mankind, 'all depraved,/Justice and temperance, truth and faith forgot' (806–7), before Noah took that action necessary to ensure the survival of God's creation. His account adds detail concerning the Flood's abatement and the Ark's return to dry land but, above the narrative, is the key lesson Michael has been instructed to teach Adam. The unimaginable cruelty and immense scale of the destruction caused by the flood was

> To teach thee that God áttributes to place
> No sanctity, if none be thither brought
> By men who there frequent, or therein dwell. (836–8)

God's Covenant with Man

The account Michael gives of the Ark's survival and the rainbow which signals a renewed covenant between God and man (870–901) restores Adam's hope and joyfully he continues to interrogate Michael in order to learn how he may live. The blind Milton ends his series of dramatic visions in the same highly visual way he began by stressing what Adam has seen, 'O thou that future things canst represent/As present' (870–1) and 'I revive/At this last sight' (871–2), but, equally importantly, he has Adam acknowledge Michael as his tutor, 'heavenly instructor' (871). Adam was of course appointed guardian by God, not just of his own race, but all created life, and so his sense of joy is as much because Noah preserves 'all the creatures, and their seed' (873) as his own kin. If you pursue your studies of *Paradise Lost* through Milton's life and psychology, you will quickly find that he was far from an orthodox individual.[5] He often exhibits a deep sympathy with characters, like Noah, whose sense of justice is so fiercely independent that it leads to their being either vilified or ostracised by their fellow men, and it is of course tempting to see this as a reflection of his own lived experience. Hence the intensity of Adam's reversal, where he forgets the loss of the thousands of souls he has witnessed but can 'rejoice/For one man found so perfect and so just' (875–6).

Reassured that the world is not lost, that man and all creation will survive, Adam asks Michael what sounds like a surprisingly trivial question, 'But say, what mean those coloured streaks in heaven' (879). He offers two ideas himself, that the rainbow is in some way indicative of 'the brow of God appeased' (880) or that it is a barrier designed to prevent further inundation of the earth, 'a flowery verge to bind/The fluid skirts of that same watery cloud' (881–2). The truth is sadly one of those delightful biblical details which used to be common knowledge but which science and secularism have trodden into disuse. Like Raphael, Michael observes that Adam is not without intelligent insight and so he tells him, 'Dextrously thou aimst' (884), punning on the Latin derivation of 'right handed' to suggest one of Adam's suggestions is correct.

The truth, Michael explains, is that the rainbow is God's covenant with man that never again will he lay waste to the earth by flood. In words very close to their biblical source, he tells Adam that God was so dismayed, 'Grieved at his heart' (887) by 'man depraved' (886) and the sight of 'The whole earth filled with violence' (888), that the Flood was his response. Only Noah's goodness, the 'one just man', (890) saved mankind, 'That he relents, not to blot out mankind' (891). It shouldn't surprise you at this stage of studying the poem to see where Milton places all the emphasis, 'Such *grace* shall one just man find in his sight' (890; my italics). Almost the entire population of the earth 'removed' (889) – the kind of Orwellian language we are more familiar with from fascist or communist ideologies – God is yet able to find enough love for his creation to grant Noah his gift of grace.

Instead, God 'makes a covenant never to destroy/The earth again by flood' (892–3) and, in an age of global warming, the rather reassuring, 'nor let the sea/Surpass his bounds' (893–4), which again uses the combination of enjambment and alliteration we noted earlier (738–9). In future, God will accompany each rain cloud with the rainbow as a sign for men to 'call to mind his covenant' (898), and a covenant, of course, is not one way. The caesura allows Michael the pause he needs to allow Adam the time to reflect on that new reality before he ends the book with his vision of the apocalypse, 'till fire purge all things new,/Both heaven and earth, wherein the just shall dwell' (900–1). In the meantime, for mankind as for Adam, life will endure, the alliterative lyricism reflecting the kind of pastoral poetry and world Milton would have been very familiar with from his classical sources:

> … day and night,
> Seed-time and harvest, heat and hoary frost
> Shall hold their course, (898–900)

The final point to make about this book is the hope and even promise contained in the very last phrase, 'wherein the just shall dwell' (901). The route to eternal salvation remains open, just unmapped.

Exercises

Lines 181–250. When Adam and Eve begin their first day's toil, a number of ill-omens appear to break any illusion they may have of continuing 'content' as Eve hoped. These natural events prefigure Adam and Eve's expulsion from Eden. Although they do not know this, Adam does realise that something more remains to be learned of their fate and, when he sees Michael approaching, he expresses this concern to Eve and requests that she retire while he speaks with Michael. Besides the ominous natural signs, Michael's appearance and behaviour is noticeably different from Raphael's. When you read this section compare Milton's depiction of Michael with his earlier account of Raphael in Book 5. How is this contrast also reflected in Adam's behaviour?

Lines 370–422. Hilltop visions are conventional biblical events and at the most basic level Milton is symbolically giving Adam a clearer view, but you may well find the lengthy catalogue of exotic, often unfamiliar place names here to be distracting or even dull. A good edition of the poem will provide you with the detailed geographical and other notes which can add to your understanding, but it is perhaps more valuable to examine how this section ends by asking yourself why Michael needs to apply a herbal cure to Adam's eyes.

Lines 467–711. This section deals with the second, third and fourth visions Michael shows to Adam. The second allows Adam to see the many forms death takes through illness and intemperance, while the third deals with the irreligious descendants of Cain and Seth and appears to Adam to offer some hope. The fourth deals with war and strife between nations and cities before the Flood, introducing the biblical figures of both Enoch and Noah. It is important for you to understand how Adam reacts to each of these dramatic scenes and then, in each case, how Michael immediately corrects him, because it is through the latter's instruction that Milton reveals his own ideas about what constitutes a life well lived.

12
Banishment and Hope

Summary

Michael restarts his narrative for Adam at the point where God has begun the human race anew with Noah and his family, but he also comments on Adam's failing eyesight, the result of seeing things divine, and chooses to conclude the rest of his narrative without the aid of visions. He starts by telling Adam that the descendants of Noah and his sons establish a time of peace and godliness until at length a new and cruel tyrant emerges, Nimrod, whose ambition is such that he subjugates all men and seeks to gain eternal fame by building a tower to reach as high as heaven, the Tower of Babel. But God, who Michael says still walks on earth amongst men unseen and unrecognised, renders the speech of the tower builders unintelligible and, such is the confusion and chaos, the tower remains unfinished, becoming a symbol of arrogance and foolishness.

Adam deplores Nimrod's pride in setting himself above all other men, stressing that God gave man dominion only over birds and beasts and not over each other, saving that role as sole lord for himself and leaving mankind free. Michael once more reminds Adam that, since his original sin, man's freedom, originally linked inherently to reason, is in thrall to lesser passions and irrational behaviours. This way, some men will always be subject to the will of others, a just punishment for Adam's original sin, and there will always be tyrants, though tyranny itself is evil. So, Michael affirms, this new antediluvian world will gradually also sink into excess and wickedness, such that God himself withdraws his grace. From Abraham – one who like Noah and Enoch remained faithful, amidst a world of idolatry – he will elect a new chosen race. Michael describes Abraham's journey to Canaan and on to

Egypt; the lives of Isaac and Jacob; their enslavement in Egypt and eventual flight to freedom led by Moses; the plagues God inflicted on Egypt; and the final destruction of Pharaoh and his entire army in the Red Sea.

In the land of the Canaanites, this new race begin a new regime under laws proscribed directly for them by God and delivered to Moses on Mount Sinai. Through this new law, man will come to know how God's design will ultimately lead to his triumph over Satan through the sacrifice of the Son. As a mark of his delight in man's new obedience, God establishes his agreement with man in the form of a sacred tabernacle, the Ark of the Covenant. Finally settled in Israel, Michael mentions the many kings and battles, wars and power struggles, the Israelites endure before Isaac succeeds in gaining control of the nation. Adam interrupts, telling Michael how much his mind is eased by the knowledge that Abraham and his sons will found a better future for mankind than that which his own sin first led him to anticipate. He asks Michael to explain why God allows so many and such varied laws to exist amongst the different races, since he keeps faith with all. Michael explains that law was given to man to expose sin, since sin will always seek to challenge law, and righteous men will from this be able to discern sinfulness in others. He tells Adam that though they might discover sin, they cannot destroy it, even through the sacrifice of animals and other proper religious rites. Through time they will then come to understand that a greater sacrifice must be made, one which will cancel out the ingratitude of original sin and appease mankind's conscience. The law is therefore always imperfect, but nonetheless points the way to the truth for man, from servility to greater freedom, and, through God's grace, man can ultimately regain his rightful place as God's own creation.

The story of the Israelites continues, through Joshua and King David to Solomon, and the prophecy that of his line man's saviour will be born. Solomon builds a permanent home for the Ark of the Covenant, the temple in Jerusalem, but a long period of disaffection follows in which God once again withdraws from the affairs of man, leaving them prey to the Babylonians. After seventy years God restores them but, through more internal, religious and political division, the sons of David lose the throne and in so doing fulfil the prophecy that Christ will be born deprived of his birthright. Michael tells Adam of Christ's nativity, born to a virgin but fathered by God himself, his humble birth attended by shepherds and the wise men.

Michael pauses when he sees that his account of Christ's nativity has filled Adam with renewed joy and Adam, overwhelmed, as by grief, interrupts the narrative once again. Adam declares his full understanding of how their saviour should yet be born a man. He praises Mary as the virgin mother, acknowledging her as his descendant and therefore in that miraculous conception, the unification of man with God. Eagerly he asks Michael how and when the Son of God, their redeemer, will fight their enemy and revenge the harm done to them by Satan. Michael advises Adam not to think of that combat in mortal or physical terms and gives a clear account of the life of Christ, his death on the cross and resurrection, so that, by following his example, man too can gain eternal life, cheating death, the penalty God imposed for Adam and Eve's disobedience. He makes it clear to Adam that only by unquestioning obedience to the father, by dying on the cross and, in effect, taking Adam's place, can Christ undo the original sin Adam and Eve committed. In this way Sin and Death are defeated and Satan cheated of his prize, the souls of men.

Michael tells how Christ returns to earth after his resurrection to instruct the disciples and how they will provide man with the means to lead a Christian life and gain salvation for themselves. He describes the Second Coming when the Son will return in triumph to heaven dragging Satan through hell in chains, where he will leave him before taking his proper place at God's right hand. Then, as the world ends and earth and heaven become one, he will judge all men, alive and dead, and those who merit salvation shall be saved. Adam rejoices effusively in this, the climactic part of Michael's story, even asking himself whether or not he should regret or celebrate his original sin, since it leads ultimately to infinite goodness. He celebrates the victory of man over Satan and of grace over anger and asks Michael, given the cruel manner in which Christ will be treated on earth, how his followers will manage once he has re-ascended into heaven. Who will guide and defend them from the ungodly? Michael tells him he is right to predict the continued persecution of the faithful but God will send his Holy Spirit down to earth as man's guide and comfort. However, over time the clergy itself will succumb to corruption and secular greed, creating false religious doctrine not based on the word of God in Holy Scripture. But all such falsehood will become known and condemned by Christ at the Second Coming when all those who have been persecuted for their faith will be rewarded with eternal life.

Adam observes how quickly Michael's epic story seems to have passed, when what he related was in fact all history, compressed. Adam then makes it clear that he has understood all Michael's instruction, and that he will depart more at peace and with a far greater understanding of how he must now live, given what time may be left to him. He acknowledges limitations on his own understanding and capacity for knowledge and lists a series of sententious rules by which he intends to lead his life, in full obedience to God. Michael affirms Adam's list by telling him that to have learned that much is to have gained true wisdom far beyond the value of knowing the names of all the things in the universe or having enjoyed immense worldly power. To Adam's learning he adds a list of seven Christian attributes, the core of which is love or charity and promises Adam that if he follows these precepts he will not mourn the loss of Paradise, but carry an inner paradise with him.

Michael finally instructs Adam that the hour of their departure from Paradise is imminent and his companions await his orders so they must descend and wake Eve, who Michael has calmed with soothing dreams. He tells Adam that when the time is right he is to tell Eve what he has learned, particularly her part as mother of the race of men leading to Christ. When they reach the foot of the hill, Eve is already awake and greets them cheerfully, telling Adam that God has been in her dreams and she is not afraid now of what may come, trusting in Adam to lead her and confirming her love for him. Though pleased with her words, Adam doesn't reply because the angels are there to lead them out of Paradise, carrying the flaming sword of God before them. Taking Adam and Eve in each hand, Michael leads them out of the eastern gate down onto the plain beneath and disappears. Looking back, they see the flaming sword guarding the gate and shedding tears, hand in hand they turn to face their new life in a new world, united in love and sorrow.

Michael Relates the History of Christianity

The final book continues the discussion between Michael and Adam while Eve is left sleeping, and a large proportion of it is taken up by an account from Michael of the period between the Flood and Christ's birth. Michael abandons using visions on the grounds that such heavenly material is exhausting for mortal eyes and proceeds from then on with pure narrative. It is best to read this section with the aid of a scholarly edition that elucidates the numerous biblical references. You may have minimal biblical knowledge but some of the figures and events, such as the building of the Tower of Babel and the escape from Egypt by Moses across the Red Sea, are likely to be more familiar. The value of this lengthy and somewhat dry genealogical narrative is that it ultimately amounts to a scholarly recreation of Christ's family tree and shows Adam how God's mercy will be fulfilled.

Christ's Triumph

When Michael reaches Bethlehem and the nativity, Adam's joy is such that it seems to justify Michael's breaking off his narrative, although it has reached its natural conclusion in the sense that it has been driving relentlessly towards this announcement. Michael still has to explain to Adam how Christ, through his suffering and death on the cross, redeems Adam's original sin, though Adam's joyful interruption provides the ideal opportunity for Michael to correct him once more.

Paradoxically, Adam's joy manifests itself 'like grief... bedewed in tears' (373) and he is almost speechless, 'Without the vent of words, which these he breathed' (374). He declares Michael 'Prophet of glad tidings, finisher/Of utmost hope!' (375–6) and leaps to conclude, yet again incorrectly, that the child born in Bethlehem will prove to be the heroic figure able to defeat Satan in combat. In his dealings with both Michael and Raphael, and to a lesser extent with God, Milton repeatedly ascribes to Adam a capacity which looks very much like intellectual curiosity, the beginnings of metaphysical speculation. It is visible here when Adam says, 'Now clear I understand/What oft my steadiest thoughts have searched in vain' (376–7).

He then refers to Christ as 'our great expectation'[1] (378) and rejoices in the connection discovered between the Virgin Mary, Christ's earthborn mother, and himself. He knows now why Christ is to be called 'The seed of woman' (379) and, in riddling language of his own, the stuff of prophecy, epitomises Christ's unique nature, since 'from my loins/Thou shalt proceed, and from thy womb the Son' (380–1), the first 'Thou' referring to Christ, while the second 'thy' refers to his mother. Finally he spells out for us the reason for his rejoicing, 'so God with man unites' (382). This climactic image is easily underestimated because it is a Christian cliché. For Adam, the protagonist of *Paradise Lost*, this realisation is the realisation of his greatest hope, born out of his love for his maker.

With intense delight he leaps to the punishment of Satan, 'Needs must the serpent now his capital bruise/Expect with mortal pain' (383–4), anticipating a battle royal between Christ and Satan, 'say where and when/Their fight. That stroke shall bruise the victor's heel' (384–5), that final phrase reminding literate readers as much of Achilles before the walls of Troy[2] as it does of Adam and Eve in the garden of Eden. Michael's job throughout this visitation has been to correct and to teach Adam. He confronts Adam's misinterpretation head on by telling him not to think of their encounter in such simple, physical terms, 'Dream not of their fight,/As of a duel' (386–7), and then continues to explain in a typically Miltonic series of negatives: God and man were not joined in order to strengthen God sufficiently to defeat Satan, and such a conflict has no meaning when Satan is already suffering a far greater hurt, 'nor so is overcome/Satan, whose fall from heaven, a deadlier bruise' (390–1). Already, Michael explains, Satan's intent to inflict death on Adam has been thwarted, 'Disabled not to give thee thy death's wound' (392), but Christ will further heal Adam 'Not by destroying Satan, but his works/In thee and in thy seed' (394–5). It is vital for a strong understanding of the poem to grasp the significance of this theological concept, that Christ will be the means by which Adam's original sin, replicated and reproduced through numerous mutations in all mankind, can finally be purged.

A caesura separates this central concept from the precise qualification that follows, 'nor can this be,/But by fulfilling that which thou didst want' (394–5). It is easy to supply the missing characteristic, 'Obedience to the law of God' (397), but less so to understand the complex syntax which then concludes Michael's lesson. Milton first reminds us that the penalty for disobedience was death and then with crystalline logic states, 'and suffering death... So only can high justice rest apaid' (398–401). The intervening two lines are parenthetic, reminding Adam that the penalty was incurred by his 'transgression' (399) and owed by all humanity, 'And due to theirs which out of thine will grow' (400). With admirable intellectual precision, Milton has delivered the promise he made at the poem's opening and brought us to the climactic moment in his theodicy. Christ, unlike man, will be an obedient son. What suffering and humiliation that entails for him and how his short life as a man relates to mankind's history, Michael now goes on to relate.

The intellectual, rational value Milton places on this section of the poem is discernible in the frequency with which single, key words are repeated in subsequent lines, clearly elucidating the process of reason which has brought him to this point: 'bruise', 'death', 'fulfil', 'obedience' and 'law' are all examples of this. Quite contrary to Adam's imagined battle royal, Michael predicts Christ 'coming in the flesh/To a reproachful life and cursèd death' (405–6) and then makes what is possibly one of the most lucid definitions of Christianity to be found anywhere:

> Proclaiming life to all who shall believe
> In his redemption, and that his obedience
> Imputed becomes theirs by faith, (407–9)

It is through faith that Adam and we, Milton's assumed Christian reader, will find salvation and escape death. If in studying the poem, you have been expecting all your big questions to be answered, I'm afraid the best any teacher of literature can possibly do at this point is refer you to St Augustine.[3] In keeping with the strict Protestant belief that good works alone cannot merit salvation, Michael ends his sentence with the rather awkward addendum, 'his merits/To save them, not their own, though legal works' (409–10).

Having corrected Adam's 'local' (387) interpretation of Christ's battle with Satan, Michael is then even more realistic about the humiliation and suffering Christ must undergo. The broken rhythm emphasises each aspect of the crucifixion tale:

> For this he shall live hated, be blasphemed,
> Seized on by force, judged, and to death condemned. (411–12)

While the ironies are etched starkly, 'nailed to the cross/By his own nation' (413–14) and 'slain for bringing life' (414), one seriously wonders if, when Milton wrote that first phrase, the thought of Charles I ever even occurred to him? The comparison certainly occurred to others and Milton was acutely aware of this.[4] Irony is the main technique in the shocking but powerful image, 'But to the cross he nails thy enemies' (415), which Michael embellishes with 'The law that is against thee, and the sins/Of all mankind, with him there crucified' (416–17). Once this single, ignominious death is accomplished, the way is open for Christians to salvation since none of Adam's 'enemies' can 'hurt them more who rightly trust/In this his satisfaction' (418–19), the latter noun having a meaning rarely used today, which specifically refers to the atonement by Christ for all mankind's sins and which is followed by a reverential caesura.

The Resurrection follows Christ's death, 'so he dies,/But soon revives' (419–20), with almost indecent haste, and Michael predicts the three-day Easter interval central to the celebration of the Christian year. The repetition of the image of dawn, 'ere the third dawning light/Return' (421–2) and 'fresh as the dawning light', announces a new beginning for mankind and plays on the conventional image of Christ as the light of the world. Where Milton departs from Calvinist or more orthodox Protestant theology is one of the liveliest debates for Milton scholars and the advice Michael gives here is a useful pointer towards a better understanding of that. Reminding Adam once again that his sin will be atoned for by Christ, 'Thy ransom paid' (424), which saves mankind from death, he then provides us with the condition:

> ... as many as offered life
> Neglect not, and the benefit embrace
> By faith not void of works: (425–7)

Although Milton did not believe in Calvin's ruthlessly predetermined world where some were saved while some were not, and nothing any poor soul did could alter that, he did believe that it was man's responsibility to 'embrace' the grace God offers and that good acts were the inseparable outcomes of such an active, purposeful faith. The caesura is followed by a curious phrase reiterating how Christ's death has replaced 'the death thou shouldst have died' (428), since 'this Godlike act' (427) implies a simile but is literally true in the sense that this act is not God-*like*, but Godly.

More significantly, this point permits Michael to return directly to Adam's original question, since with 'sin for ever lost from life' (429) it is this specific, sacrificial action by God that:

> Shall bruise the head of Satan, crush his strength
> Defeating Sin and death, his two main arms, (430–1)

The satisfaction to be gained being even greater since the punishment Satan suffers is far worse than merely temporal death,

> And fix far deeper in his head their stings
> Than temporal death shall bruise the victor's heel, (432–3)

The image is both redolent of the confrontation Satan had with Death in Book 2 (688–727) and of the insight Milton has provided throughout the poem into Satan's envious psyche. His key instruction done, Michael offers Adam and all men of faith those 'whom he redeems' (434), a gentler image of death as 'like sleep/A gentle wafting to immortal life' (434–5), the lyrical rhythm and soft sounding syllables combining to soothe the reader and offering a marked contrast with the staccato, alliterative harshness of 'And fix far deeper'.

Adam's Renewed Faith

Michael, at God's instruction (XI, 113–17), has taken Adam on a narrative journey from the murderous action of his own offspring, Cain, to the end of the world, on the way providing him with everything he needs to know to defeat Satan and gain eternal life. That narrative has taken Adam to emotional extremes, from despair to joy, but ultimately brings him to a point where he is able calmly, and lucidly, to summarise what he has learned from Michael (552–73).

The 'last replied' phrase (552) is a literal statement in the sense that these are the last words in *Paradise Lost* we will hear Adam speak. The phrase will be repeated shortly (574) to indicate the end of Michael's dialogue too. The 'prediction' (553) Adam speaks of also signals this because it consciously refers back to Michael's task, which at the start he told Adam was 'To show thee what shall come in future days' (XI, 337). Adam is left with a quintessentially human perspective on time, the period of Michael's narrative having covered so much and yet taken up so little, 'How soon hath thy prediction, seer blest,/Measured this transient world' (553–4), while 'beyond is all abyss' (555). The rhythm lingers on 'transient world, the race of time' (554) but comes up against a dead stop after the final three, stressed syllables in 'Till time stand fixed' (555), which is counterbalanced by the lyrical 'beyond is all abyss' (555). Adam's reflection on time concludes with an equally skilful, single line where the repetition of the two different 'e' sounds contained in the first word, 'Eternity' (556), are repeated but perfectly balanced in 'end', 'eye' and 'reach'. It is not least this acute awareness of sound and the relationship between words (how many poets would hear the connection between 'beyond' and 'abyss'?) that makes Milton's prosody such a pleasure to study.

Michael's visionary teaching is acknowledged by Adam when he says 'Greatly instructed I shall hence depart' (557), but it has also brought him to a calm acceptance both of his own limitations as a mortal and of the lessons he has been taught. Adam's choice of 'vessel' (559) to describe himself works on two levels, both as a receptacle and as a ship, the first holding only what knowledge God has provided and the second having come to the end of a turbulent voyage with Michael. This moment is one of the most powerful in the entire poem because it is here that Adam demonstrates the change wrought in him by the Fall and by his penitent response to God's punishment. His belief that he aspired too high, 'Beyond which was my folly to aspire' (560), takes on huge significance when followed by his promise 'Henceforth I learn that to obey is best' (561) because it links confession and sorrow, the latter a condition of sincere contrition.

The next few lines (561–73) echo a number of biblical quotations and in unison sound credibly prayer-like. In effect, what Adam produces here is a litany.[5] After obedience comes a promise to 'love with fear the only God' (562), which links God's omnipotence to Adam's punishment, which leads very naturally onto 'to walk/As in his presence' (562–3). Unlike Satan, whose resentment of God's omnipotence was unbalanced, Adam sees God's power as beneficent, merciful and eternally forgiving, 'Merciful in all his works' (565). The litany proceeds with a list of divine paradoxes: 'good still overcoming evil' (566–7), 'by small/Accomplishing great things' (566–7), 'by things deemed weak/Subverting worldly strong' (567–8), 'worldly wise/By simply meek' (568–9), and, ultimately, 'death the gate of life' (571). It's also important to understand that Adam has learned all this not from Michael alone, but from 'my redeemer ever blest' (573). And there is one part of this litany which captures perfectly this principle of Christ's teaching because it also offers us a paradigm of his life and death, 'that suffering for truth's sake/Is fortitude to highest victory' (569–70).

Michael Confirms God's Will

Milton repeats the very literal phrase he used earlier to signal he is coming to the end of this immense enterprise, 'thus also the angel last replied' (574), but more significantly for us it also signals the close of Michael's narrative and the didactic process underpinning it. Like all skilled teachers, Michael reiterates his lesson in a condensed form. He affirms Adam's understanding, telling him he 'hast attained the sum/Of wisdom' (575–6), adding a brief list of unknowable goals:

> ... hope no higher, though all the stars
> Thou knewst by name, and all the ethereal powers,
> All secrets of the deep, all nature's works,
> Or works of God in heaven, air, earth, or sea, (576–9)

The Puritan Milton steps in to add to this scientific list, 'all the riches of this world' (580) and 'all the rule, one empire' (581). None of these known or attained, Michael tells Adam, can bring happiness. Instead he offers him the Puritan's touchstone, 'Deeds' (582), which implies not simply actions but healthy labour, a concept which became deeply insinuated in the national psyche.

To deeds Michael adds a brief catalogue of essential qualities he advises Adam to cultivate, 'add faith,/Add virtue, patience, temperance, add love' (582–3), that last given the additional refinement, 'By name to come called charity, the soul/Of all the rest' (584–5). Michael's list can fuel lively debate, the isolation of 'love' and the ease with which Milton redefines it as 'charity' (584) is certain to be contentious. In sinning we have seen Adam offend, though he has never lost God's love, yet how we perceive that quality will depend heavily on how we respond to God's actions after the Fall and therefore to Milton's entire theodicy. In many ways this section of the poem is one of the most crucial for serious students of Milton to comprehend since not only does Michael state categorically that here is 'The sum/Of wisdom' (575–6), but after a caesura which signals we should take note, he links it ineluctably to happiness:

> ... then wilt thou not be loath
> To leave this Paradise, but shall possess
> A Paradise within thee, happier far. (585–7)

Turning to more practical, narrative matters, Michael instructs Adam to descend the hill they climbed in order to gain a better vision, which he calls with something approaching humour, 'this top/Of speculation' (588–9), bringing them, in several senses, down to earth. This shift is emphasised when he alerts Adam to the other angels who await his orders by the gate of Eden, through his adopting military diction: 'guards' (590), 'encamped' (591) and 'remove' (593), a military term for departure. Adam is instructed to 'waken Eve' (594) and all risk of further debate or discussion is entirely removed by the 'gentle dreams' (595) Michael has granted Eve, 'Portending good' (596), which have 'all her spirits composed/To meek submission' (596–7). Not only is Eve removed from those visions and lessons in faith that Michael gives Adam, she is 'calmed' (595) and the former independence which she exercised so effectively on the morning of the Fall (IX, 205–403) is deliberately neutered. There may be many reasons, narrative as well as psychological, why Eve is treated in this way and Milton does use a caesura to emphasise that she is not denied Michael's instruction, the key difference is that Adam will be her teacher, 'thou at season fit/Let her partake with thee what thou hast heard' (597–8). Michael himself raises the link between his instruction and Eve's faith, advising Adam to ensure Eve connects Christ's birth to herself, through the virgin mother, Mary:

> Chiefly what may concern her faith to know,
> The great deliverance by her seed to come. (599–600)

Michael's final few words also strain to unite Adam and Eve: 'That ye may live' (602) refers to them both and 'Both in one faith unanimous though sad' (603) consciously plays with the paradox of their being two *beings*, united in one future. It is almost as though Milton feels himself the unresolved nature of their marriage and makes a last ditch effort to reconcile these two, highly distinct characters that his own dramatic skill has so richly brought to life. Their future together is envisioned by Michael as one

> With cause for evils past, yet much more cheered
> With meditation on the happy end. (604–5)

For Milton, ultimately, redemption and immortality are immutable future events.

Michael Leads Adam and Eve out of Paradise

In this, the final section of the poem to be analysed in detail (606–49), Michael leads Adam and Eve out of Paradise and into an uncertain world. When contemplating this quite remarkable poetic project, Milton must have conceived of, and rejected, a number of possible titles before settling on *Paradise Lost*, a phrase of such resounding familiarity four centuries later, that it is all too easy to underestimate its meaning. It is no accident that the poem ends with the expulsion of the guilty pair from that realm God had created purely for them and for their delight. The entire narrative has been leading us to this tragic moment in the history of mankind, in which we all share the loss of happiness uncorrupted by human frailty. In Christian thinking it is from Adam that we all inherit our capacity for sin and hence damnation.

The first thing you may notice is the shift to the present tense, 'He ended, and they both descend the hill' (606), which is immediately followed by a return to the past, 'Descended' (607). The use of the present tense often signals dramatic immediacy or intensity of action, and here it may have that momentary effect, but what may also strike you is the sudden lyricism, created largely by the similarity of sound between 'ended' and 'Descended'. Milton may have wished clearly to signpost the onset of the poem's final phase through this distinctly memorable tautology. Adam's rush to wake the sleeping Eve in 'the bower' (607) hints at an improved relationship, but Eve is already awake and prepared for the encounter, 'with words not sad she him received' (609). Her fourteen lines are the last words spoken in the entire poem (610–24). The sonnet form itself lifts them above the surrounding narrative and imbues them with value and power. Initially it may be difficult to conceive in what way her words are 'not sad' but close analysis reveals this.

Milton's fondness for a combination of alliteration and internal rhyme is evident in Eve's opening exhortation to Adam not to explain his departure, 'Whence thou returnst, and whither wentst, I know'

(610). She follows this witty opening with words which even convey a degree of excitement, since her divinely inspired dreams, 'For God is also in sleep, and dreams advise' (611), are 'propitious' and presage 'some great good' (612). The excitement is partly achieved through contrast with that mood in which she fell asleep, 'since with sorrow and heart's distress/Wearied I fell asleep' (613–14). Milton's syntax makes it clear that Eve slept, 'Wearied' by her own sadness and distress, which elicits our sympathy. She pauses mid-line before demonstrating in quite spectacular terms the truth of Michael's statement (595–7) about her new found submissiveness. Although this speech by Eve is far shorter than the lengthy dialogue she had with Adam in Book 9, which led ultimately to her unguarded encounter with the serpent (IX, 205–384), it invites comparison. Whereas formerly she argued skilfully and emotionally, now she is eager to stress her compliance in briefer, but no less eloquent, terms. 'In me is no delay' (615), she urges, before using a riddling paradox to convey her utter and complete indifference to Adam's decision. The riddle is in two parts. The first is 'with thee to go/is to stay here' (615–16) and the second is 'Without thee here to stay,/Is to go hence unwilling' (616–17). The riddle might not impress, but the reason she gives for articulating it might, 'thou to me/Art all things under heaven, all places thou' (617–18). Eve's dream seems to have included the knowledge that their expulsion from Eden is imminent because she links her declarations of fidelity and guilt to Adam's banishment, 'Who for my wilful crime art banished hence' (619). However we respond to the poetic techniques she uses, it is difficult not to be struck by the dramatic contrast with her former wilfulness, or to imagine a more chastened individual than Eve.

In the final quatrain of her sonnet, Eve offers the only consolation she can, her role in the long sequence of events which will lead to the birth and death of Christ, and consequently man's salvation. Continuing the inexorable theme of expulsion borne by the word 'hence', Eve tells Adam, 'though all by me is lost' (621), there is the future promise of redemption, 'By me the promised seed shall all restore' (623). Parenthetically she also acknowledges her guilt once again and God's generosity, 'Such favour I unworthy am vouchsafed' (622). In fulfilment of his wish to 'justify the ways of God to men' (I, 26), Milton closes Eve's lips emphatically with the Christian promise of eternal life with God, 'shall all restore', and instantly connects all his readers to her, and therefore to that promise, 'So spake our mother Eve' (624).

Adam, though 'Well pleased' (625), does not speak. And indeed it is difficult to imagine how Eve's poignant sonnet could be answered except as it is, by their sad departure from Eden. Time has caught up with them, and they watch as the cherubim, sent to guard Eden 'all in bright array' (627), glide, 'metéorous, as evening mist/Ris'n from a river o'er the marish glides' (629–30). The unusual word 'marish' simply means 'marshy' and, however we respond to the intriguing coinage, 'metéorous' (629) must connote the kinds of unexplained luminous light associated with marshes and bogs in the popular imagination of the time and often linked to spirits of one kind or another. As a whole, the simile is as interested in the concept of hurrying home as darkness falls, as it is in foreboding, since it continues, 'And gathers ground fast at the labourer's heel/Homeward returning' (631–2). We are reminded that Adam is now merely a labourer in the fields as he leaves the safety of Eden's garden for the uncertainty of agricultural life on earth. The description is also rhythmically appropriate, the long, soft consonants combining effectively with a number of lengthy 'i' and 'e' vowels to suggest the slow but insidious movement of mist across the marsh surface. Against this slow rhythm, the sudden burst of short stresses in 'gathers ground fast' (631) contrasts very distinctly and suggests the unpredictability and danger of such events to benighted travellers that Milton's readers would have understood far better than we do.

With 'The brandished sword of God' (633) going before them, and blazing 'Fierce as a comet' (634), Milton connects the images through astronomy, but also contrasts the damp marsh world with the 'torrid heat' (634) created by the sword which begins 'to parch that temperate clime' (636). For the first time Adam regards the angels as frightening and dangerous, and Michael's urgency seems to imply the fear is justified, 'In either hand the hastening angel caught/Our lingering parents' (637–8), who seem to be transfixed by the sight. Their final departure from Eden is shockingly pre-emptory:

> ... and to the eastern gate
> Led them direct, and down the cliff as fast
> To the subjected plain; then disappeared. (638–40)

The plain below is 'subjected' (640) in the sense that it is appropriately beneath or lower than Eden, but it is Michael's immediate disappearance which is so shocking because it leaves Adam and Eve starkly and dramatically alone. As Milton himself might have put it, undefended, unhoused and uncertain.

As Adam and Eve look back, they are in no doubt that the way back is barred forever, 'all the eastern side' (641) being 'Waved over by that

flaming brand' (643). The sword of God has been transformed into a terrifying firebrand surrounded by 'dreadful faces' and 'fiery arms' (644).
The angels have not changed. In the battles with Satan we saw how
readily Milton gave them heroic, martial qualities. It is Adam and Eve
who have changed and, in so doing, they lose the higher level of discourse and amity they shared with angels in Eden. It is also important
to note that Milton's emphasis on fire and flames is a reminder of the
choice that humanity faces. It is really an oddly unbalanced critical position to adopt when dealing with *Paradise Lost* to admire everything he
describes in terms of Paradise and heaven, but ignore the reality of hell
and damnation.

Reduced to Lear's 'thing itself; unaccomodated man is no more but
such a poor, bare, forked animal as thou art'⁶, Adam and Eve shed 'natural tears' at their loss 'but wiped them soon' (645) before setting forth
into their new domain. The rhythm of these last few lines is halting
and contemplative, the lengthy stress which falls on 'all' (646) matched
by the lengthy stresses throughout the penultimate line, 'They hand
in hand with wandering steps and slow' (648), which is another of
those beautifully balanced, single lines in the poem. Milton captures the
loneliness and expanse both in the image of 'The world was all before
them' (646) and in the idea that in all that vast space their first act
would be 'to choose/Their place of rest' (646–7) for themselves. What
can seem an unremittingly bleak prospect is lifted by two details. The
first is the mention of 'providence their guide' (608) and the second
the quintessentially human detail of their holding hands. Their joined
hands not only suggest a renewed intimacy, but are symbolic of their
shared faith, an idea reinforced by Milton's choice of 'solitary' (649) as
an adjective to describe their joint path. But perhaps the most poignant
detail in this genuinely pathetic scene, is the faltering, uncertain manner in which they set forth 'with wandering steps and slow' (609). The
phrase is easily overlooked but captures powerfully the absolute nature
of the blank page before them. They have no destination, no route and
no guide other than the spiritual advice Michael has given them. It is
that, and that alone, which will sustain them in this new world, devoid
of the presence of their creator.

Exercises

Lines 436–551. Michael proceeds to describe the role of the disciples
and the Second Coming, Satan's final defeat, before a lengthier section
devoted to the religious controversy of Milton's own era. Adam's joyful

reception of this vision of a restored Eden creates a logical difficulty because, as he himself explains:

> ... Full of doubt I stand,
> Whether I should repent me now of sin
> By me done and occasioned, or rejoice
> Much more, that much more good thereof shall spring. (473–6)

There are two useful tasks you can pursue having read this section. The first relates to Adam's dilemma. To what extent does his apparent joy impact on your understanding of Milton's theodicy? The second relates to Milton's own religious background and opinions. How does his account of the inheritance of the Christian faith by the disciples, and thereafter his descriptions of the clergy and their behaviour on earth, compare with the lessons Michael has taught Adam about the pathway to a good, Christian life?

Notes

Introduction: Milton and His England

1. As a fully qualified scrivener who had served a lengthy apprenticeship, Milton's father would have produced a wide range of legal documents and managed an equally wide range of property and commercial transactions for customers.

2. Charles Diodati was almost an exact contemporary of Milton's at St Paul's school and arguably his closest friend until his death in 1638 when Milton was abroad in Italy. He was from an Italian Protestant family living in London and it may well have been Milton's contact with Charles's family which gave him an advantage in learning and speaking Italian.

3. William Chappell was a Fellow at Christ's College who earned a reputation as a prominent Arminian who converted many pupils to his views. Milton was probably among them.

4. Gordon Campbell and Thomas N. Corns, *John Milton, Life, Work and Thought*, Oxford, Oxford University Press, 2008, Chapter 7, p. 109.

5. Ibid., Chapter 11, p. 222.

6. 'Cromwelling' involves the simple act of selecting an MP's name from an online list on the website 'You've Been Cromwelled', which then automatically sends that MP an email telling them another voter has expressed a desire to see them resign. The website keeps a tally of how many votes of little confidence each MP has earned. At the time of writing, Labour MPs, mostly cabinet ministers, occupied fifteen of the top twenty-five slots.

Chapter 1: Religious Mythology

1. Milton was appointed Secretary for the Foreign Tongues by the Council of State, which took control of the country after executing Charles 1, on the strength of his skill with Latin, the international language of diplomacy at the time.

2. There are a number of high quality recordings of the poem available as audio books or online.

3. One of the central tenets of Puritanism is a distaste for lavish ceremony, artifice or architecture.

4. The onset of Milton's blindness was around 1644 when he was only thirty-six; ten years later, he was totally blind. See Campbell, Gordon and Thomas N. Corns, *John Milton, Life, Work and Thought*, Oxford, Oxford University Press, 2008, p. 212.

5. Dante Alighieri, commonly called Dante, is arguably the greatest Italian poet, whose great work, *The Divine Comedy*, was written during the Middle Ages. In it he travels through hell and purgatory to paradise guided by Virgil, the great Roman epic poet, and his idealised lover, Beatrice.

6. William Shakespeare, *King Lear*, Act 5, ii.

7. William Shakespeare, *Othello*, Act 5, ii.

8. Book V, 520–43.

9. John Calvin, a French preacher and theologian, who settled in Geneva from where he became one of the most influential figures of the entire European Reformation and of Puritanism. In many ways he was the dominant force behind the English Revolution in which Milton played a role, and to whom the latter owes much to his thought and writing.

10. Stanley Fish, for example, established his critical reputation with his 1967 book, *Surprised by Sin: The Reader in Paradise Lost*, Cambridge, MA: Harvard University Press, which in some ways sought to reconcile the two sides of this debate.

11. Neil Forsyth, *The Satanic Epic*, Princeton and Oxford: Princeton University Press, 2003.

12. Jacob Arminius was a Dutch preacher and theologian who gave his name to a branch of Protestant thinking, Arminianism, which gained notoriety principally for objecting to Calvin's severe interpretation of the doctrine of predestination. Arminians (and Milton is frequently described as one by critics) believed that it is an individual's faith, rather than God's unknowable election of all redeemed souls, that is central to their ultimate salvation.

13. Hugo Grotius was a Dutch jurist, theologian and philosopher, whose work is generally regarded as having created the foundations for modern international law.

14. William Shakespeare, *As You Like It*, Act 5, i.

15. William Shakespeare, *King Lear*, Act 5, iii.

16. Much of the interest in Homer's great epic poem, *The Iliad*, revolves around a comparison between Achilles and Hector, their characters, courage and martial skills.

17. William Shakespeare, *A Midsummer Night's Dream*, Act 2, i, 141.

Chapter 2: Epic Voyage

1. 'and lead us not into temptation but *deliver* us from evil, amen.'

2. These trials, which took place during 1692–93 and ended in the execution of fourteen women and five men, provided Arthur Miller, the American playwright, with the narrative for his famous play, *The Crucible*.

3. In some ways perhaps the most fundamental of all Christian beliefs is the idea that God exists as three persons, Father, Son and Holy Spirit, known since the earliest centuries of the Christian Church as the Holy Trinity. Later in the poem Milton will treat the Father and Son as distinct characters.

4. The term 'Cavalier' was used by republicans like Milton to denigrate Royalists, originally horse soldiers and largely aristocrats, who Puritans associated with the greed and excesses of the court of Charles I.
5. Orpheus, the archetypal musician and poet in Greek mythology, travelled to the underworld to recover his dead wife, Eurydice.

Chapter 3: Redemption and Free Will

1. William Shakespeare, *As You Like It*, Act 5. iv. 90–6.
2. One of the main attacks Milton employed in his polemics against Charles I was the fact that his wife, Henrietta Maria of France, was Catholic.
3. Martin Luther argued that salvation was entirely and wholly dependent on God's will, not man's, and in so doing gave rise to the troublesome concept of *predestination*: just as some souls are saved, some are damned, without their will playing any part in the process.
4. Arminians believed that free will did indeed have a part to play in individual salvation, rejecting Calvin's rigid division of souls into the elect and the damned.
5. Echoing the language and ideology of Calvin.
6. New Testament, John 3:16.
7. Jesus, of course, asks the disciples to give up everything to follow him.
8. Martin Luther was especially critical of what he saw as the excesses of the Catholic church and advanced a far simpler, less materialistic form of worship.
9. A reliquary is a sacred vessel designed to contain the remains of a saint, or some object associated with them, and used as an object of veneration by Catholics. These were often extremely valuable objects, combining precious metals with jewels; many were destroyed or melted down during the Reformation.
10. See the exercise at the end of this chapter on lines 416–612.
11. The originator of the Big Bang Theory, Georges Lemaître, was ironically a Catholic priest and member of the religious order most hated by Milton, the Jesuits.
12. Judas Escariot betrayed Christ to the soldiers seeking to arrest him by a kiss on the cheek.

Chapter 4: Paradise Perturbed

1. See for example Neil Forsyth, *The Satanic Epic*, Princeton and Oxford: Princeton University Press, 2003.
2. Christopher Marlowe, *Dr Faustus*, Act 1. iii. 73–4.
3. A concept captured perfectly by the slogan of a well known cosmetics brand, 'Because you're worth it'.
4. Classical poetry by Hesiod, Ovid and Virgil contains different versions of the same myth in which an idealised human existence was imagined, analogous to the state of innocence and joy Adam and Eve share in Eden.

5. A good example is Diane Kelsey McColley analysis of Eve's free will in "Shapes of Things Divine: Eve, Myth, and Dream", in *Milton's Eve*, Urbana: University of Illinois Press, 1983, pp. 63–109.
6. This style is exemplified in portraits of Charles I by the great Dutch portrait painter, Anthony Van Dyck.
7. Genesis, 2:23; Corinthians, 11:9.
8. In most versions of the Greek myth, Narcissus was a handsome youth famed for disdaining his lovers. Falling in love with his own reflection in a pool, he becomes so obsessed with the figure he sees in the reflection, he cannot drag himself away and dies pining for it.
9. Jupiter and Juno, the chief God and Goddess in Roman mythology, have equivalents in Greek myth, Zeus and Hera. Classical literature is replete with stories of their loves, squabbles and infidelities.
10. In the Greek myth, Pandora, far from being intent on evil, accidentally opens a box or jar, releasing all the evils into the world, trapping only hope inside.
11. Anna Beer, *Milton: Poet, Pamphleteer and Patriot*, London, Bloomsbury, 2007, pp. 151–3.

Chapter 5: Wilful Transgression

1. His pamphlets, *The Tenure of Kings and Magistrates*, and *Eikonoklastes*, both published after the execution of Charles I in 1649, were two of the most crucial defences of the commonwealth, the former attacking Presbyterian opponents who baulked at the idea of trying Charles, the latter arguing for the regicide after it had taken place and written directly to counter the potent mood of regret Charles's own posthumous publication, *Eikon Basilike*, was having on the English populace.
2. *Paradise Lost* first appeared in print in 1667, some seven years after Charles II had been restored to the English throne and republicanism had become an untenable ideology.
3. The seven deadly sins have an ancient pedigree but were formally designated cardinal, or mortal sins, by Pope Gregory I in AD 590. Pride is one of them, and it figures significantly in Dante's *Divine Comedy*.
4. John Milton, *Eikonoklastes*, ch. 27. www.michaelbryson.net/miltonweb/eikonoklastes.html; accessed 3 November 2008.

Chapter 6: War in Heaven

1. The links between Milton and Shakespeare are enticingly unclear. Milton wrote a eulogistic poem, *On Shakespeare*, which was published in the Second Folio of Shakespeare's plays and his father was a trustee of the playhouse at Blackfriars. The safest thing to assume is that Milton was at least very familiar with Shakespeare's writing, perhaps even primarily as a theatregoer.

2.   It is not at all unlikely that Milton saw something of himself and his own history in Abdiel.
3.   Much of Homer's *Iliad* is taken up with attempts to persuade the sulking Achilles to rejoin the conflict.
4.   William Shakespeare, *Macbeth*, Act 5, viii.
5.   New Testament, John, 15:13.
6.   'Reins' is an archaic term for kidneys.
7.   Critics have often noted the sexual punning that accompanies the devils' use of artillery in the poem. Sexual innuendo or insult was a common form of invective used by both sides during the civil war and the implication is that Milton uses it here in a similar fashion.

Chapter 7: Genesis

1.   Urania is best understood as the muse closely associated with astronomy and hence astrology. Foretelling the future is a key aspect of her role.
2.   It is generally accepted that Milton met Galileo in Florence in the late 1630s. See Gordon Campbell and Thomas N. Corns, *John Milton, Life, Work and Thought*, Oxford, Oxford University Press, 2008, Chapter 7, p. 112.
3.   The older meaning of 'fond' as foolish or credulous is what is meant here.
4.   New Testament, John 1:1–3, 'In the beginning was the Word, and the Word was with God, and the Word was God'.
5.   At its simplest, semiotics is the study of signs and meaning.

Chapter 8: Divine Love and Love Divine

1.   In Greek mythology Icarus and his father Daedalus attempt to escape captivity in Crete using wings made from feathers held together by wax, but when Icarus flies too close to the sun, the wax melts and he drowns.
2.   William Shakespeare, *Anthony and Cleopatra*, Act 2, ii.
3.   Saint Augustine is one of the most deeply influential of early Christian theologians and his writings, notably *Confessions* and *On Christian Doctrine*, have been of huge significance to Puritans and Catholics alike.
4.   New Testament, Matthew, 19:6.

Chapter 9: Wiles and Wilfulness

1.   'At school John had learned to read verses aloud, to recite themes, to link his learning of Latin with his mastery of rhetoric. At Cambridge, this oral performance based education continued, if anything becoming more central.' Anna Beer, *Milton: Poet, Pamphleteer and Patriot*, London, Bloomsbury, 2007, p. 23.

Chapter 10: Crime and Punishment

1. *The Eumenides* is the title of a play by the Greek tragedian, Aeschylus, the final play in his trilogy *The Orestiea*.
2. Hamlet calls it 'a consummation/Devoutly to be wished'. William Shakespeare, *Hamlet*, Act 3, i, 63–4.
3. Ibid., 65–82.

Chapter 11: Loss of Paradise

1. Voltaire's great satire, *Candide*, was published in 1759.
2. See Alastair Fowler (ed.), *Paradise Lost*, London, Pearson Longmann, 2007, p. 612. Shakespeare famously bequeathed his second best bed to his wife in his will.
3. Ibid.
4. See Joe Nutt, *John Donne: The Poems*, Basingstoke: Macmillan, 1999, pp. 133–4.
5. The latest biography by Anna Beer, *Milton: Poet, Pamphleteer and Patriot*, London, Bloomsbury, 2007, makes every effort to position him as the complex writer, theologian and hands-on political activist he was.

Chapter 12: Banishment and Hope

1. An admittedly brief research effort could find no connection between the title of Dickens's great novel *Great Expectations* and *Paradise Lost*.
2. Achilles, the Greek's greatest warrior in the struggle against Troy, had only one weak spot, his heels. His mother, Thetis, dipped him in the river Styx as a child to protect him but held him by his heels.
3. Saint Augustine is arguably the greatest writer who has tried to address the many and difficult questions that the concept of faith provokes in most rational minds. His key work, *Enchiridion: On Faith, Hope, and Love*, can be found easily online at www.tertullian.org/fathers/augustine_enchiridion_02_trans.htm.
4. The famously popular defence of Charles, *Eikon Basilike*, which Milton was employed to refute in *Eikonoklastes*, in many ways relied on a comparison between Charles and Christ.
5. A litany is a series of prayers bound into a single sequence by rhythm, often recited by a priest and then repeated by members of the congregation.
6. William Shakespeare, *King Lear*, Act 3, iv, 108–10.

Bibliography

Armitage, David, ed., *Milton and Republicanism*, Cambridge: Cambridge University Press, 1995.

Beer, Anna, *Milton: Poet, Pamphleteer and Patriot*, London: Bloomsbury, 2007.

Brown, Cedric, *John Milton: A Literary Life*, New York: Palgrave Macmillan, 1995.

Bryson, Michael, *The Tyranny of Heaven*, Newark: University of Delaware Press, 2004.

Campbell, Gordon, ed., *A Milton Chronology*, New York: Macmillan, 1997.

Campbell, Gordon and Thomas N. Corns, *John Milton, Life, Work and Thought*, Oxford: Oxford University Press, 2008.

Carey, John, *Milton*, New York: Arco, 1969.

Corns, Thomas, N., ed., *A Companion to Milton*, Oxford: Blackwell, 2001.

Demaray, John, G., *Milton's Theatrical Epic*, Cambridge, MA and London: Harvard University Press, 1980.

Dobranski, Stephen and John P. Rumrich, eds, *Milton and Heresy*, Cambridge, UK: Cambridge University Press, 1998.

Emma, Ronald David, *Milton's Grammar*, The Hague: Mouton & Co., 1964.

Fish, Stanley, *Surprised by Sin: The Reader in Paradise Lost*, Cambridge, MA: Harvard University Press, 1998.

Fish, Stanley, *How Milton Works*, Cambridge, MA and London: Harvard University Press, 2001.

Flannagan, Roy, *John Milton, A Short Introduction*, Oxford: Blackwell, 2002.

Forsyth, Niel, *The Satanic Epic*, Princeton, NJ and Oxford: Princeton University Press, 2003.

Geisst, Charles R., *The Political Thought of John Milton*. London: Macmillan, 1984.

Herman, Peter C., *Destabilizing Milton*, New York: Palgrave Macmillan, 2005.

Hill, Christopher, *Milton and the English Revolution*, New York: Viking, 1977.

Lewalski, Barbara K., *The Life of John Milton: A Critical Biography*, Oxford: Blackwell, 2000.

Lewis, C.S., *A Preface to Paradise Lost*, New York: Oxford University Press, 1956.

Lieb, Michael, *Milton and the Culture of Violence*, Ithaca, NY: Cornell University Press, 1994.

Lieb, Michael, *Theological Milton*, Pittsburgh, PA: Duquesne University Press, 2006.

McColley, Diane Kelsey. 'Shapes of Things Divine: Eve, Myth, and Dream', In *Milton's Eve*, Urbana: University of Illinois Press, 1983, pp. 63–109.

Miller, Leo, 'Milton's Clash with Chappell: A Suggested Reconstruction', *Milton Quarterly* 14, October 1980, pp. 77–87.

Newlyn, Lucy, *Paradise Lost and the Romantic Reader*, Oxford: Oxford University Press, 1993.

Norbrook, David, *Writing the English Republic*, Cambridge: Cambridge University Press, 1999.

Patrides, C.A. *Milton and the Christian Tradition*. Oxford: Oxford University Press, 1966.

Patrides, C.A., ed., *Milton's Epic Poetry: Essays on 'Paradise Lost' and 'Paradise Regained'*, London: Penguin Books, 1967.

Poole, William, *Milton and the Idea of the Fall*, Cambridge, UK: Cambridge University Press, 2005.

Porter, William, *Reading the Classics and Paradise Lost*, Lincoln: University of Nebraska Press, 1993.

Rumrich, John P., *Milton Unbound*, Cambridge: Cambridge University Press, 1996.

Shawcross, John T., ed., *Milton: The Critical Heritage*, London: Routledge & Kegan Paul, 1970.

Shawcross, John T., *John Milton: The Self and the World*, Lexington: University Press of Kentucky, 2001.

Steadman, John M., *Milton's Epic Characters*, Chapel Hill: University of North Carolina Press, 1968.

Tillyard, E.M.W., *Studies in Milton*, London: Chatto & Windus, 1951.

Walker, Julia M., ed., *Milton and the Idea of Woman*, Urbana: University of Illinois Press, 1988.

Wilson, A.N., *The Life of John Milton*, Oxford: Oxford University Press, 1983.

Wittreich, Joseph, *Feminist Milton*, Ithaca, NY: Cornell University Press, 1987.

Zunder, William, ed., *Paradise Lost*, New York: St Martin's Press, 1999.

Index